Savannah on My Mind

Bettye Clary Toomey with Katherine Wood Wolfe

Bettye Clary Toomey
Katherine Wood Wolfe

Warren Publishing, Inc.

ISBN 978-1-886057-19-7

Library of Congress Control Number: 2008943009

Manufactured in the United States of America
First Edition
17039 Kenton Dr. 101-B
Cornelius, North Carolina 28031

To the dear Lord who whispered in my ear and gave me these memories.

And

To our families who have loved and supported us.

Acknowledgments

This book could not have been written without the help of many people. A personal thank you is extended

To those who read early drafts and offered valuable suggestions—Mike Rouse, former editor of the *Goldsboro News Argus*, Irv Metz Jr., former Executive Director of the Savannah Chamber of Commerce, Reverend Bill Brettman, retired Episcopal minister, Judy Hogan, founder of Carolina Wrenn Press, who asked the right questions and gave us direction, and Gini Vose Nicoll, loyal friend whose input was priceless.

To Savannah friends, Nita Potter and Eleanor Blood, who consoled us when we were overwhelmed, Dr. Irving Victor, who explained the Savannah game of *Half Rubber* to us, and John Lassiter and his wife "Dot," who helped with family history and photographs.

To Goldsboro friends, Dr. Brad Brenton and Dr. Linda Brenton, who struggled to no avail to get a clear picture of Thelma.

To the library staff at Mount Olive College—Pam Wood, Director, for her support, Susan Ryberg for obtaining Interlibrary Loan Materials, Heather Braswell for her computer expertise, Cynthia Hughes for help with scanning photographs, and Nathan Stancil for reading the final draft and offering astute comments.

To other authors for sharing their writing and publishing experiences, especially, Patti O'Donoghue, author of *The Stanhope Trilogy*, Karen Dodd, author of *Begin Again Quinn*, and the Goldsboro Writers Group.

To the *Savannah Morning News* for permission to use articles and photographs.

To Cathy Brophy and Pace Clem of Warren Publishing for their support and patience.

To all our children and grandchildren for reading and rereading "the book," listening to our concerns, and always being there with encouragement, advice, and insight.

And, lastly, to our husbands, Ollie and John, who have endured.

Contents

Foreword

"How can one make a life out of six cardboard boxes full of tailors' bills, love letters and old picture postcards?"
Virginia Woolf

In 2005 my friend "Betsy" Clary Toomey began sharing stories about growing up in Savannah. Betsy is a master storyteller. When she begins one of her tales, her eyes sparkle and there is an excitement that is infectious.

Our storytelling time became "Tuesdays at Betsy's." We sat at a table in her den, ate Nabs, and drank tea or Coke as she introduced me to the Clarys of Savannah and the history of her father's famous drugstore on Abercorn Street. It is now Clary's Café referred to in John Berendt's book, *Midnight in the Garden of Good and Evil,* as a place he visited regularly to eavesdrop on the city's eccentrics. I was hooked!

Each Tuesday she had a new story, a new photograph, a letter, or something from her boxes of memories. Her stories became chapters in what we first called *The Book.*

Betsy's memories provide a unique picture of life in Savannah during World War II and beyond. She grew up in Savannah during the 1930s and 1940s and is part of what is sometimes referred to as the "greatest generation." She had a friend who warned her not to date a serviceman or she might end up leaving Savannah. She ignored her friend's advice and married a serviceman from Ohio, but said, "I've always kept *Savannah on my Mind."*

My part of the book has been to listen, to read her hand written stories and prepare the manuscript. It has been a labor of love and friendship

-----Katherine Wood Wolfe

Preface

"Writing is the hardest work in the world, other than heavy lifting."
Peter Hamill

This book had been a part of me for the last fifteen years. I found myself writing on little slips of paper, the back of grocery bills, and anything I could get my hands on until finally I knew the story had to be written. I called my friend Katherine Wolfe and asked her if she would like to share the adventure. Without hesitation, she replied, "Yes," and our work began. We have laughed and cried as the story came alive.

So that you won't get confused during the story, I would like to tell you a bit about me. I'm an ordinary girl who experienced an extraordinary time in history. One of my daughters once said to me, "Mother, I wish I had been born in your generation and been your friend."

I have never understood why my mother ever named me Betty with an *e* on the end. To make matters worse, in true southern style, it was Bettye Lorraine. Our household help called me "Miss Bet," and my school chums drawled Low-raine. College brought another name for me to add to the list, Georgia, due to my strange Savannah accent. Finally, my husband said, "You're none of the above. You're just my Betsy," and so it has been for the past sixty-two years. When I answer the phone and someone says, "Lorraine," I know it's a Savannah friend. "Georgia" tells me it's someone from my college days.

It's been a wonderful life, and I'm so delighted that you've chosen to relive it with me. Katherine and I invite you to enjoy *Savannah on my Mind.*

-----*Bettye Clary Toomey*

Chapter One
The Knowing

The day I entered Savannah High School in the fall of 1940 all was right with my world. I lived in Savannah, the most beautiful city in America. I had good friends and the best mother and daddy in the world. What more could a girl want? Little did I know then that a few weeks later this was all about to change.

Have you ever had a *knowing,* a *knowing* that deep inside in your spirit that something terrible is going to happen? This happened to me on October 27, 1940. Mother and I were eating Sunday dinner alone because my father was too ill to come to the table. Suddenly, my food seemed to stick in my throat. I felt a horrible *knowing* engulfing me. Tears began to pour down my cheeks. Mother took me in her arms and tried to console me. "Bettye Lorraine, it's perfectly normal for a person to get sick once in a while. Soon your father will be better." She kissed me. "Go dry your eyes. I'll check on your father."

But I knew she was wrong. Daddy never got sick. He was always at work at Clary's Drugstore even on Sunday, so in spite of Mother's reassurance, I broke my date with a football player on Savannah High's team, telling him my father was sick. He asked if it would be all right to come over and sit with me. I said, "Yes."

Late in the afternoon Mother asked Daddy if there was anything she could get for him. He said, "Cold orange juice would sure taste good."

Mother drove to the only market that was open on Sunday night to get some oranges. While she was gone, I crawled up into bed with Daddy. We talked and talked. I wish I could remember every word he said. It was something to the effect that he loved me, and he knew I would never do anything to make him ashamed. Then he laughed, "I think your mother had to go to Florida for those oranges."

My date arrived about eight o'clock. While we were sitting on the sofa in the living room listening to Glen Miller records, I heard my mother scream. I jumped up. My big football player grabbed me, but I had super human strength. I pushed him away and ran to the bedroom. The horrible *knowing* had come true. Daddy was lying very still with a slightly blue look. Without thinking, I fell to my knees and began to pray, "Oh, Lord, please don't take my precious daddy. We need him so. We love him."

I heard Mother call the doctor. Then she dropped the phone, crying hysterically.

1

Dr. Quatlebaum arrived quickly. His home was a short distance away from us in Ardsley Park. He placed his stethoscope on Daddy's chest, felt his pulse and slowly turned toward my mother, "Clara, he's gone." Mother fainted and Dr. Quatlebaum turned his attention to her.

I got up from my knees and ran to the front door. I went outside and began running. There was a thick, heavy fog, no stars or moon. The streetlights gave a faint, eerie yellow light. I ran as fast as I could. Finally out of breath, I stopped and slowly, mournfully started walking back. When I arrived home, the sight that greeted me made my blood run cold. Several men were bringing a large covered bag down our front steps. I stood there crying. I was Daddy's girl and my daddy had died.

News spread quickly and soon the house was filled with neighbors, friends and relatives. In those days the body was brought back to the house. Daddy's open casket was placed in the living room in front of the fireplace. I leaned over the casket and kissed his lips. They were cold as marble. Mother was given a sedative and put to bed. My greatest comfort came from Thelma and Lulline, women who over the years had worked for us and cared for our family. They served food to the endless stream of people who came to pay their respects to my father, Dr. Clary, as they called him.

Suddenly, tears were streaming down my cheeks. I had to get away. I slipped into my bedroom, closed the door and threw myself on the bed sobbing. When my tears subsided, I began to think about the stories my parents had told me about their lives in the *olden days,* as they called it, and how they fell in love and came to Savannah.

Daddy had told me about his first train ride to Savannah when he was a young man—about the train belching smoke and shooting fiery red sparks. He was on his way to Savannah to study pharmacy with his uncle, Mr. Will Knight. He was so happy he could hardly contain himself. He pinched himself to see if it was real. He was leaving behind the farm in Odum, his mother, his father, eight brothers and two sisters. As the oldest, he worked from sunup to sunset, but he still found time to dream and study pharmacy by mail.

When the train backed into the union station, Daddy grabbed his valise and rapidly made his way down West Broad Street. He stopped under a street light, pulled a slip of paper out of his pocket and checked the address. He quickly found the three story frame house. Although it was past midnight, he pounded on the door of the dark house. Eventually, a woman in her nightgown and a wrapper cracked the door open. A joyous young man said, "I'm Luther Clary."

The woman opened the door. "I'm Mrs. Harold, your landlady. I was expecting you."

2

Daddy worked in his uncle's drugstore on Broughton Street. Finally, he completed the Georgia State requirements and was able to go to Atlanta to receive his certificate in pharmacy. His Uncle Will was a stern teacher and task master and always a shrewd businessman. He hired Daddy to work full-time with only an occasional weekend off to go home to Odum.

Odum was only fifty-seven miles from Savannah, but it was so different it could have been a million miles away. Savannah was a seaport town and Odum was a tiny flat town with a railroad running through it. It was on a visit to Odum that my father met my mother at church. He found the buxom, vivacious Clara charming, so charming that he invited her to go home with the Clary family and have dinner. Even though Daddy was eleven years older, Mother was at once attracted to the auburn-haired man who carried himself with quiet dignity and purpose.

Mother lived on a farm with her parents, three brothers: Ezra, Arthur, and Quinen and four sisters: Cora, Claudia, Ada, and Ida ("Billie"). Life on the farm was hard. Mother's oldest sister Cora was talented in sewing, so she was allowed to spend her days sitting while she stitched and mended the family's clothes. My grandmother chose Mother, the second oldest, to be her kitchen helper. Mother resented the hard labor of cooking on a wood stove, three meals a day for ten people, but she loved her sisters, particularly Claudia and Billie. Her father, David Carter, could be stern, but he enjoyed showing off his five girls.

Like every other young girl in love, Mother dreamed of spending the rest of her life with her new found love and could hardly wait for Luther's visits. After a short courtship, my mother, age twenty, married Luther Clary in 1917.

The wedding was celebrated with Daddy's family, the Clarys, because my grandmother Carter would not attend the wedding. She did not approve of the older man who was stealing her kitchen assistant. The Clarys lived on a farm several miles from Mother's home in Odum and were fun loving people. My grandmother Clary was an energetic woman with eleven children, nine boys and two girls.

Mother delighted in now being a part of the Clary family. She and Daddy rented a small apartment in Savannah on West Broad Street. While Daddy worked at his uncle's drugstore, Mother explored the city. Sometimes she strolled along Broughton Street perusing the millinery, dress, and notions shops.

There was a large black population in Savannah, most employed in domestic work. Mother told me one day an unthinkable act occurred while she was in one of the millinery shops. A black woman boldly walked in and took

3

one of the hats off display and placed it on her head. She looked in the mirror. Then with a defiant glance set the hat on a table and pranced out. A shocked clerk quickly picked up the hat, took it to the back of the store and disposed of it. Such acts by blacks were rare. They usually stayed on West Broad Street for their shopping and were so aware of their position in Southern society that they stepped off the street when they saw a white person approaching them. Mother, as most white people of that time, did not question this established custom or the actions of the clerk in the millinery shop, even though she did not feel comfortable with such treatment.

In her explorations of Savannah, Mother discovered Colonial Cemetery at Abercorn Street and Oglethorpe Avenue. Some of the graves were rectangular cement slabs that looked like stone beds to her. She said she spent hours scanning the names and inscriptions on tombstones. From local visitors, she learned the names of famous people buried there and about the desecration of the cemetery when General Sherman occupied Savannah. Union soldiers heard rumors that the vaults contained silver and jewels. In their search for treasure, headstones were broken and bones were scattered.

Mother was fascinated by Savannah and the way General Oglethorpe had laid out the town in squares. She returned home each day with new tales of her exploits. One day while she was in Wright Square staring at the large stone dedicated to Tomochichi, chief of the Yamacraw Indians and a friend of Oglethorpe, an old gentleman tipped his hat to her and said, "Good day, young lady, did you know this stone will talk to you?"

Mother was excited, "No, I didn't."

"All you have to do is walk around the stone three times and ask Tomochichi, what are you doing? He'll answer."

Mother followed his instructions. She walked around the stone three times. Then asked, "Tomochichi, what are you doing?"

After Mother waited a few minutes for an answer, the old man asked, "What did Tomochichi say?"

"Nothing," Mother answered.

"That's what he always says." The gentleman smiled and tipped his hat again as he walked away.

Daddy also smiled as Mother related the story.

"I felt so embarrassed!" She exclaimed.

"Don't worry about it. It's just a joke locals play on newcomers in Savannah."

My mother never forgot this. She was becoming a local and passed this joke on to me, and I would pass it on to my children.

Her travels around Savannah extended to streetcar rides to the waterfront area at Thunderbolt Harbor on the Wilmington River, where she watched the shrimp boats come in. She went to Bonaventure Cemetery, which is on a bluff overlooking the Wilmington River. She said Daddy told her, "Savannah is the only city built on a bluff and its main street is Bull Street."

Having grown up on a farm, the waterfront area and the activity of the city provided an unending source of entertainment for her. She told Daddy, "I love this place. It weaves a spell over me. I want this always to be my home."

My father was delighted that Mother was happy living in Savannah; so happy that in the early 1920s he started his own business. He borrowed money from his Uncle Will and opened a drugstore at 242 Bull Street and Perry Lane. It included an eating area where breakfast and lunch were served. It would be the 1930's before he opened his second drugstore on Abercorn Street where Clary's Café is located today and where the characters in John Berendt's book *Midnight in the Garden of Good and Evil* (1994) came alive.

Daddy worked hard and was an innovative businessman. His employees cooked chickens for chicken salad and made his special Clary chocolate. He taught the soda jerks to make popsicles by putting a scoop of vanilla, chocolate, or strawberry ice cream on a tongue depressor. Then they dipped them into the special chocolate syrup and placed them straight up in the fountain's ice cream compartment. No one could tell by looking at the chocolate covering what flavor ice cream was underneath. To elevate sales, he made fewer strawberry popsicles and advertised that anyone who got a strawberry one received a free popsicle. People in Savannah flocked there and his business prospered.

Most of the people who frequented the original Clary's went inside, but Daddy also provided service outside by hiring curb boys. Customers pulled into parking spaces on Bull Street, honked their horns, and the curb boys, wearing starched white jackets and hats, sprinted out to get orders.

Inside, the store was long and narrow, with a black and white tile floor and a high decorative tin ceiling. It had a long marble soda fountain with a mirror behind it and stools that swiveled around and were attached to the floor. Customers who sat at the fountain or at the marble tables were cooled by paddle fans and enjoyed Clary's chicken salad sandwiches, sodas, and popsicles.

My father never tired of the people who came into the store to ask for his advice as a pharmacist. They called him Dr. Clary, and for some he was the only doctor they had. He listened to their ailments and prescribed over the counter medicine. A porter was always available to deliver their prescriptions. I can still see him standing at his prescription counter mixing medicine in his huge mortar and pestle. No simply counting pills in those days.

I was startled out of my memories at the sound of a slight tap at my bedroom door and slowly it opened. Thelma stuck her head in and said, "Miz

Bet, I brought you a plate of food. You know you've got to eat. People are asking to speak to you."

I rubbed my eyes and remembered that my father had died. I took the plate of food from Thelma and begged for a little more time. Thelma nodded and left the room. I had so many happy memories. How could I bear all this sadness now?

From the time I was a little girl Daddy took me fishing. He would tie a rope around my waist and tie the other end to his leg. If I fell over he said he would pull me in.

He was gone now. He would never be there to pull me up again.

Chapter Two
Claudia and Billie

Mother's two sisters, Claudia and Billie, stayed with Mother and me for a week after Daddy died. They lifted our spirits and kept us busy. At night, we sat in the den and invariably one of them would say, "Do you remember?" I loved hearing their stories.

Claudia told about coming to live with Mother and Daddy after Mother's first baby, a baby boy, died in 1923. His neck was broken in birth. Mother was devastated by the death, but even more by the news that she couldn't have any more children. She had always dreamed of a large family. My sweet father's chief aim in life was to make his wife happy, so he agreed to have Aunt Claudia and her husband come to live with them on Drayton Street.

Aunt Claudia and her husband were a welcome addition. Daddy hired Claudia as a cashier at Clary's Drugstore on Bull Street, and she became his right hand in running the store. Mother enjoyed having her sister with her, and gradually the pain of my baby brother's death began to heal.

Mother joined several "spend the day" bridge clubs and had a wide circle of friends who loved to have a good time.

Aunt Claudia was Mother's best friend as well as her sister. Laughter and love filled the house as they reminisced about their younger days.

A story Mother and Aunt Claudia enjoyed telling was about Mother and her first dime. When Mother was a chubby little girl, she often visited her grandparents' house, which was just down the road from hers. She liked going into her grandfather's bedroom and gazing at the scattered money on the dresser. Her grandfather had a habit of emptying his pockets on his dresser. The pieces of silver fascinated her. Money was scarce, and she had never had any. Finally, the temptation became too much. She looked all around to make sure that she was alone. Then she quickly placed a shiny silver dime in her pocket. She ran outside to the Scuppernong vine and walked under the arbor where she carefully took the dime out of her pocket. Then she threw it into the air. It landed at her feet. She picked it up and happily skipped home.

At home, she went to her mother and said, "Look what I found!"

"Well, aren't you the lucky one. Finders, keepers, losers weepers. It's fine for you to keep the dime," her mother said. But somehow the money didn't bring happiness. Clara began to feel sick. That night she tossed and turned in her bed, not able to sleep.

The next morning bright and early she told her mother that she was going to Granddaddy's. Once there, unobserved, she quietly went into the bedroom and put the bright shiny dime back on the dresser. It was at that moment Mother said she knew she could never live a life of crime. Aunt Claudia and Mother laughed many times in years to come about Mother learning at an early age she could never be a criminal.

A year after Claudia came to live with my parents, Mother became pregnant in spite of doctor's warnings. Because her pregnancy was such a high-risk one, she spent the last weeks before giving birth in Telfair Women's Hospital. It was at the south end of Forsyth Park on Gwinnett Street, which was across from their apartment on Drayton Street. The nurses provided constant attention, the best of food, and most important, their concern. On September 17, 1924, my mother gave birth to me—Bettye Lorraine Clary—a small, red-haired baby girl.

Claudia and her husband, George, continued to live with us after my birth. Her husband was a traveling salesman, a fast talker. In fact, he talked so much he was nicknamed "Polly," like Polly, the parrot. He knew how to charm anyone he met, and his charms certainly worked on me.

I delighted in my Uncle Polly's attention. I liked him because he always had time for me. Some nights Uncle Polly and Aunt Claudia took me for walks in the Big Park.

******

Life was going along smoothly until Mother's baby sister, Ida, nicknamed Billie, left Odum, Georgia, and knocked on Mother and Daddy's door. When Mother opened the door, there was Billie with her boyfriend, Stanley.

"I've left home for good," Aunt Billie said. "I want to go to Florida with Stanley. We want to get married at your house."

Mother told them to sit down and ran to get Daddy. "What can we do?"

"Try to talk them out of it!" Daddy answered.

Daddy tried to convince my Aunt "Billie" she was too young to get married, but to no avail. Billie said, "I'll just go with Stanley without getting married if you don't help me!" Daddy couldn't allow that, so he and Mother let them be married in our living room on Drayton Street, in spite of the objections they knew Mother's father would have. He would erupt like a volcano when he learned of the flight of his favorite child.

I remember the song Mother always sang about Billie. "She was a wild sort of devil, but dead on the level was my gal Sal." Aunt Billie was different. She knew it and liked it. She wasn't what you would call beautiful, but she had style. Her black hair was bobbed, and her wedding dress was mod 1920s. She left for her honeymoon dressed in stylish knickers and a white blouse with a man's tie. Mother kept wailing, "She's so young!"

Daddy said, "That girl has a mind of her own. There's no stopping her." And I, at five, found it all thrilling. I would have gladly followed her anywhere.

After the wedding, Mother and Claudia went to Odum and faced their parents' wrath. After the initial shock, their father said, "You did what you could. Thank you for seeing that she is a married woman. I couldn't stand it if she ran away without getting married."

Billie's husband, Stanley, had a job with Maus Brother's Department Store in Tampa, Florida. He was a hard worker and after a short while there, Maus Brothers hired Billie. She was placed in fashions, and with her sense of style, she soon became a top clerk. Stanley was so proud of her that he said she could sell a kangaroo a wedding dress.

Chapter Three
Life Goes On

A few days after Daddy's funeral, Aunt Claudia and Aunt Billie left. Mother and I were alone. The house felt empty, but not as empty as the hollow feeling in my heart.

Going through Daddy's closet was a job that had to be done. We started it, but the sight of his blue and white seersucker and white linen suits filled me with pain. I hugged the sleeves of his jackets, smelling crushed drug potions, seeing him standing at the prescription counter with his mortar and pestle. It was too much. We put off removing the clothes for awhile.

Nightly, Mother and I sat in the den trying to console each other. Mother sat there smoking one cigarette after another. Finally, one night she held the pack of Camels out to me and said, "Smoke one with me."

It seemed right to share our grief together. I was sixteen. I slowly took the cigarette. I put it between my lips. Mother handed me her silver cigarette lighter. I put the flame to the cigarette. Tears burned my eyes. I choked but I kept on. Somehow it seemed important to share that moment with my mother. It was then that our relationship changed. No longer were we mother and child. We were two close friends, sharing our lives and sorrow together.

Mother must have felt it too, because she squared her shoulders and, with flashing eyes and a quiver in her voice, said, "I'm going to work."

I couldn't believe my ears. My mother had never worked a day outside her home, but I knew that, when she said something, she meant it. As we sat there smoking, the plan was formed. I was to go to school and Mother would take over my father's drugstores. These would be our jobs.

Mother said, "It's not proper for you to be at home alone at night. Thelma will be here all day; but since I won't be home from the drugstore until almost midnight, we need someone to be with you at night. Let's think about this."

I first knew Thelma as a nursemaid when I was a baby. She was a tall, slender, light-skinned black girl of fourteen when she first knocked on our front door. She said her name was Thelma, and she was looking for work. Mother interviewed her and even though she was very young, she assured Mother she loved children and she could cook. Her father was a preacher and her mother was a midwife. "I'm honest. I can learn, and I need work," she said.

Mother was impressed with Thelma's determination, so right then Thelma came to work for us. Thelma grew into a good-looking woman and was better educated than most black women of her day because her father taught her at home. She stayed with our family off and on for over forty years.

Thelma became an excellent cook and was gifted in serving dinner parties. Many guests wanted her recipe for deviled crab, but she had a secret ingredient she refused to reveal. I wanted to know what it was, so one night when I was ten, I hid in the kitchen while she was preparing for a party. Before she put the last ingredient in the deviled crab, she looked around to make sure no one could see her. Then she quickly threw a block of cream cheese in the mix. I learned the secret ingredient, but I never said a word.

Mother was good about inviting playmates for me, but once in a while I'd be alone. I was glad to have Thelma. She always planned a way to keep me entertained. One way was to pin a huge towel around me, put me on a little stool at the bathroom sink and give me small things to wash, like handkerchiefs. I scrubbed and rinsed. I thought it was great fun. Then we'd put them out on the line to dry. Eventually, she'd place me on a stool at the ironing board. I'd iron and iron under Thelma's watchful eye. Her famous words were: "No cat faces, Miss Bet." She made me practice until I could iron anything without a single wrinkle or "cat face" as she called it. Even today when I iron and see a wrinkle, I'll say to myself, "No, no—no cat faces, Miss Bet."

******

The next morning Mother kissed me good-by and left in high gear. She was off to Clary's Drugstore to talk to the pharmacist and start learning the business. I'll never know how she did it, but she was determined. That night she told me that we had a housekeeper coming. She had remembered an elderly pharmacist and his wife who had fallen on hard times. Mrs. Day was happy to spend the night with me, knowing she could go home every morning and be with her husband while I was in school.

It came as a great shock to Mother to learn how much money was owed to Daddy. How could it be collected? Mother said, "I have to succeed in running the drugstores. Everything we have is tied up in them."

Things were going along all right until Thelma came to Mother one day and said, "Mrs. Clary, something funny is going on. Sheets and towels are missing and food seems to be floating out the back door." What a shock! Sweet, genteel Mrs. Day was stealing us blind. That was the end of Mrs. Day.

Not to be outdone, Mother hired another housekeeper. Her credentials were good. We were relieved. Mrs. Katz had thin, orange frizzy hair. She was a large fleshy woman, not at all like little Mrs. Day. Mother said, "You can't judge a book by its cover."

Mother hired two good pharmacists who assured her that they could run Clary's on Bull Street. The Abercorn Street store was still in good hands with the pharmacist Daddy had hired.

Business was good. Life was going well until one day when Mother was sitting on a stool at the soda fountain. The cashier called her to the phone. Somehow, as she turned on the swivel stool, her foot caught, and she was thrown onto the tile floor. Her wrist was broken, a bad compound fracture. I was called, and I rushed to the hospital. What bad luck when things were going so well! They operated on Mother's arm and put it in a cast.

The next day after school I went home to get the car to drive to the hospital. As I opened the front door, I heard moaning. I rushed to the kitchen. There was Mrs. Katz sprawled out on the kitchen floor. I said, "I'll call a doctor."

She replied, "Oh, no, no. I'll be all right, just help me to bed."

After a short struggle, we made it to the bed. She said she would be all right, so I left for the hospital. Mother was grumpy because I was late. I didn't tell her about the problem.

When I arrived home, Mrs. Katz told me to fix her supper. It was Thelma's day off. What was I going to do with two sick women and school? I didn't know how to cook. Then I knew. I called Aunt Billie in Orlando, Florida. She assured me that she would hop on the next train for Savannah. Mrs. Katz screamed, "I need to go to the bathroom. Get me a bedpan!"

"Oh, Lordy," I said. "Help me get through the night."

The next morning I left poor Thelma to look after Mrs. Katz. She wasn't too happy about this, but there wasn't much else she could do. I told her Aunt Billie was on the way.

Aunt Billie arrived later that day and immediately took charge of the situation. She phoned Dr. Penn who arrived about supper time. He took one look at Mrs. Katz and said, "Get out of that bed!"

Then he turned to us. "She is one of Savannah's biggest dope addicts. She's a sly one, sly enough to take advantage of your situation."

Mrs. Katz meekly got out of bed, and gathered her belongings. Aunt Billie and I drove her to a relative's house. She kept wailing, "I have no place to go."

Too bad, we thought.

When we finally brought Mother home from the hospital, we had a family "pow wow." Aunt Billie, Mother, and I agreed that I was better off looking after myself at night. Never mind about propriety. That was the end of the nighttime housekeepers.

Chapter Four
Drifting Back

When Mother went back to work, Paul and Roy Hussey who lived in the apartment upstairs were like dear, loving brothers. They truly looked after me until the day I married. They were so concerned that they rigged up a security system. They bought a loud doorbell, and the button was installed right beside my bed. If I pushed the button, the buzzer would go off upstairs, and one of them would grab our key and dash downstairs. Only once did I get frightened and ring the bell. It turned out nothing was wrong, but the good part was that I had someone close by to call. My security system really worked.

When I was alone, my mind would drift back to my childhood in Savannah.

There were many places that stood out in my memory. There was Forsyth Park—the Big Park with its beautiful fountain—the park that I thought was "my park" until we moved away from Drayton Street when I was seven. And then there were daytrips to places close to Savannah. Bethesda was one of those places.

When I was six I remember hearing Mother faintly singing, "Lazy Mary, will you get up? Will you get up?" I yawned and rubbed my eyes. From my open window I could hear the melodious voices of Negro vendors hawking their wares in a sing-song voice. "Yea, shrimp! Yea, crab! Come and get your shrimp. Come and get your crab."

Mother said, "It's a beautiful Savannah day and we're going to Bethesda Orphanage."

Fear gripped my heart. Why were we going to an orphanage? An orphanage was for orphans. I knew about orphans from the newspaper comics Daddy read to me on Sundays. When he read about *Little Orphan Annie,* it made me sad. I didn't want to be an orphan. I pouted and pleaded not to go. I said I could stay home with our maid but Mother won the battle. We were soon on our way in Mother's car, a stylish 1929 four-door black Hupmobile. Bethesda is about fifteen miles from Savannah. Usually, I sang with Mother when we went for a ride, but not this day.

When we got to the gate, we were directed to the matron's house. I was surprised Bethesda was such a beautiful place. There was a quaint brick chapel, a large building or two, and scattered small cottages. Everything was green and flowering. Great oak trees were draped with Spanish moss.

Mother had a friend named Janet who had taken a job there. She greeted us and invited us into her small neat cottage. Janet smiled and attempted to make friends with me, but I shied away from her. She turned to Mother, "Clara, since this is your first visit to Bethesda, let me tell you a bit of Bethesda's history."

Charles Wesley and James Oglethorpe had a dream of establishing an orphanage in Georgia. The Reverend George Whitfield and James Habersham were to oversee the project and raise funds for it. In 1739 a grant of five hundred acres was obtained. In 1740 the first children arrived from Savannah.

"But that's enough history. Let's go for a walk."

We strolled across the green to the largest brick building. We went upstairs into a huge, bright dormitory room. There were neatly made white cots, one after another in a line. The walls were painted white and the old, clear-paned glass windows let you see the moss waving in the breeze. Next we went to the chapel. How peaceful it was!

Janet said, "Bettye Lorraine"—she drawled the Lorraine so it sounded like Low–rain—"it's time for you to meet some of the children, so you can play awhile."

I didn't want to play with orphans. I tried to hide behind Mother, but she pushed me away. "Come along," she said. "You'll have a good time."

We walked across the green to a boisterous ball game. The children were curious about me, but they smiled and called me to play. I shook my head, and clung to my mother.

Next we went to the creek where a group of children were laughing and crabbing. I loved water. This looked like fun, but I still refused to take part in the activities. About that time a huge bell rang, and children from all directions started running to get cleaned up for lunch. Suddenly something seemed very strange to me. The children were all boys. Lunch was nice, except the boys kept watching me.

After lunch, there was a rest period. Everyone disappeared, so we went back to Janet's cottage. She gave me crayons and a coloring book and left me in her living room. Then Janet and Mother went out on her screened in porch. I could hear them talking and laughing before my eyes grew heavy. The salt air had made me sleepy.

My heart jumped with joy when Mother came in and whispered into my ear, "It's time to go home." Then it all came clear to me. Bethesda was a boys' orphanage and I was a little girl. Mother wasn't going to leave me there. I wasn't going to be an orphan. How foolish I had been. We sang all the way home.

******

From the day I was born I had a black nursemaid. Of course, no one used the word *black* then. They were simply referred to as nurses or if color was mentioned, they were referred to as "colored." To me they were my playmates, storytellers, and a beloved part of my family.

My first nurse was Tuba. Her real name was Cora, but when I tried to say Cora, it somehow came out as Tuba. She was a small, wiry woman with skin that looked like the chocolate covering on Daddy's popsicles. I was fascinated by her addiction to snuff, but in order to work for my mother she had to use it discreetly, never letting anyone see her spit out any of the tobacco juice that built up in her mouth.

When I was a baby she wheeled me all over Savannah in my white wicker carriage. When I was a toddler, she took me for outings in Forsyth Park. It was across the street from our apartment at Drayton Street, and I thought the park belonged to me. Sometimes Tuba packed our lunch, and we ate sitting on the large roots that grew out of my favorite tree, a huge moss-draped oak tree that looked hundreds of years old. Tuba was a perfect playmate. We dug in the sand together, ran and skipped, and she even taught me to do the "black bottom," a variation of the Charleston in which I learned to wiggle my hips while moving down to the ground and patting my bottom. When we rested, she told me stories. She never tired of telling me the story of the gypsy woman who tried to steal me when I was an infant.

Sometimes we went to Chippewa Square near Daddy's drugstore, Clary's at 242 Bull Street. Tuba and all the nurses were dressed in gray uniforms with white aprons. They sat on park benches while their children played in the park. One of our favorite pastimes was hiding from each other around the large monument with a statue of General Oglethorpe on top that stood in the center of the square. Often Daddy sent ice cream cones to the park for everyone. I have an early memory of being in the park carefully licking my cone and having a young boy my age, "Doc," reach over and try to take it. In the struggle he bit my arm. Tuba jumped up yelling, "Miss Bet, bite him back, bite him back!" I didn't want to do it, but Tuba made me.

That night when Doc went home, his mother, who had already been informed of the incident by his black nurse, asked him, "Well, Doc, what did you do at the park today?"

He replied, "I bite Bettye, and Bettye bite me."

Tuba was my protector and taught me how to take up for myself. I believed she would never leave me. She was part of my family, but one day Mother told me she had left us and was never coming back. My mother said to be happy for her because she was going to a better place. Even though I was only four years old, I remember riding with Mother one day to take Tuba home and seeing her unpainted, shanty house, one of many row houses on an unpaved street on the west side of town. I remember seeing several half-starved dogs running around the yard and her huge, unkempt husband sitting on the front porch. Later I overheard my mother say Tuba's husband got drunk and shot her in the head. Life was not fair to Tuba. I hoped it was true that she was in a better place.

After Tuba's death, Thelma was my nursemaid, but sometimes she took what my mother called a *sabbatical*. That's how my beloved Lulline came to our house. She was half-Negro and half-Indian. I thought Lulline was beautiful, particularly her long black hair. She parted it in the middle, braided it, and wound it in two large rolls over each ear. She was a perfect grown-up playmate for a seven-year-old, gladly cutting paper dolls with me on rainy days.

When all the other children could roller skate and I couldn't, it was Lulline who taught me how to balance on the skates in the kitchen. Then we waited until night when everyone was inside. She hung on to me as I practiced on the front walk. Soon I was skating like a streak of lightning. All the other children were impressed, and Lulline was proud. When it was time for supper, she stood on the porch and called me with a special Indian call. I answered back with my own Indian call.

During one of Thelma's sabbaticals, Rosa came to work for us. My earliest memory of Rosa is seeing her standing at the kitchen stove on Sunday, frying chicken loudly singing "Swing Low, Sweet Chariot" in her rich, husky voice. She never worked for long periods, but she kept reappearing when Thelma needed a substitute. I tried to stay out of her way as much as possible because she scared me.

When I was in high school and had "gentlemen friends," she dug out her Tarot cards for each young man to cut. Then she read them and hastened to let Mother know if the young man was a proper companion for me.

Chapter Five
Early Memories

It was a major adjustment to get used to Mother working. I didn't like coming home without her there, but I knew that was the way it had to be. The drugstore was important to me too. I had happy memories of Clary's on Bull Street when I was a little girl. Each year Savannah had a big celebration on Confederate Memorial Day. All the parades came down Bull Street right in front of Clary's Drugstore. I remember Daddy taking a small wooden box out to the curb and telling me to sit until the parade came by. When I heard the band playing "Dixie" I clapped my hands and tapped my feet. I was a fierce rebel! I waved to the Confederate veterans who rode by in an open car. They smiled and waved back. They were my heroes, but they were very old and would soon be gone. The crowd cheered, but a tear rolled down my cheek.

Sunday was an especially busy day at the drugstore on Bull Street. The First Baptist Church was just across Chippewa Square, and St. John's Episcopal Church was two blocks away on Bull Street. Sometimes Daddy took me to work with him, and I was allowed to be out front with the curb boys. When the church bells chimed, it sent shivers down my spine. I wanted to be in Sunday school like the other children, but there was no one to take me.

Mother did not take me to church because she helped Thelma prepare a big dinner in the middle of the day on Sunday. Daddy worked long hours – 8:30 a.m. through 11:00 p.m. Monday to Saturday. On Sunday he closed the drugstore by 2:00 p.m. so the family could have dinner together. This was a big occasion for Mother and a special time for me. Mother had a cook to prepare the food, but she fixed flowers for the table and made sure the house was festive and inviting because she often included guests for dinner.

When I was eight, Daddy hired a relief man, another pharmacist, two nights a week. Then he could take me to Trinity Methodist Church on Wednesday nights. But he still worked on Sundays, so no Sunday school for me.

Clary's Drugstore on Bull Street became a well-known hangout for high school students because Savannah's Chatham High was just a short distance away. Students cut classes and dashed through Chippewa Square to the drug store where they drank Cokes, (or "dopes" as they called them), smoked cigarettes, and socialized. As a child, I took it all in with amazement and thought they were very sophisticated. I couldn't wait until I could cut classes and hang out at Clary's, but that day never came for me. My daddy would have skinned me alive.

Daddy bought a drugstore on the corner of Abercorn and Jones Street in the early 1930's. Jones Street was filled with doctors' offices housed in old Savannah houses. Daddy felt there was a need to have a pharmacy close to these offices. His business instincts proved to be correct because the store at 404 Abercorn took off.

Daddy hired a pharmacist, a tall, slender, gray-haired man customers referred to as Dr. Cauldwell. Daddy did not add a café to the drugstore at this time although he did have a soda fountain. He stayed at the Bull Street Store and let Dr. Cauldwell manage the Abercorn Store. It was twelve years after Daddy's death before the Bull Street and Abercorn Street drugstores were consolidated into one drugstore at 404 Abercorn Street.

Mother worked long hours at the drugstore. I guess it helped her deal with the loss of my father. But I was dealing with the loss too. I treasured the times we had to sit and talk together. We talked about Daddy, and we also talked about the Carter and Clary families.

******

The oldest daughter in Mother's family was Aunt Cora. She was jolly and short with a tiny waistline. There is a saying "opposites attract." This certainly proved true in her case because she married a man who was exceptionally tall. At seven, the top of my head was even with my Uncle Seymour's waist.

Aunt Cora lived in Odum, Georgia. Every summer Mother drove me there to spend a week. Odum was so small, Daddy said, that if you blinked your eyes, you would miss it, so I kept my eyes wide open. I knew I was there when I saw the bright yellow train depot and the railroad tracks which split the town. Near the depot was a large white house where a prominent Odum family lived. Next we passed Uncle Seymour's General Store, the only general store in town, the barber shop, the drugstore, a café, and one or two other businesses.

Then we crossed the tracks to go to Aunt Cora's house which was a big gray house surrounded by a white picket fence. Inside the fence, flowers exploded everywhere. Aunt Cora was head of the Garden Club, and she took that job very seriously.

My visit to Odum was a big event. Aunt Cora and Uncle Seymour had four children—two boys and two girls. My cousins, Eugene, Aubrey, Katherine, (nicknamed Kitty), and Margie were always at the door to greet me with hugs.

I had another aunt in Odum, Aunt Ada. She lived with my grandmother (whom we called "Donnie"). Grandmother's house was on a street across the railroad tracks from Aunt Cora's. It had a large wrap-around porch with wisteria vines that draped over the porch rails and provided luscious purple blooms and shade in summer. Aunt Ada had a son, John Winburn (whom she called "Winburn"). Winburn came to Aunt Cora's to spend the week also.

Mother left all kinds of instructions about what I could do and what I couldn't do—no bare feet and I must wear a sun hat. Mother was no more than out of sight when my shoes came off and my dress was exchanged for overalls and a huge straw hat. I fitted right in with my country cousins.

Fast trains rumbled by on the railroad tracks in front of Aunt Cora's house three times a day, in the early morning, at noon, and at midnight. I never tired of watching them. At night when the midnight train came through there was a low mournful whistle. It always gave me shivers. One morning I was looking out of the window while I brushed my hair. I heard the train's whistle far away. There was a herd of handsome black and white cows on the tracks. They heard the whistle and started to run, but the train was already too close. One cow got hit. I saw its head roll to the side of the tracks. I almost fainted. Next I was sick. I'll never forget how the other cows gathered at the spot where the cow died, put their noses up to the sky and gave low moaning cries. That was a sad day, but most of the days in Odum were happy days.

Kitty and Margie had a pony and a cart. We enjoyed galloping around the whole area. We even rode out to Uncle Seymour's farm, where we saw a hired man ploughing a field. I was so fascinated we stopped and sat on the fence to watch. When the two big mules came to the end of the row where I was sitting, the man pulled back on the reins. The mules opened their mouths, and I saw their huge, slimy green teeth. I fell over backward into a briar patch. How the cousins laughed!

Aunt Cora was a devout Baptist, and it seemed that my visit always coincided with the revival at her church. The visiting preacher stayed at her house. The dining room table sagged from the weight of the food served: fried chicken, red rice, potato salad, field peas, okra, turnip greens, corn bread, biscuits with Aunt Cora's homemade butter, and sweet tea. Then desserts were served, peach or blueberry cobbler with thick whipped cream or three-layer lemon cheesecake.

The revivals lasted three days. I remember the church bells ringing to call us to the morning and night services at the white clapboard church, and Aunt Cora yelling, "You children, get in here. We don't want to be late."

After going barefooted, it was hard to get our swollen feet back into shoes. Reluctantly, we put on our best clothes and followed Aunt Cora to the church. There was no air conditioning in the 1930s. To get a breeze, windows were opened, which let in flies. We used cardboard fans on a wooden stick provided by the local funeral home to stir up some air and keep the flies away. The services were long, and I found myself nodding off and then being awakened by the choir as they broke into "Beulah Land, Beulah Land," or "Trust and Obey." My cousins and I were thankful when the revival was over and we could go back to our mischief.

Once when the four of us were on the back porch in the hammock swinging to the moon (as we called swinging high), we used Aunt Cora's long flower box full of new plants to push off to make the hammock go higher. Well, we pushed too hard and over went the flower box. Aunt Cora came charging out with fury in her eyes. She stopped, surveyed the damage, and looked at us. I guess we all looked so scared that she ended up laughing. Life was good again!

The only time Aunt Cora ever got really angry with us was one morning when the four of us got into a pillow fight. Feathers were flying everywhere. We were shouting insulting remarks at each other, "You're a Yankee!" "You're a buzzard!"

Aunt Cora yelled, "Behave, all of you, right this minute!" We ignored her. Then, I heard her coming up the steps. I quietly got off the bed, slipped out into the hall, and sat on the floor looking like an angel. She sailed right past me and gave each of the others a sound smack. Amazingly, the cousins didn't get mad with me. In fact, they admired my quick thinking, but I felt ashamed.

I enjoyed going to Aunt Cora's, but I was always happy to get back home. Savannah was a wonderful place to grow up, especially in the summer. Tybee Island, Savannah Beach, was only eighteen miles from the city. We often went to the beach for a week or just for the day. I always had to wear a big hat because of my red hair and fair skin. I hated that!

******

The only part of summer in the 1930s that was unpleasant was the polio scare. Polio was a dreaded disease that struck many children during the summer months, sometimes leaving them paralyzed. There was no cure. It would be 1953 before the Salk Polio vaccine would be discovered and 1954 before it was tested.

In hopes of preventing the dreaded Polio disease, the common practice of most parents at that time was to see that children rested more during what was known as the "Polio" season. In summer children were sent to bed after lunch for a rest period. They believed the additional rest would make the children stronger and keep the killer Polio away. I always went to bed with a stack of books, which one by one were taken away by one of the maids with "Go to sleep, Miss Bet."

20

Early Memories

******

In 1931, when I was seven, my parents moved away from my park, Forsyth Park. They moved to 610 East 49th Street. It was in a section known as Ardsley Park about three-and-a-half miles from Clary's Drugstore on Bull Street. We moved into a two-story, duplex apartment building. Our apartment was on the first floor and had a living room, sunroom, dining room, kitchen, breakfast room, three bedrooms and, as most apartments in the 1930s did, one bath.

The Al Hussey family lived upstairs. I wondered how I would like them. Mother told me Mr. Hussey had been married twice and both his wives had died. He had two sons by each wife. After his second wife's death, the grandmother, Mrs. Ryan, came to live with them. One of the boys, Roy, was my age. I had never had any playmates except for my black nurses. I was excited and a little nervous. There was also another son, Paul, a year-and-a-half older than me. We got along fine and were soon playing our favorite game, "The War Between the States."

Paul and Roy gathered all the other neighborhood children together, and our front lawn became the scene of the Great War. I was always the nurse and took care of the wounded. Nasturtium leaves made great bandages. No one wanted to be a Yankee and the very word *Sherman* made me angry. I was a fierce rebel.

That first summer on 49th Street was fun. All the children lived outside. Our maids even brought our lunch out to us. We ate under the branches of a huge camphor tree. I loved the way the wind blew the bright shiny leaves. Sometimes Margaret, a next-door neighbor, joined us. She became a great girl friend. We played dolls, cut paper dolls, and eventually saved movie star pictures, which was a favorite children's pastime during the 1930s. We cut pictures of movie stars out of movie magazines and traded them with our friends to try to get our favorites. We even wrote to Hollywood asking for pictures with autographs.

******

When we moved to Ardsley Park in 1931, Aunt Claudia and Uncle Polly moved there with us. Aunt Claudia had an easy-going disposition and seemed willing to accept life just as it came. Uncle Polly never provided very well for her financially, but that didn't seem to bother her. She had a good job with my daddy at the drugstore and was content.

Imagine my mother's surprise when one day Claudia called Mother from the drugstore and said, "Can you come downtown and take me somewhere?"

Mother replied, "Of course, but what's wrong?"

There was something terribly wrong. Claudia's voice had a hardness that was completely out of character for her. Claudia said, "I can't live with him anymore. George has been keeping another woman." Being a traveling salesman made it easy for him to have an affair with a woman in another town.

Mother asked, "Where do you want to go?"

"I want to go to a lawyer. I want a damn divorce!" This would be the first divorce in our family. Claudia never cried. She was just downright mad!

Daddy was furious. How could this man live in his house, eat his food, and act this way? Daddy said I could never see Uncle Polly again. Uncle Polly cried and so did I. I loved him. Polly packed his things and he moved out, never to return.

The drugstore became Aunt Claudia's life. She had a winning personality. I know many people came to Clary's because of her. She was also Daddy's watchdog. Her cashier's post was right at the front of the store on Bull Street. She greeted everyone who came in with a sunny smile. The soda jerks and curb boys liked her, but they knew she wouldn't put up with any foolishness. Daddy was usually in the prescription department mixing up his potions. He didn't worry about what was going on in the rest of the store as long as Aunt Claudia was on duty. I think it was out of love and respect for Daddy that Claudia took on more and more responsibility. He was a father figure to her.

One day a few years after Claudia's divorce, Daddy told Mother, "I think Claudia has an admirer. A nice-looking young man comes into the store a dozen times a day. It's for a Coke, a milkshake, gum, or cigarettes." Shortly after this, the man asked Claudia to go out with him. His name was Louie Brittain. Claudia got excited and nervous when she went out with him. I didn't understand her trepidation. It seemed silly to me.

One Sunday afternoon as Claudia was nervously dressing for a date with Louie the zipper in her girdle got stuck. She couldn't get it up or down, nor could she get out of it. She called Mother, but Mother couldn't move the zipper either. Claudia became frantic. In her mind she had to be on time for her date. Mother said, "We'll have to call Luther."

Since she was a very modest person, Claudia was horrified at the thought of Daddy seeing her in her girdle. Mother calmed her by wrapping a robe around her. Then Daddy, pliers in hand, came to the rescue. As he left, we heard him chuckle quietly under his breath. Claudia was on time for Louie.

Louie's business eventually took him to Chattanooga, Tennessee. We thought the romance was over, but he asked Claudia to marry him. I thought, how could Claudia leave us, the drugstore, and Savannah? But she did accept his proposal. She and Louie were married in our living room in 1936. I was twelve years old. Mother and I cried. How we would miss her! My second mother and Mother's best friend was leaving us.

******

In the fall of 1931, I entered Charles Ellis Elementary School which was six blocks from our house on 49th Street. Every morning I walked to school with several other children who lived close by. Sometimes one of the mothers walked with us, but most often it was one of the maids. I didn't start school until I was seven because of the mastoid operations I had when I was five and six.

My first-grade teacher was Miss Christianson. I thought she was beautiful. Sometimes she wore a red knit dress that I thought was particularly beautiful. I was envious that she could wear a red dress. Red was my favorite color, but I was never allowed to wear it because of my red hair. Every morning, Miss Christianson opened our class with the Pledge of Allegiance. Then we sat down and our teacher took out a small, black Bible and read a Psalm to us.

I liked everything about school, but I especially looked forward to lunch at eleven o'clock. In the lunch room, for a dime, you could get a plate of spaghetti or one of two kinds of sandwiches, peanut butter and jelly or pineapple. Sandwiches and milk were five cents each. I always had the pineapple. Lunch was early and light, as the Savannah custom was to have dinner at two o'clock and supper late in the evening. My daddy had dinner at the drugstore, but most businessmen came home for dinner and a nap. Many northern people thought we were lazy. We weren't. Our life style was leisurely. Perhaps, the hot humid days contributed to our way of living.

My only problem with school was that if I had a cold or even a sniffle, I was kept home and put to bed. My parents had a great fear that I might develop a third inflammation of the mastoid and become deaf. Since there were no antibiotics in those days, my doctor used to say, "Bed rest and plenty of fluids." Sometimes he prescribed a croup kettle filled with a smelly substance that I breathed to keep my nose open. I thought it was horrible! Aunt Claudia was sympathetic. She would bring me Nancy Drew mysteries which sold for fifty cents each. I acquired a large collection over the years and read them over and over.

23

At Charles Ellis, I met Betty Laine Jackson who changed my life. Her father was a minister, The Reverend Arthur Jackson. Betty Laine asked me if I would like to go to First Baptist Church with her on Sundays. Of course, I said "yes." Her family picked me up on Sunday mornings. Oh what joy! Now, I was like other children.

In the fourth grade a new girl came to our school, Catherine Monsees. She was from the tiny White Bluff School. We became close buddies. She was much larger than I was, so everyone began calling us Mutt and Jeff. Catherine's family lived on the creek at White Bluff and her mother sometimes invited me for the weekend. Mother returned the hospitality and had Catherine visit us. It was a great arrangement.

Catherine liked to come to town, and I loved visiting the country. She had a big white playhouse with a porch. It was located in her back yard facing the creek. We spent long hours playing house and sitting on the porch rocking our dolls. As we got older, we spent time on the water in a bateau, a flat-bottomed boat. We crabbed, rowed, and went swimming. Once we heard that mud treatments would make your skin beautiful. We waited for low tide and immersed ourselves in the mud, feeling sure we would become raving beauties. When Mrs. Monsees saw us caked with mud, she stayed calm, bless her. She simply made us strip and used a water hose to wash the mud off. The mud treatment didn't make us raving beauties, but it did give us something to laugh about in years to come. We became lifelong friends.

******

It seemed that before we knew it, we were in seventh grade and leaving Charles Ellis Elementary School for Richard Arnold Junior High School where I attended seventh, eighth, and ninth grades. It was mid-town on Bull Street and 34th Street. Daddy always drove Paul and Roy Hussey, Margaret Siems and me to school in his Packard coupe. The boys sat in the rumble seat.

Richard Arnold Junior High was different in many ways from elementary school. We had home rooms, some men teachers, and tea dances twice a month in the gym. I was most impressed by my social studies teacher, Mr. "Goat" Oliver. He was tough, but he could also be kind. Students usually listened when he spoke, however. One day the class was so rowdy when he asked for their attention and didn't get it, that he picked up an eraser and threw it across the room. Everyone got quiet. Then he told this story.

"There was a long freight train coming down the track. Some of the cars moved along smoothly and quietly while others bumped up and down making a loud noise." He then turned to us and asked, "Why are some freight cars quiet and why are some noisy?" He didn't wait for an answer. "They are just like people, just like you. The empty ones make all the noise." We got very quiet.

At Richard Arnold I made many new friends, but one in particular became my best friend, Juanita Cole. To my surprise she lived on 48th Street, within walking distance from my house. Mother was glad for me to have this new friend. "Nita," as she was called, spent many nights with us. We talked about growing up and our new interest in boys. We only had one thing we didn't agree on. She liked to go to sleep early, while I wanted to talk half the night. She woke up early, and I could barely get up in time for school.

One night we were at home alone for awhile, and we became frightened. We heard noises, then boards creaking. We just knew that someone was in the house prowling around, ready to rob the house or kill us. I ventured out of the bedroom and went to the kitchen where I got the biggest butcher knife I could find. I placed it between the twin beds. Next we put trinkets and glass vases on the window sills so that if anyone tried to come in we'd hear them. We couldn't pull down the windows as it was a hot steamy Savannah night. Our last acts for security were to balance a small, metal Buddha incense burner on the doorknob and put a coat hanger through my tennis racquet and hang it on the door frame. Whoever opened the door would be in for a surprise!

Feeling somewhat secure, we finally went to sleep. We were awakened by loud noises as the tennis racquet and the Buddha incense burner fell to the floor. I grabbed the knife and sat up in bed, knife held high. Mother, Daddy, and Daddy's brother, Uncle George, the Methodist preacher, were standing in the doorway looking. Nita and I felt so foolish we didn't sleep much that night.

The next day Nita and I went on one of our long walks, a favorite pastime. We thought nothing of walking three-and-one-half miles from my house to Daddy's Bull Street Drugstore. We walked to Victory Drive, then over to Bull and straight through the Big Park. On arrival at the store, Daddy gave us our favorite treat, a chocolate Coke and a Baby Ruth candy bar. Nothing could have been better. Then we walked the three-and-one-half miles back home, talking and laughing all the way.

Nita and I shared many good times together and spent all our free time together until Nita met a boy and fell in love. It all began at a Richard Arnold Junior High School tea dance. She came rushing over to me and said, "Bobo"—her nickname for me—"I've just seen a boy with the most beautiful blue eyes in the world. I wish he'd ask me to dance." It must have been mental telepathy because he walked over and asked her to dance. After that she fell hard for him, and he felt the same way.

As for me and boys, I liked anyone who was a good dancer. I was thirteen and in the eighth grade when I had my first date with a boy in my class. He invited me to go roller skating. We double-dated with Betty Laine Jackson and her boyfriend and rode to the skating rink in her boyfriend's chauffeur-driven car. Junior high days were so good we could hardly wait to go to high school.

Chapter Six
Remembering Depression Times

As Christmas approached, the first Christmas without Daddy, I thought about other Christmas times. Savannah has always been known as a party town. Even in the 1930s, when money was scarce, there were still good times. I remember adult house parties when the rugs were rolled up and the victrola played for dancing. I peeped from the sidelines.

I especially remember Mother's Christmas Eve parties. Even though times were not easy, Daddy insisted that Mother still keep our maid Thelma who prepared and helped serve the Christmas Eve supper parties.

The dining room table was filled with a smorgasbord of delicious foods: roast turkey, ham biscuits, sweet potato soufflé, corn pudding, spoon bread, marinated vegetables, celery stuffed with cream cheese and olives, and fruit cake soaked with bourbon.

At midnight Santa appeared and gave out the presents under the Christmas tree. I was always prepared with my little blunt scissors so that I could open packages quickly. One present I looked forward to was a tall paper bag from Uncle Polly. It contained fireworks. Shooting off fireworks was an exciting part of Christmas in Savannah.

Santa always left with a "Ho, ho, ho," and a "Merry Christmas."

Savannah never seemed to let the Depression get it down. Sometimes there were street dances, always held in front of the DeSoto Hotel, which was a Savannah landmark. There was a huge covered porch across the front of the hotel. Tourists enjoyed sitting in the rocking chairs and watching the Savannah sights. I liked the water running out of the mouth of the lion's-head fountain in front of the hotel. Lights were strung across the street and a band played. It was a short walk from the drugstore.

Daddy would say to me, "How would my favorite girl like to go to the dance with me?" I had the best daddy in the whole world.

I thought it was exciting to go to the dances. Everyone danced, young and old. Little children jumped up and down. Everyone had a good time!

Savannah was a dancing town. My maid Tuba had taught me the "black bottom," and the porter at the drugstore taught me how to "truck" and how to tap. I also took dance lessons from Miss Gertrude Williams.

I never knew how hard times were during the Depression until my daddy told me I had to stop taking dancing lessons. I loved dancing. I went every Monday for tap and floor work. Fridays we did ballet. The last Friday in the month we dressed up for ballroom dancing. It was scary to wait to see who would ask you to dance. The tall girls worried about having to dance with a shrimp of a boy, one worry I didn't have because I was so small. I looked forward to classes each week, so I was crushed when Daddy told me I had to stop taking lessons. Reluctantly, Mother told Miss Gertrude about Daddy's decision. To my joy, Miss Gertrude said, "I won't have it! You can pay me when things get better."

******

What would Christmas of 1940 be like? My girlfriends, Betty Durrance and Betty Eitel, knew I was sad. They wanted to do something to get me out of my blues, so with a laugh and a wicked twinkle in her eyes, Betty D. came up with the idea of "the contest." She said, "Let's pick out a cute boy that none of us know and see who can get the first date with him."

We thought this was a shocking but wicked idea and one that would be fun. We all agreed and the ground rules were that whatever information we obtained must be shared.

Arm in arm the three of us walked the halls of Savannah High School for several mornings saying, "How's that one? No, not him, never!" Finally, we saw "him." He had dark, thick wavy hair. He was tall, but not too tall, and he wore the uniform of an officer in the R.O.T.C. We all agreed he was handsome and perfect for the contest. We crossed our hearts that we didn't have a clue who he was. The race was on.

Our high school building was so huge that a person had to be a super sleuth to track anyone down. After several days, I just happened to see him at his locker. I kept going, but after he left, I went back. The locker number was 219. I quickly shared the information with the other Bettys. His real name was Sidney but we called him "219." Betty D. learned his homeroom was Room 100, so I started walking past that room swinging my hips with my "Shetland Pony" walk, as my friends called it. I got his attention because he started smiling at me, but before we got a chance to speak, school was out for the holidays. The contest would have to wait.

Christmas in Savannah was usually chilly but not cold enough for snow. The only snow was the fake snow in our decorations, and there was plenty of that. The whole town got decked out. Even the fountain in the Big Park was decorated with Christmas garlands and bright red bows. There were parties for young and old, and a feeling of joy filled the air. Mother and I went through the motions of decorating for Christmas, putting up a tree and mistletoe, but without Daddy our hearts were not in it. Aunt Claudia and Uncle Louie called to say they were coming to spend Christmas with us, so we would not be alone.

Once Aunt Claudia and Louie arrived, it seemed more like Christmas. Thelma was in her glory baking all kinds of goodies, especially her fruit cake, pound cake, and lemon cheese cake. The house had a sweet aroma.

Christmas Eve afternoon I went downtown to do some last minute shopping. As I came out of a store on Broughton Street, I saw Sidney, the boy we called "219." My heart skipped a beat. He waved and walked over to me. We stood there in the cold laughing and talking. Finally, with a stammer, he said, "My youth group, M.Y.F., is going Christmas caroling. Are you busy tonight?"

I answered quickly, "No, I'm not busy. I'd love to go." I gave him my address. I hoped he couldn't hear my heart pounding. What would I wear? I settled on a green long sleeve cardigan buttoned in the back, a string of pearls, and a plaid wool skirt that covered my knees and had a kick pleat in front and back. On my feet I wore dirty saddle shoes with white socks folded down to my ankles. This was the style of the day.

When Sidney arrived, he complimented me on my outfit. We had a terrific time. We laughed. We sang and laughed some more. I felt giddy. At my front door we said good-night, and he asked if he could come over the next day. I said, "Oh yes, Mother is having her annual open house." We said good-night. I couldn't wait to tell the two Bettys about Sidney and that I had won the contest. I closed the door thinking, "Joy to the World!"

Christmas 1940 and the year that followed was a new beginning for me. It's amazing what love can do for you. After I started dating Sidney, I felt happy again. Everything seemed bright. Now, I knew how my friend Nita felt about Alvis. My friends, the two Bettys, were pleased with the outcome of the contest and not one bit jealous. What good friends!

Every morning Sidney came by and drove me to school, even though S.H.S. was only two blocks away. My days were full. My beloved dance teacher, Gertrude Williams, asked me to be an assistant on Monday, Wednesday, and Friday after school. Gertrude was getting old and relied on helpers. I remember she often wore red lounging pajamas. She sat in a white wicker chair and pounded out the rhythm with her cane. If a student performed poorly, she stuck the cane out and caught an ankle.

Gertrude was a tyrant, but a beloved one. On Saturday nights she opened up her dance studio on Drayton Street to teenagers. For twenty-five cents, Sidney and I could dance to her juke box from 7:30 until 10:30, but I didn't get to dance with Sidney very long because there were usually more boys than girls. The boys who came stag stood on the sidelines surveying the girls, and then they broke in on girls they fancied.

29

I was always glad when intermission time came. The young men invited the girls to stroll through Monterey Square. Sidney and I would hold hands and walk past the monument to the Polish Count Casimir Pulaski, in whose memory Fort Pulaski was named. We would pass Temple Mickve Israel and the Mercer House. There would be just enough time before we had to return to stop at Solomon's Drugstore for a treat, usually a Coke and a candy bar for five cents each. It was good clean fun and the price was right. Being with my first love made it seem like all was right with the world.

Sidney and I had many good times together. One of the most memorable was a visit to see *Sweet Daddy Grace*. Going to see Daddy Grace all started with Thelma telling me about about a "Black Messiah" named "Sweet Daddy" Grace. She said he was holding a service in Savannah on the following Saturday night. I told my friends, and six of us, three couples, decided it would be fun to see what all the talk was about. That Saturday night we drove over to the west side of town and went down an unpaved street to a huge, barn-like building.

Just as we arrived, a big black limousine drove up. Two young men got out of the car and unrolled a red carpet. The back door of the car opened. A large black man stepped out. Two men crossed their arms and made a seat. Daddy Grace plopped himself down on their arms. With great care he was carried down the red runner to a large chair on a platform inside the building. There were rows of people on either side of the aisles chanting, "Oh, Daddy, oh, Daddy—Hey there, Sweet Daddy."

We followed at a distance and were directed to seats that were marked off for whites. The six of us and two elderly women were the only white people in the whole building. We sat down quietly.

Daddy Grace sat upon a throne-like chair. I couldn't take my eyes off him. I was fascinated by his appearance. His skin was smooth, the color of milk chocolate. His long silver hair was parted in the middle and combed into the style of a pageboy. He wore a mammoth white linen, cut-away coat with tails. With his long slender hands he made waving gestures, the bright lights bounced off the gold and diamonds on his ring-covered fingers. As the band played, the crowd went wild, lifting their hands high and swaying to the tempo of the Negro spirituals.

I inched closer to Sidney on the plank seat and took his hand, feeling a little frightened. Then the music stopped. Daddy Grace made his way to the podium. A hush fell over the crowd. He began speaking. "Daddy has something for you that will take away whatever hurts you. No more pain. I have this little book that you can read. If you can't read, that's all right. You can put it under your pillow at night. It will take away all your troubles, all your pain, and Daddy will let you have it for just $10.00. Immediately, ten dollar bills were waved in the air. The music roared and men distributed the books, carefully collecting the money. Daddy Grace sat smiling on his throne with a gold tooth flashing. At last he stood up and said, "Daddy sees that some of his children look sad 'cause they don't have $10.00. Well, Daddy's gonna let you have the book for $5.00." There was pandemonium. This time $5.00 bills waved in the air.

When there were no more bills, Daddy came forward again. "I just happen to have some more of these miracle-working books, and I can't stand to see my children sad. Out of the goodness of my heart, I'll let them go for $1.00 each." The crowd chanted, "Thank you, Daddy, thank you."

When all of the books were sold, he stepped forward, opened the Good Book and started to preach. He preached and preached. It was getting late, and we wanted to leave. We looked at each other rolling our eyes, but we were apprehensive, afraid that we might offend Daddy Grace.

At last, the two women who were in our section started down the aisle to leave. It was our chance. We stood up. Then the unforgettable happened. Daddy Grace shouted, "White children, stay!" My bottom hit the bench so hard that my teeth rattled.

Daddy Grace continued, "Those old ladies should go home. You children need some of Daddy's religion." So we sat and sat. It was after midnight, when with fear and trepidation, we quietly tried to leave once more. Not a word was spoken to us. We were ignored as we made our way down the long aisle and finally through the door.

Once outside, we hung on to each other and gave a sigh of relief. Hallelujah!

Chapter Seven
World War II

December 7, 1941, my care-free high school days ended. Every detail of that day is still alive in my memory. The day started out with excitement because my friend Catherine was flying back to Savannah from a trip to Chicago. Catherine had attended the National 4-H Club Conference where she was named the National Health champion. I wasn't surprised because she was a gorgeous teen-age girl with blonde hair, blue eyes, and flawless skin. I referred to her as a "golden goddess."

Roy Hussey, my friend from the apartment upstairs, agreed to drive me to the airport to meet Catherine. We left about noon. Roy played the radio loudly as he streaked down the highway in Mr. Hussey's brand new Chrysler. We were singing along to the popular song *"Tangerine."* Then the music abruptly stopped. "We interrupt this program. Pearl Harbor has been bombed by the Japanese. This is an alert. All service men report to their units immediately. We repeat, we are being bombed by the Japanese. This is an alert."

Roy and I were stunned. What was happening? Where was Pearl Harbor? What were they talking about? I was suddenly afraid. I'll never forget that moment.

The next day, December 8, 1941, President Franklin D. Roosevelt announced that the United States had declared war on Japan. There was a general state of confusion in Savannah, and I suppose the whole country. Young men gallantly signed up to go to war, ready to defend our nation. What could the rest of us do? What could I do? Somehow, we tried to go on with our normal lives. We went to school. We went to work. We listened to our leaders, gladly doing whatever was asked of us.

We learned that Pearl Harbor was on Oahu, one of the Hawaiian Islands, that the Japanese had executed a plan for a sneak attack to destroy our battleship fleet based there. On December 7, 1941, at eight o'clock a.m. (Hawaii Time) eight of our battleships were sunk, and 2,400 Americans died. The American people were outraged and shocked, but they rallied together. Women with sons who enlisted in the military put a blue star in their windows. The blue star was exchanged for a gold star if a son was killed. We started down a long path of sacrifice and resolve.

On December 11, 1941, the United States declared war on Japan's axis partners, Germany and Italy. President Roosevelt gave weekly fireside chats on the radio. I thought they were inspiring and informative. Young and old, we

32

all sat by our radios, listening and gathering courage. The President was our leader, and we believed his words: "America was suddenly and deliberately attacked by naval air forces of the Empire of Japan, but we will gain the inevitable triumph, so help us God."

I was only seventeen years old, but I wanted to do my part. The Red Cross wanted wool scarves, so I learned to knit. The scarves were one foot wide and six feet long. They were made of the ugliest olive green wool I had ever seen. I never knew how they could aid the war effort, but I kept on knitting.

As the men enlisted, women went to work in droves all over the U.S. to replenish the workforce. In Savannah there were huge shipyards, and women learned new skills, replacing the men. There were jokes about "Rosie the Riveter," but also immense pride in what these women could do. We were on a long, hard journey.

Every man, woman and child had ration stamps for coffee, sugar, beef, shoes, and many other things. The big shock to civilians was the rationing of gasoline. Gas was needed for the armed services. We walked. We rode buses and bikes. We car pooled, but no one grumbled. We were told, "Zip your lip. You could sink a ship. Idle talk might aid the enemy."

Women sadly gave up their nylon stockings. Parachutes had to be made. Leg make-up was the alternative, at least in the South. It was a creamy, thick, tan colored lotion that was applied to your legs. It didn't look bad once you learned how to apply it. The drawback was that if you were sleepy at night and didn't wash your legs, the make- up came off on your sheets and left ugly tan stains.

Every school child felt like he had a part in the war. President Roosevelt said: "Every single man, woman, and child is a partner in the most tremendous undertaking of our American history." Children emptied their piggy banks and bought stamps for U. S. Savings Bonds. Each stamp cost ten cents. The stamps were put into a book which (when filled) could be exchanged for a war bond which matured in ten years. Then its cash value was twenty-five dollars. They were investing in the war and in the future.

That summer, the summer of 1942, I took the train to Orlando to visit Aunt Billie and Uncle Stanley. I loved Orlando with all its beautiful lakes. Aunt Billie was fun. There always seemed to be excitement wherever she was. She gave her all to the war effort, working as a nurse's aid at the hospital.

One day while Aunt Billie was at the hospital I took a long walk, ending up at Lake Eola. I'll never forget that day. The sky was a brilliant blue with clouds like huge marshmallows. Graceful swans and their babies were gliding across the lake. Water was gently lapping at the shore. I wanted to cry and I did cry. How could everything be so peaceful here and in another place across the ocean there was only horror and death? I knew then and there that it was true—war is hell.

These were wild times. We partied. We laughed with others, but when alone we prayed to God that the madness of this war would soon end. We sang *When Johnny Comes Marching Home, Hurrah! Hurrah! And we'll all be gay when Johnny come marching home*, and *Hello to Love*, but there would always be an eternal sadness for those who had given their lives. Over two hundred young men were on the list of Savannah's dead. Our fervent hope was that this would be the war to end all wars.

Chapter Eight
Savannah and the War Effort

In 1942 the war was raging. Savannah was important in the war effort as a port, a ship-building center and a location for nearby military bases. There were two air bases in Savannah, Chatham Air Field and Hunter Air Force Base. Fort Screven, located at Tybee Island, helped guard the coastline. Parris Island, a training base for Marines, was just across the Savannah River at Beaufort, South Carolina. Camp Stewart at Hinesville, Georgia, was about forty miles away. It was called "Swamp" Stewart because it was in the middle of nowhere.

When soldiers had a pass, they flocked to Savannah. The city was crowded. Businesses were booming. Mother stayed busy at the drugstores. Wives came to Savannah to be close to their husbands, and the plea went out for the city to open their homes to them. Mother took in a young sergeant and his wife. Helen, the sergeant's wife, and I became great friends. She was good company for me while Mother was working.

People were urged to plant a victory garden and grow their own vegetables. Mother hired a man to come with a mule to plough up the lovely St. Augustine grass in our side yard. Mother recalled her days on the farm in Odum as we planted butter beans, squash, okra, onions and green beans. What a change it was to see Victory gardens all over town!

I thought for a long time about what else I could do for the war effort. Suddenly I knew. The U.S.O. was begging for young Savannah ladies to dance with the soldiers. That was right up my alley. I applied and was accepted.

The U.S.O. dances were held in the old armory on Bull Street just down the street from the drugstore. Going alone the first night, I felt strange. I had never gone to a dance without an escort. I stepped slowly up the staircase. At the top of stairs I had to check in with a U.S.O. representative. After giving my name, I strolled down the hall and checked my appearance in a huge mirror. I smoothed the flared skirt of my formal, green and white taffeta strapless gown and ran my fingers through my long auburn hair that tumbled to my shoulders. I decided I looked quite grand. This gave me courage to go through the archway into a huge ballroom.

The ballroom was a sea of military uniforms. Even the musicians in the orchestra were soldiers. Immediately, a young soldier asked me to dance. We glided across the floor. It was only a short time before a young man tapped him on the shoulder, and I was in the arms of another soldier. I made small talk, danced, and eventually drank a cup of punch to catch my breath. I went to the armory many times during the war years.

All the soldiers seemed to like the jitterbug, but each one had a different style. I got so I could tell what state a soldier was from by the way he danced. One of their favorite songs was "Deep in the Heart of Texas." It was an action song. At one place the music would stop and everyone clapped their hands. It was wild and funny. We all knew every word.

Sometimes on slow romantic songs, I could almost feel my partner slip away into another time, another place thinking of another person. These were hard times for everyone. I liked to think I was doing my bit for the morale of the troops. Sidney was not happy about this. It caused us to break up.

Not long after Sidney and I parted, a friend, Betty Hubert, called me. Her boyfriend Jack, a soldier from Fort Scriven, wanted to see her that night and asked if she could get a date for a friend. She assured me she had met Jack's friend and thought I would enjoy him. This was my first date with a serviceman.

I was pleasantly surprised to see that my date was a very handsome young man named Danny. We spent the evening playing records, joking, and laughing. Time rushed by and when it was time for them to leave in order to make their curfew, Danny lingered a moment. He shyly asked if he could call me. I said, "Yes."

As I closed the door, my heart skipped a beat. I thought Danny was the nicest, most handsome young man I had ever known. He was of medium height, had blonde hair, a golden tan, deep blue eyes, and the whitest teeth I had ever seen. I went to bed that night humming a popular World War II song, "*I'll be seeing you...*"

True to his word, Danny called and asked for a date as soon as he could obtain a pass. I hoped it would be soon, and it was. On our first date alone we went to a movie and then spent the remainder of the evening getting to know each other. He was from Hampstead, North Carolina, a small town near Wilmington, North Carolina, and had enlisted as soon as he graduated from high school. He played the trumpet in the band of the 252nd Coast Artillery. His friend, Jack, who had been in school with him, also played in the band.

Danny said, "If I can get a pass for you, will you come to some of the dances at Fort Scriven?"

I answered, "Yes."

Soon we had a group of young women who went to the Fort on Saturday nights. Our dates met us at the gate. Then we had some time to visit before the dance began. We strolled around the post. The gentle ocean breeze blew and palm tree fronds waved in the breeze. All too quickly it was time for Danny to take his place on the band stand and the music began. I never had a lack of dance partners, but Danny and I kept eye contact. Occasionally, he broke away and danced with me. Even if he hadn't told me, I would have known he was from North Carolina. He did a mean Carolina jitterbug.

Things rocked along like that for a couple of months until one Sunday morning I got a frantic call from Danny. He said, "We're shipping out, and we're confined to the post. Can you come down this afternoon so we can say goodbye?"

My voice quivered as I said, "Yes." At that moment the war became real and hideous to me. I may never see him again. I didn't tell him that I felt terrible and that both my ears were hurting. I called Betty, and we drove one last time to Fort Scriven. What an afternoon! The post was mobbed with wives, mothers, fathers and sweethearts. We held hands, walked around the post, sat on benches and looked at the ocean. As the wind blew, I clutched a scarf over my aching ears.

All too soon, it was time to say goodbye. Everyone tried to laugh and smile, all the time fearing what was ahead. I think I kissed everyone in the band goodbye. We prayed that they would all be safe. They left the next day at dawn.

I cried all night which made my ears ache even more. The next morning Mother called Dr. Maner, my ear doctor. She feared the worst because of my near death experience in 1929.

Even though I was only five, I can still remember throbbing pain in my ears as Mother wrapped me in a blanket and carried me down the steps of our Savannah apartment on Drayton Street. Daddy drove us to Telfair Hospital where a huge woman in white chopped off my long red curls. Then she picked up a straight razor and with rough, jerky motions began shaving my head. In horror, I witnessed her actions in a mirror above the dresser in front of me. My daddy was close by and finally said, "If it has to be done, I'll do it."

When Daddy finished, another nurse came in. She smiled and said, "I hear you like to cut paper dolls."

"Oh, yes, I do," I answered, perking up.

"Well, get on this table, and I'll roll you into the paper doll room." She rolled me into a room with bright lights. Then someone put a strong-smelling cone over my nose. I was the paper doll. The surgeon made an incision behind both ears to scrape the mastoid bones and remove infection that could have killed me or caused me to become deaf. In 1929 there were no antibiotics to cure infections.

Mother said that after the operation my head was completely bandaged, except for my eyes, nose, and mouth. And, unlike today, there was no IV in my arm. Necessary fluids had to be given by mouth, but my teeth were clenched tightly together. I had a raging fever, and my doctor said I couldn't live unless

I took nourishment. Mother stayed by my side, even though the doctor and my daddy tried to get her to leave.

She told Daddy, "I'm not leaving. Go to the drugstore and get some pineapple sherbet for me."

When Daddy returned, Mother dipped a spoon into the sherbet and began rubbing it on my lips. She stayed by my side rubbing sherbet on my lips the rest of the night. At daylight my fever broke. My tongue came out and began to slowly lick the spoon. How did she know that sugar and water in the sherbet would save my life? That is essentially what is in glucose given intravenously today. I call it a miracle.

Dr. Maner was amazed. Dehydration that would have killed me was prevented. He said she truly saved my life in 1929!

This time (in 1942) when Dr. Maner examined me, he laughed and said, "Thank the Lord it is not your ears. You have a full blown case of the mumps."

I wailed, "I've sabotaged the army!"

******

In the days to come I feared for Danny and all the soldiers, but I went on with school as usual and teaching at Gertrude's School of Dance. Sidney heard about Danny's leaving and invited me to a movie. We went out and eventually made up. Sidney was a good and loving friend, and the best part was we had such fun together.

Eventually, letters from Danny started coming regularly, but I had no idea where he was. His letters had words or whole sentences blacked out. He begged me to write, so I started writing every night. What strange times! My high school days went on with ball games, friends, studying, and Sidney taking me to high school affairs. I tried to live a normal, happy school life, but underneath there was sadness. We all knew that nothing was normal. At night the whole country listened to their radios to hear H. V. Kaltenborn. I held my breath awaiting his first sentence which was either, "There's good news tonight," or "There's bad news tonight."

One day our door bell rang and the postman smiled as he handed me my usual letter and then a small, flat package. I tore it open. It was a small book about Trinidad. I knew this was Danny's way of trying to tell me where he was. I was happy and thankful that he wasn't in Japan or Europe where the fighting was fierce.

Chapter Nine
B. B. Kelley (Bad Boy Kelley)

The stress and worry of overseeing two drugstores during the busy war years caused Mother to seek more help in managing the businesses. She decided to place an ad in the pharmaceutical trade paper and The Atlanta Journal for a pharmacist with managerial experience. I thought this was a good idea. She would be able to leave the store early, and we could spend more time together.

Mother had several replies to her ads. There was one she particularly liked. It was from a man named Benson B. Kelley. He came to Savannah from Atlanta for an interview. He was well over six feet tall, slim, wore glasses and had his light brown hair slicked down with Brylcreme which was the fashion of the day. Mother hired him to take over immediately.

I was delighted and looked forward to more time with Mother, but this didn't happen. In fact, it was just the opposite. I had less time with her because she still stayed at the store every night, claiming that she couldn't leave because there was so much to do.

Kelley wanted to change everything. When he began to attack the drug department, it was too much for me. He threw away all the old antique bottles that held drugs, putting the medicine in ugly clear, modern containers. I decided right then and there that I didn't like this cocky, know-it-all man.

As time went on, Mother and Kelley began to go to Johnny Harris' Supper Club for a late dinner after they closed the drugstore. It was strange to have my mother dating at the same time I was. I told my boyfriend Sidney how miserable I felt seeing my mother acting like a lovesick school girl as her long courtship with Kelley began. I missed my daddy now more than ever.

My daddy was a friend of Johnny Harris when he opened his first restaurant in 1924. It was in a long, low white building on Victory Drive with sawdust on the floors and booths with curtains. Behind the building there was a small zoo with wild animals in cages. I suppose that was to entertain the children.

Eventually, Johnny Harris moved to its present location on Victory Drive. The main dining room had a dance floor. The ceiling resembled the sky, dark blue with stars that twinkled. There was a bar and kitchen with a huge open spit.

Sidney tried to comfort me saying, "Kelley's really not so bad."

Then my imagination got hold of me, "I know what he's up to. He wants to marry my mother and take the stores that Daddy worked so hard to acquire." I had a hard time being pleasant to Kelley, but I had to get used to it because the courtship continued all through my high school years.

One of the reasons I particularly disliked Kelley was the way he brought Mother home at night. Holding hands, they often came into my room and woke me from a sound sleep, expecting me to be happy to see them. I wasn't. I hated it. Kelley was not a good influence on my mother. I knew this because I learned from our long time favorite waiter at Johnny Harris's that as soon as Kelley came in, the waiter hustled over to bring a fifth of Old Overholt (or as he called it "Old Overcoat") rye whiskey to their booth. Kelley liked his liquor straight up, a shot glass filled with alcohol, chasing it with water. He urged Mother to do the same. She had never been a drinker. She would have an occasional social drink, even though Savannah was a hard drinking town. Kelley fit right in.

I had never hated anyone in my life, but I came close to it. I decided to take the bull by the horns and have a talk with my mother. My chance came on a cold, rainy night when Mother finally decided it was a perfect one to stay home and spend some time with me. We settled down with our cigarettes for an evening together. With a pounding heart, I told Mother I thought she was going overboard in her relationship with Kelley.

Mother immediately began to tell me what a hard, unhappy life Kelley had lived before meeting her. Then she dropped the bomb. She said he had been an ordained Methodist minister, happily pastoring a small church in a small town in north Georgia. I gasped, "What happened?"

"Well, he and one of his parishioners fell in love and had an affair. She divorced her husband. Kelley was defrocked. They married, but they were never happy. I think he felt guilty. Eventually, they got a divorce. After the divorce, Kelley went wild, drinking and carousing for a while. Then he pulled himself together and went to pharmaceutical school. He's a good man who wants to make a new start."

I was dumbfounded. How did we ever get into this mess? I could see Mother was all starry eyed, thinking that she could help him become a man like my father. This was serious. I knew I had to somehow help her see the folly of this relationship, but how?

I wasn't the only one worried about the situation with Kelley. Several of Mother's old time, good friends came to see me. They were concerned about Mother and the talk that was going on about her. I was told about a statement that was going around in the pharmaceutical group about Kelley. It was being said that his name was Benson B. Kelley and the B.B. stood for "Bad Boy Kelley." I had to agree. He truly was a bad boy.

******

B. B. Kelley (Bad Boy Kelley)

Christmas of 1942 Kelley lived up to his name of "Bad Boy Kelley." My aunts, Claudia and Billie, tried to get mother to see Kelley as others saw him.

The Christmas holiday started with excitement. Mother liked a full house at Christmas, so as usual we had my aunts come. We looked forward to seeing Aunt Claudia, Uncle Louie, Aunt Billie and Uncle Stanley. The house had seemed empty because Helen and her sergeant husband had left. His unit had been shipped to the conflict in Europe. She had gone home to stay with her parents. She would have a sad Christmas, but I was excited. I loved family.

Finally, the day came when the aunts and uncles arrived loaded down with packages. The house was filled with laughter and love. Thelma, our maid, was in her glory. All kinds of savory smells emanated from the kitchen. Mother and I had been saving our ration stamps, so that we could have a feast.

Christmas morning we all gathered in the living room. There was only one fly in the ointment. Kelley had arrived early to join us.

The honor of giving out the gifts piled high under the Christmas tree was always given to Thelma. She wore her best black uniform, a small white apron and a starched white head piece. It was with pride and dignity that she passed out sealed Christmas cards to each of us. They were signed, "Yours for service, Thelma." How grateful I was for Thelma's years with us. I loved her and thought of her as part of our family.

On Christmas morning I still wore a ribbon around my neck with a small pair of scissors attached, a trick that I learned in my childhood. It helped me quickly open my presents.

Thelma quietly left us to tend to her cooking. She eventually called us to a hardy breakfast: fresh squeezed orange juice, platters of bacon, sausage, eggs, grits (which we always called "Georgia ice cream"), hot biscuits, and pots of steaming coffee.

Mother and I had not had coffee for months because of the rationing. We had hoarded our supply for this occasion. We lingered at the table laughing and talking. Finally, Mother agreed to read our coffee cups. This was quite a ritual. First, we all emptied our cups. Then we carefully held them above our heads, moving the cups three times in a circle. All this was done with great anticipation. Next our cups were turned upside down on our saucers.

Mother sat up with her back as straight as possible and seriously eyed the dried grounds of coffee that remained in the cups. We listened intently as she said: "Oh, I see someone coming soon. I see a winding road. You will take a trip. Oh no, I see sadness and tears. An important letter will arrive soon. There's a woman with a large face and curly hair coming to see you." I don't know where she learned this trick but she was very convincing. It was great fun, and she took it very seriously. Perhaps, it was because Savannah had more than its share of belief in psychics and the supernatural.

Because of the huge breakfast, Mother announced that Christmas dinner would be served at six o'clock that evening instead of the traditional two o'clock in the afternoon. After our late breakfast, friends dropped by and were offered mixed drinks and snacks. My friends and I enjoyed Par-T-Pack, a delicious orange drink. The day flew by and before we knew it we were all seated at the table again.

Mother asked Kelley to sit in Daddy's chair at the head of the table. She took her usual place at the foot. Bile filled my throat. How could she do this? But what could I do? There was a sudden rush of conversation. The rest of the family sensed my anger. Thelma quietly began serving all of the traditional food. It tasted like dust to me. Then the unbelievable happened. Kelley went face down in his plate of food. How disgusting! He was drunk, out cold! He proved he was "Bad Boy Kelley."

Sidney came over that night in his family's car. We went to a drive-in, the Triple X, for Cokes. I poured out the whole outrageous story about Kelley. I cried and Sidney assumed his usual role as my comforter.

Later, at home that night when we were all in our night gowns, my two aunts and I went into Mother's bedroom. We crawled up into her bed and settled down for a talk. We had agreed before we went into her room that we would confront her about her relationship with Kelley.

We reasoned and pleaded with Mother to realize that Kelley had a drinking problem. Aunt Billie even got up the nerve and said, "Clara, I know Kelley's about fifteen years younger than you are. That's too much difference." It didn't seem to faze Mother at all. She smiled at us and said, "The age difference doesn't matter." She said she loved us, appreciated our concern and knew that what we were saying was out of love for her, but she had everything under control. "Kelley's drinking is not a problem. Tonight was just an unfortunate accident," she said. "I'm sure it won't happen again, so stop worrying and go to sleep."

What more could we do?

After my aunts and I failed to convince Mother to end her relationship with Kelley, there was nothing I could do but accept life as it was and try to make the best of it.

******

After Christmas our lives settled back into a normal routine, except that Thelma seemed to be happier than normal. She was even singing while she stayed busier than usual cleaning and polishing brass and silver. Mother knew the signs. She said to me, "I'm afraid that Thelma is planning a sabbatical." Her prediction came true. One morning Thelma just didn't show up for work. This bout with alcohol was a long one.

When Thelma finally reappeared, Mother said, "Don't you think that it is time that we do something about this?"

Thelma was ashamed. She hung her head and said, "Mrs. Clary, I can't seem to help myself."

Mother's reply shocked me. She said, "Thelma, I think you need to get out of Savannah and make a fresh start. A change will do you good."

Surprisingly, Thelma agreed to Mother's suggestion and applied for a job up north as a live-in cook. There was a great demand for experienced household help. Mother provided a reference, and Thelma was quickly hired. That was when Thelma out of her love for us introduced us to Alma. Her words to Alma were, "You take good care of my people until I can come home again." With that, we said a tearful good-by to Thelma and welcomed Alma into our lives.

Alma was a laid back, pleasant person. Her light colored face was round, and she had large deep brown eyes with golden flecks. Her black hair was straightened, and she wore it in a short page boy style. She immediately won a place in my heart when she established the tradition of making a cake every Friday for the weekend. My favorite was a three layer white cake with chocolate filling and icing. What could be better than to come home from school and find a cake!

Chapter Ten
Sweet Lorraine

During the early part of 1943, World War II was in full force. Shoes were added to the list of rationed items. Each person was limited to three pairs of shoes a year because of a shortage of leather for soles. President Franklin Roosevelt said, "Peace can come to the world only by the total elimination of German and Japanese war power." I listened intently to the news of the fighting in the Pacific, France, North Africa, and Russia, always thinking about Danny.

One Saturday afternoon I almost fainted when I answered the door bell and there was Danny grinning at me. He laughed at my shocked expression, pulled me into his arms and soundly kissed me. We walked inside with arms around each other. All I could think of saying was, "The war isn't over. How can you be here?"

He replied, "Long before I left Fort Screven, I applied to O.F.S (Officer's Flight School). Several days ago my commanding officer told me the good news that I had been accepted. My orders were to return at once to the states. I was able to obtain a flight to Savannah, so here I am. I just had to see my girl!"

"How long can you stay?" I asked.

"I'll be here tonight, but I have a flight home to North Carolina tomorrow. After I see my parents, I'll leave for flight school."

I hated that our time together would be so short but was grateful to be with him no matter how brief the time. "Let's call Mother," I said, "and tell her the wonderful news."

After giving her all the details, she said. "Tell Danny he is welcome to stay overnight with us."

I thought this was terrific of her, but Danny said he had to report back to the base that night. His flight was leaving early in the morning. Mother seemed sorry. We hung up, but in a few minutes she called back and said we could have her car for the evening.

Danny and I were excited. We decided we should make our one night special by going to Johnny Harris'.

When Mother came home, she warned us not to use too much gas. I excused myself and headed for a long hot bath, all the while pondering what to wear. I had to look my best. I finally decided on a black velveteen knee length dress with three quarter length sleeves. It had a fitted waistline and was trimmed with heavy embroidered white lace. After one last look in the mirror and a dash of Tabu perfume, I walked into the living room.

Danny stood up. The look on his face told me everything I hoped for. He joked, "I could plum eat you with a spoon."

We drove down beautiful Victory Drive looking at the moon, feeling like the two happiest people in the world. Since it was Saturday night, there was a three piece band at Johnny Harris'. After our dinner we danced the night away.

While we were dancing, I noticed women flirting with Danny, which always happened when we were together. He ignored them, but it made me wonder what he saw in me. As a small child, my mother told me I wasn't pretty, but I was sweet. This made it hard for me to understand how a young man as handsome as Danny could choose me above all the raving beauties that surrounded him.

In the midst of our dancing, I heard a voice say, "Hey, you two." It was Mother and Kelley. We asked them to join us. What an unforgettable night—first, the flirty girls trying to get Danny's attention and then being seated in a booth with Mother and Kelley.

Danny excused himself. He went to the band leader and asked him to play "Sweet Lorraine." (Mother called me Bettye Lorraine, but my friends called me Lorraine.) Then Danny asked me to dance and held me close as we listened to the words.

Finally, it was time to call it a night. It had been all too short. We drove home and Danny came in to call a cab. When we said our final good-bye, he told me that he would be leaving for Midland, Texas, after he saw his parents. I was happy he would be in the states, even though Texas seemed like a million miles away.

The taxi arrived. We had one last kiss and he was gone. My heart broke again. It seemed that we were always saying "good-bye."

Chapter Eleven
The Lonely Graduation

In the final months of my senior year I found it hard to believe that graduation was approaching. There were term papers and projects to turn in as well as dreaded exams. The war in Europe, the Pacific and around the world was always before me as I walked past young men in R.O.T.C. uniforms. I knew they would enlist in the military service as soon as they graduated. I worried about where they would be sent, but I was young and refused to dwell on the negative. I turned my thoughts to the two big affairs of that semester—the Spring Swing Dance and the Military Ball.

The Military Ball and the parade that preceded it will always stand out as one of the most thrilling events in my life. Sidney was a captain in the R.O.T.C., and he asked me to be the sponsor for his company. The whole school turned out for their final parade. When the troops passed in review, the sponsors, dressed in Sunday dresses and clutching bouquets of red roses, stood on a flag-draped platform while the Savannah High School Marching Band played and the color guard and troops marched in review. There were fifty to seventy-five young men in each of the companies. Their precision marching was a splendid sight, but it was also sad. What would life hold for all of us after graduation? This was the end of our carefree days, but for that moment everyone loved a parade.

The Military Ball was elegant. The air was perfumed with the sweet smell of gardenias and magnolia blossoms. It was a night to remember with the girls in their formal gowns and the young men in their uniforms. It was the highlight of my school days.

After the ball it was back to studying, projects and final exams. Then, at last, graduation day arrived. I could hardly contain myself. The sun was shining. The birds were singing and truly all seemed right with my world. To add to my joy Aunt Billie came for the big event. The clock seemed to tick slowly that day, but finally it was time to go to the high school for one last event.

Mother said, "You're not going until you eat a bite of supper," so I went to the breakfast room where Alma had a plate prepared for me. She said, "Come on, Miss Bet, you gotta' eat something."

About that time the door bell rang. It was Kelley. He was laughing. He had a paper bag in his hand, and he held it up and said, "I brought a little something to help celebrate this fine day."

"Oh no," I groaned inwardly. "Why is he here?" Of course, Mother welcomed him warmly. When I left, Mother, Billie, and Kelley were sitting in the living room having a highball. Mother kissed me and said, "We'll be there in plenty of time." I believed her.

My high school graduation class had two hundred sixty-three students graduating. In our caps and gowns we were a sea of blue. Before long every seat was filled in the large Savannah High auditorium. On the stage the seniors, in alphabetical order, stood on risers. Because I was a Clary, I was on the front row.

At last it was time for the graduation ceremonies to begin. The heavy velvet curtains were opened. The audience rose and applauded enthusiastically. My eyes searched for my family, but I couldn't see them. I thought maybe they were in the back row or even in the balcony. One by one we received our diplomas; and finally, it was over. We tossed our mortar boards into the air, laughing and hugging each other. Parents with proud looks embraced their sons and daughters. There was pandemonium, but for me there was no one. I stood alone. I smiled, even though I wanted to cry. Maybe Mother, Aunt Billie and Kelley were still in the balcony, but I lost hope as the auditorium began to clear. I stood like a stone statue. Then, I felt loving arms around me. It was Sidney and his parents. Sidney said, "I'll come over to your house as soon as I take my folks home." I nodded and left.

When I arrived home, the lights were burning brightly. Mother, Kelley, and Aunt Billie were seated at the breakfast room table. Their empty dinner plates were in front of them. They were smoking and laughing. As I walked into the room, there was silence. The realization struck them that they had missed my graduation. Mother jumped up and threw her arms around me crying, "I'm so sorry Bettye Lorraine. How could this have happened? The time just got away from us."

I turned and without a word went to the phone and called Sidney. I told him I couldn't go to the graduation party. He pleaded with me. Then he understood. My heart was too heavy.

I went to my room and slowly undressed. Then, throwing myself on the bed, I began blaming Kelley. "Why had he invaded my life?" I wanted my father. He had been my best friend, but he was gone. This was supposed to be my big day. Twelve years of school completed, but who cared? I buried my face in my pillow. Tears finally came, and I cried myself to sleep.

Things are supposed to look brighter in the morning light. They didn't. Then I heard a faint rap on the door, and Mother and Aunt Billie poked their heads into my room. They looked terrible. It had not been a good night for anyone.

Mother began by apologizing. "How could I have hurt you like that? I love you more than anything in the world."

I could see the pain on her face. Then she went on, "Billie and I have been talking. We wonder if you'd like to go home with her for a visit."

I nodded my head yes. It seemed like a good idea. We began making plans. A few days later, Mother drove Aunt Billie and me to the train station to board the Silver Meteor to Orlando, Florida. We purchased our tickets, and Mother got a pass to go through the gate with us. Trains in Savannah didn't just pull in; they backed into the terminal on West Broad Street. It was fun watching the giant train hissing white steam as it slowly backed into the station. When the train stopped, the conductor jumped down and placed a step stool for passengers to use as they stepped on board. He smiled as he assisted passengers.

A few moments before we left, Mother put her arms around me. With a quiver in her voice she said, "I can't bear for you to go away angry. I'm sorry. Can you forgive me?"

We were instantly in each others arms sobbing. We kissed. It seemed like a million-pound weight had been removed from my heart. All too quickly, the conductor cried, "All aboard!" And Aunt Billie and I were on our way. Smiling, I waved to Mother as the train pulled out of the station.

Chapter Twelve
Orlando - A Visit with Aunt Billie

In Orlando, Aunt Billie and I quickly settled into a routine with Uncle Stanley leaving early in the morning to open his business, a fabric and drapery store. Business was prosperous, as many women were making their own clothes because of the war.

Aunt Billie and I were happy to be lazy for a while. The days were hot. How grateful we were for afternoon showers that brought a short respite from the heat! I loved to lie on a couch, a fan circulating the air, and read historical novels or take walks to the near-by lake.

One day when Danny's daily letter arrived, I yelled to Billie that I was going down to the lake. Sitting on a bench, I tore into the letter. As usual, Danny wrote in detail about his training, poking fun at the regimentation, and the stress that he was under and reassured me of his love. But the last part of his letter was different. It was an invitation to his graduation from flight school. At his graduation he would receive his commission and his bombardier's wings. He wanted me to come to Midland, Texas, and pin his wings on him. I was thrilled. I sat there reading and rereading his letter.

I raced home to share the letter with Aunt Billie. That night I called Mother to ask if I could go to Texas. There was silence for a few minutes. Then she said, "Bettye Lorraine, I realize how much you would like to go, but it just isn't possible. It's a long trip for a young girl alone. I would worry."

I knew she was right. Travel was difficult with the steady movement of troops, but that didn't take away the disappointment. I tried hard not to mope. I was sick of the war. Then too, I was afraid. Where would Danny be sent after graduation?

Aunt Billie and I became close friends while I was in Orlando. We talked for hours. It was like a spigot had been opened. I had someone to listen to me and I took advantage of it.

Aunt Billie asked me about my plans for the future. I told her I wanted to attend Armstrong Junior College in Savannah. She had other ideas. She suggested we take a tour of Rollins College which was located in nearby Winter Park, Florida. Rollins was not large, but it was a beautiful college situated on Lake Virginia. There were tall palm trees and huge live oaks covered with moss which provided a shady, peaceful campus.

Aunt Billie urged me to apply. I did, never dreaming that I would be admitted, but within a few weeks, I received an acceptance letter.

During that summer Aunt Billie became just Billie, my best buddy. I was intrigued by her many talents, interests and concern for others. She loved to socialize and have a good time, but she was also giving and generous. She opened her house for the military and served delicious dinners. She aided the war effort by working at the hospital. She took art lessons and painted, but her greatest talent was attracting people.

Wherever Billie went, there was always excitement and fun. She was an expert seamstress. We scanned fashion magazines and shopped for material for my college wardrobe. One day while we were shopping, we stopped at a street crossing. As Billie stepped down from the curb, the button at the waist of her under panties came loose causing them to slide down to her ankles. Without blinking an eye, she stepped out of them, left them lying on the street and continued on our way. We giggled all the way down the street. Panties with buttons instead of elastic were one of the sacrifices made during World War II. The elastic was needed for the war effort. Women like Billie took it in stride and went on their way, never complaining.

Another afternoon, we stopped at Uncle Stanley's store. He laughed as we tried to juggle all our packages. "How would you two like for me to take you to dinner?"

In unison, we answered, "Yes!"

We left the store and stopped at a downtown supper club. The room was crowded, but we found a table beside the small dance floor. A three piece band belted out the latest songs. I thought the club was glamorous and exciting. As we sat there laughing and talking, I was surprised when a young air force captain came to our table and spoke to Uncle Stanley. He asked if he might have the pleasure of dancing with his daughter. Uncle Stanley liked his polite manners and gave his permission explaining that I was his niece. I was delighted. My foot had been tapping under the table as the band played Glenn Miller's, "In the Mood."

After several dances, we walked back to the table where Uncle Stanley asked him to join us. The captain seemed grateful for the invitation. We were all aware of the loneliness that plagued the military. Being away from friends and family was no fun.

The captain's name was Jerry. He was assigned to the Adjutant General's Office at the Orlando Air Base. Before we left that night, I agreed that he could call me.

Shortly after that, we were dating several nights a week. We went to the Officer's Club, to concerts, and plays. Occasionally, Billie would invite him to have a home-cooked meal with us.

It turned out to be a good summer for me, but by August I was ready to see Mother. I wanted some time with her before I had to leave again to go to Rollins in the fall.

Chapter Thirteen
Rollins College

When I arrived at Rollins my freshman year, it was a bee hive of activity. Parents and students were frantically unpacking cars. They were moving their belongings into Cloverleaf, the three story freshman dorm. The front was graced with a splendid veranda with white pillars. It was named Cloverleaf because it had three wings that jutted out behind the veranda. Cloverleaf had an air of elegance and mystery. I wondered what secrets it would impart to me.

Billie and I carried my suitcases up the three flights of stairs to my room. I felt like I was in a castle. My room had floor-to-ceiling windows which offered a captivating view of Florida's blue skies and Lake Virginia. I placed my suitcases on the single bed. Billie sat down at the desk and rested. I walked across the hall and found a communal bath and shower room. I thought I was lucky to be so close to it.

All freshmen had received a notice to gather at five o'clock p.m. for our first dorm meeting. I said goodbye to Billie and thanked her for getting me settled. Then I quickly made my way down the stairs to a large parlor and found it filled with excited girls. Everyone seemed friendly and eager to meet and mingle. It was then that I met my suitemate, Gini Vose from Lowell and Marblehead, Massachusetts.

With a laugh and a twinkle in her eye, Gini said, "My name is spelled Gin with an "I" at the end."

I was mesmerized by Gini. She was pretty and sophisticated.

Just then a lovely, silver-haired lady walked into the room. She wore a blue dress with a white lace collar anchored by a diamond bar pin. Immediately, the room was quiet, and we all rose to our feet. She introduced herself as Mrs. Wilcox, our house mother. She welcomed us to our dorm and went over the house rules with us.

A few of the rules were: We must wear dresses for dinner at night. We must observe curfew hours which consisted of being in every night by ten o'clock p.m. except Saturday nights when we could come in at eleven. We were granted one extra hour a week which we could use at our own discretion.

Mrs. Wilcox continued, "Now, let's get to know each other. Please stand and give your name, city, and home state."

One by one, the girls introduced themselves. They all seemed confident and poised. I was surprised to learn that most of them were from northern states. When it was my turn, my heart pounded and my face flushed, but I managed to say, in my thick southern accent, "I am Bettye Lorraine Clary from Savannah, George-gah."

With a chuckle, Gini said, "From now on, your name is Georgia." And it was. There was one other southern girl there. She was from Alabama. She became known as "Bama."

We moved into our daily routine, and I was very happy. I thought everything about Rollins was perfect. My classes went well and I never tired of walking around the lovely campus. It was a mixture of old and new. Most of the buildings were of Spanish architecture, soft, off-white stucco buildings with red tile roofs. The buildings were connected by loggias.

There were few men on campus because of the war. The ones there had a military draft classification of 4F (which meant they were ruled physically unfit for the military). The others were part of a select group of soldiers known as the A.S.T.P, Army Specialized Training Program and were quartered in fraternity houses on campus. They were part of the college, yet they were separate from the rest of the students. They marched past Cloverleaf early each morning, loudly singing, "Good morning to you, good morning to you, good morning dear girlies—get it out of bed."   They were specialists on their way to war. We never got to know them.

Gini Vose became my best friend, even though we were complete opposites. Gini was highly intelligent, cultured, tall, slim and flat chested. I, on the other hand, was an average student, short, big bosomed, and had an hour-glass figure. Gini sounded like Boston, and I sounded like a character out of *Gone with the Wind.*   Gini had many talents which included being an accomplished artist. She had a throaty laugh and was full of mischief.

We had fun together and became lifelong friends. I think the main reason for our long friendship was that we needed each other, helped each other, and were loyal to each other. Shortly after I met Gini, I learned that she was admitted to Rollins at age sixteen because of her high IQ. Underneath her confident outer appearance, I think she was a little frightened, and she often made bad decisions. I had common sense, born of a few hard knocks in life, and after all, I was eighteen, two years older. Together we made a good pair.

Rollins was known as a party school, and Rollins girls were in great demand.   Even though there were few men on campus, there was AFTC, Armed Forces Tactical Center in Orlando and the Naval Air Station in Sanford.

Because my days were crammed full, I kept my mind off things at home. I enjoyed sorority rushing. There was one party after another. Gini and I pledged Alpha Phi. The sorority girls were wonderful. They seemed to take us under their wings. We looked forward to moving into the sorority house the next year.

I still dated Jerry from the Orlando Air Base. For me, it was a comfortable relationship. He knew I was in love with Danny and was receiving his letters regularly, so it came as a shock to me when one night he hemmed and hawed and then blurted out, "I'm in love with you. Will you marry me?"

I was stunned! He had told me he had a girlfriend back home. I sat there, not knowing what to say. Finally, I said, "Thank you for your proposal, but I can't marry you."

He blurted out, "It isn't because you don't love me. It's because I'm a Jew."

"That's not true. It's because I only want to be your friend. You know I have a serious boyfriend."

He snarled, "So you want to be friends. All right, you get me a date with a Jewess, and I'll get you a date with a Gentile."

By this time, I was angry. "Fine! Would Saturday night be okay?"

He nodded and walked me to the door of Cloverleaf. Without another word I went inside.

******

If Jerry wanted to date a Jewess, I knew just the right one for him. She lived down the hall from me. She was lovely.

When Saturday night arrived, we waited in my room until we heard a message over the intercom, "Georgia, Jerry is here."

I turned to Jerry's blind date who was feeling a bit apprehensive and smiled. "Here we go!"

When we arrived in the parlor, I introduced her to Jerry. I looked around for my date. There wasn't anyone else there. What a dirty rotten trick! He just wanted to spoil my Saturday night. "Have a wonderful time you two," I said. Then I turned to leave the room.

"Georgia, wait a minute." Jerry said, "Don't you want to meet your date? He's in the car."

Oh no, I groaned to myself. My date's so bad he doesn't know enough to come in. We walked to the car and sure enough there was a man sitting in the back seat. To his credit, he did get out as we approached. (Later I learned that Jerry, as a senior officer, had told Ollie to wait in the car). I was surprised to see that he was quite nice looking, a second lieutenant, and very polite. Jerry hustled us into the car saying that we were going to the Flamingo, a swanky supper club.

During the course of the evening, I found out that my date was from Dover, Ohio. He said that his name was Oliver Ralph Toomey, but everyone called him Ollie. "My parents wanted to name me Ralph Oliver Toomey, but my initials would have been ROT," he joked.

Ollie was not much taller than I was. His most distinctive feature was a strong chin that jutted out. His dark brown hair was closely cropped, and I thought he was cute. We found much to talk about which didn't seem to please the captain. Ollie was a good dancer, and we both liked to jitterbug. Jerry eyed us with a scowl on his face.

Finally, Jerry asked me to dance. Once on the dance floor, he scolded me. "You don't have to act like you're having such a good time."

I laughed. "Well, I am having a good time." I had learned in moments of stress to either laugh or cry.

When I got back to the dorm, Gini was still up, waiting to ask me how my date was. My reply came out so quickly it surprised me. "Oh, he was all right. What's strange though is I have a horrible feeling that I'll end up marrying him." I don't know what made me say that. He was just another soldier and a nice date. After Gini left, I settled down to write my nightly letter to Danny.

Several nights later Ollie called and invited me to a movie. That evening I found out he had graduated in 1941 from Colgate University in upper New York State. Then he was drafted into the Air Corps as a buck private. Later, though, he went to OCS and received his commission as a second lieutenant. He was six years older than I was and joked about robbing the cradle. Maybe being older made him different. I don't know, but whatever it was I liked it. His manners were perfect. He wasn't pushy in any way and even went to the library with me when I had to study.

The more I saw Ollie the more impressed I was with his thoughtfulness. I mentioned I could hardly speak into the phone that served the second and third floors of Cloverleaf because it was mounted so high on the wall. Shortly after that, he brought me a present. It was a box that had a pull out step I could stand on and speak directly into the phone. The box was stained a nice wood tone. On top, in bold black letters, was one word—Georgia. I loved it, and so did the other Cloverleaf girls.

Then there was the night we went to the Coliseum. Before the big dance started, the Air Corps band played "The Star Spangled Banner." Everyone sang. Goose bumps ran up and down my spine as I looked at Ollie and all the men in uniforms singing in their strong male voices. Surely with all our fine servicemen we would win the war.

That same night I lost one of my favorite earrings. It was green crystal. Ollie looked under the table for the tiny object but didn't find it. He asked me if he could have the one I still had. I forgot about it until several nights later when he appeared at Rollins with a small gift wrapped box. When I opened it, there was a pair of earrings exactly like the one I lost. He later confessed that he had searched all over town to find matching earrings. He made me feel special.

Chapter Fourteen
My Worst Nightmare

Life was going well for me socially at Rollins, but I faced challenges in my school life and home life.

My major was theatre arts. In speech class my professor informed me I had to lose my southern accent. He might as well have asked me to stop breathing. That would have been easier, but I had to do it to pass. I struggled until finally I realized I had a habit of going up at the end of sentences in a sing-song manner. Our textbook discussed this problem. I read every word over and over. Then I practiced until I acquired a generic accent which was the goal for the theater.

One day I was in front of my speech class proudly reading, minus my southern accent, when the classroom phone (which was only used for emergencies) rang. Professor Allen answered and handed the phone to me. I walked to his desk and nervously said, "Hello."

I was not at all prepared for what I heard. My mother said, "Bettye Lorraine, I have some wonderful news." Her voice sounded light and airy, not at all like an emergency. "Kelley and I were married last night." I couldn't move. I was a statue; only statues don't have tears sliding down their faces. I never believed she would marry him. My worst nightmare had come true.

Everyone was staring at me sensing my tension. Somehow, I uttered a few sentences of congratulations to Mother and said I would call later. As I hung up, Professor Allen looked at his watch and said, "Class, that's all for today." I thought, God bless Professor Allen.

I ran to my room, closed the door and cried.

When Christmas vacation came, everyone was excited about going home for the holidays. I tried to pretend I was too, but it was no use. I wanted to see my mother. I did not want to see Kelley, but the first sight I saw when the train backed into Savannah was Kelley waving his hands with Mother beside him.

I embraced Mother, and we made our way to the car. Driving home I realized I may not have missed Kelley, but I had missed my beloved Savannah. I was met at the front door by Alma smiling and saying "Christmas gift," the traditional greeting of black Savannahians. I was home.

We celebrated Christmas in our usual way. Mother had open house that afternoon and served her special egg nog. The only difference was there were few of our old friends. Most of the people were Kelley's friends, and there was no Sidney. He had enlisted in the Air Force and was in flight school.

How I missed him and my aunts and uncles who weren't with us this year! To make matters worse, Kelley was drinking far too much.

After everyone left the open house, Alma announced dinner was ready. Kelley walked into the dining room with my father's smoking jacket on. I was in shock! It was the most insensitive act I had ever witnessed. Kelley had come into my father's home with only a suitcase. Now he was head of the household and Daddy's drugstores. I'll never know how I managed to sit there. I ate, but I tasted nothing.

That night my mother and I had the biggest argument of our lives. I cried. She cried. We broke a family rule—never go to bed angry with anyone. I cried myself to sleep.

The next morning when I woke up someone was shaking me, but I didn't want to wake up. Mother said, "Wake up! Don't be sad. There's someone here to see you." She opened my bedroom door and there stood Danny in the hall. My eyes were red and puffy. I didn't care. I dressed as quickly as I could and ran into the breakfast room where Danny and Mother were having coffee. Thank goodness, Kelley had left early to open Clary's.

This was the first time I had seen Danny in his officer's uniform. He was handsome with his bombardier wings shining on his chest. He explained to us he had a furlough and he wanted to see his family and me before he was sent overseas. He felt sure he would be sent to the European theater.

"I just had to come and deliver my Christmas gift," he said. It was a huge bottle of Prince Matchabelli perfume. I immediately put some on, but Danny was my real Christmas gift.

It was an absolutely perfect day. It was hard to believe it was December. We filled every moment of the day. The beach seemed to be calling us, so we drove to Tybee and parked there and looked out at the ocean. The beach was virtually abandoned except for the noisy sea gulls, circling and searching for food. We walked the beach. Danny and I talked and talked. Then we sat quietly watching the crashing white-crested waves. I'm sure that we were both thinking about the fact that soon he would be crossing that huge, gray sea.

I wanted Danny to have happy memories to take away. I suggested that we go home, get cleaned up and go to a late movie, then have supper in a downtown restaurant.

I didn't know a thing going on in the movie. I was afraid for him, but I tried to laugh in the right places. When the movie ended, we went to a small café off Wright's Square on Bull Street. The place was crowded, but we found a booth. As we finished our supper, a loud wailing siren went off. Savannah was in complete darkness. It was scary. There had been rumors that German submarines were off the coast of Savannah. Everyone became quiet.

Danny put his arm around me. We hung on to each other, not speaking a word. After what seemed like an eternity, the all-clear signal sounded. The lights came on. We blinked our eyes, and everyone breathed a sigh of relief and applauded.

Finally, it was time for us to go home and say one more goodbye. We both knew in our hearts that this could be the end of what might have been. In my mind I kept hearing a line from a song:
For all we know we may never meet again.

******

After Christmas I returned to Rollins and soon became so involved in school activities that I had little time for my thoughts to linger on Danny.

I was never very athletic, but at Rollins, we were required to participate in some form of physical fitness. I decided on golf. This turned out to be a poor choice because I didn't like being in the sun, and I couldn't hit the ball very far. The one good thing was that the pro had a sense of humor. He said, "You have a great swing. Your form looks wonderful. I just don't understand why you have no distance." He would leave my partner and me with a bucket of balls and tell us to practice.

My partner was just as bad at golf as I was, so we both hated the game. We devised a plan. After the pro left, we took the buckets of balls and walked down the fairway scattering the balls, leaving us free to sit under a palm tree. After awhile the pro would return. He seemed pleased at our efforts. We chuckled to ourselves and kept our secret, but we were glad when the course ended.

My next attempt at athletics was more successful. I tried horseback riding and loved it, even excelled in it. To my utter delight, Ollie told me he enjoyed it too. He said his father had Tennessee walking horses, and he had been riding all his life. We seemed to keep finding things that we both enjoyed. Occasionally we rode together on weekends.

Gini had suffered rheumatic fever as a child and was excused from all physical activities. Some may say she was lucky, but it turned out to be unfortunate for her. It gave her free time that she did not always use wisely. Once after a glorious afternoon of riding, I came back to my room and still in my jodhpurs, started studying. Suddenly, a breathless, white-faced Gini rushed into the room.

Gini wailed, "Oh, Georgia, I'm in trouble. I went to Harper's Bar with several girls. We all had rum and Coke. On the way back, I was walking along the side of the road, still sipping my drink when a car started to pass us.

Right at that time I got an insane desire to throw the glass into the street. Suddenly, we heard a loud crunch. The car ran over the glass and a tire blew. The driver jumped out of the car and started yelling and chasing us. He chased us onto the campus but didn't catch us. The last thing we saw was him heading toward the dean's office."

About that time, a girl stuck her head in my room and said, "The dean is on the warpath. She's checking every girl at Cloverleaf to see if she's been off campus drinking."

I thought what Gini had done was awful. Due to the shortage of rubber, tires could not be replaced. All a person could do was patch and patch a tire as long as possible. But even though I didn't approve of what Gini had done, she was my friend. I couldn't let her be caught and sent home. I said, "Gini, go jump in the shower and pour shampoo on your hair." She followed my command.

I settled down with my book and tried to look peaceful. Dean Cleveland who had a tall, imposing figure walked into my room. Immediately, I stood up. She said, "Georgia, where is your suitemate, Gini?"

I calmly looked up and said, "She's washing her hair."

The dean went into the bathroom and saw Gini with suds all over her head. Dean Cleveland left.

Shortly, Gini came into my room and collapsed on my bed. "Georgia, I've never been so scared in my life. If Mother knew, she would kill me!"

I would not have blamed her mother, but I didn't tell Gini that.

We survived Gini's mischievous exploit, but more trouble followed. The third floor of Cloverleaf had a wide ledge outside our ceiling-to-floor windows. Springtime was the mating season for the many pigeons that graced Rollins. The third-floor wide ledges were so attractive to them they built nests there. They cooed and laid tiny eggs. We thought this was exciting and enjoyed watching their daily activity.

How could we know that our innocent pigeon watching would cause us so much pain? It began with itching, and several of us went to the school nurse to get relief. We were horrified when she determined that the cause of our itching was lice. She examined all of the third-floor girls and said lice were everywhere. We were the laughingstock of the campus. She gave us bars of Octagon soap with instructions to bathe all over and wash our hair twice a day. This was humiliating. Everything in our rooms was scrubbed and sprayed. My enchantment with pigeons was over forever.

I was thankful when we were declared lice free, and we could turn our attention elsewhere. For me, that was the theater. I loved it and was fortunate enough to get a part in a major Rollins production. My character was not southern. Hoorah! I was not typecast. Rehearsals were every night for three weeks. They were intense and kept me busy.

The play ran for three nights. Ollie came to every performance and cheered me on. When the final curtain went down, I received a bouquet of red roses from him, but the biggest surprise of the night was when my mother came backstage.

The following night Ollie took all of my family to the Officer's Club. This man certainly knew how to treat a girl!

Shortly after the play, Ollie received orders to go to Dalhart, Texas. At first we wrote regularly, but gradually I was so caught up in college life that our correspondence stopped. I hardly realized it at the time.

Chapter Fifteen
New England Bound

I loved life at Rollins. Unlike some of the girls there, I was not anxious for the spring semester to end, but Gini changed that feeling when she rushed into my room waving a letter from her mother. "Georgia, Mother has told me to invite you to come home with me." Then she paused a few minutes. "For the whole summer. If you say yes, she will write your mother."

I was overwhelmed with joy. This was an answer to my prayers. I wouldn't have to spend my vacation with "Bad Boy Kelley." I jumped up and threw my arms around Gini saying, "Yes, yes, yes!"

Mother gave her permission, and Billie was almost as excited as I was. She took me shopping and helped me get ready for my visit to Massachusetts. I had never been to the northern part of the U. S. except once when I went to Washington, D.C. with Roy and his family (my upstairs neighbors in Savannah).

Finally, the day arrived for our trip North. We began with a visit to New York City. We rode the train, and as it clickety-clacked along the tracks, I had to pinch myself. I couldn't believe this was really happening to me. My family had never traveled anywhere except Florida. As soon as the train pulled into Penn Station, Gini took charge. She had been to New York many times. I marveled at the way she handled our luggage, hailed a cab and whisked us away to the Barbizon, a hotel for women only. Gini's mother said it was her treat.

Gini was determined I was going to see as much as possible of New York. We took a city tour, visited museums, and saw the Empire State Building. We boarded a ferry to view the Statue of Liberty in her glory. I felt like dancing a time step and singing, *East Side West Side All Around the Town.* We ate at Schraff's, which was like a ladies' tea room. The waitresses wore frilly uniforms. It was famous for its sweets and candy. But my greatest thrill was seeing the precision, high-kicking dancing of the Rockettes.

My head stayed in a whirl as the two of us toured the city, but all too soon it was time to leave for Boston. Gini's mother met us at the train station. She welcomed me warmly and then hustled us into the car. I climbed in the back seat and sat quietly enjoying the camaraderie between Gini and her mother. I liked listening to their precise New England accent.

When we arrived in Lowell, Massachusetts, Mrs. Vose turned into the driveway of a large Victorian home. As we entered the house, we were met by

Gini's cat, Snookie. Gini swooped the purring cat up into her arms and whispered, "I'm home."

Mrs. Vose said, in her commanding voice, "Girls, go upstairs and unpack. I'll have dinner ready shortly." We obeyed.

Mrs. Vose set a lovely table and served lamb chops, baked potatoes, green beans and salad. The dessert was a first for me, meringues with vanilla ice cream in the center and hot chocolate sauce on top. Everything was so different from my home. It was a culture shock.

After dinner we settled down in the living room with our coffee and chatted. The furniture was antique Victorian except for one small rocker that became my chair. Mrs. Vose wanted to hear all about school and New York, but more importantly, she was ready to plan the rest of our summer vacation. "For the next several days, we will take Georgia sightseeing. We must introduce her to our heritage, first Boston and then Marblehead."

Looking at me, Mrs. Vose said, "Georgia, we have a house at Marblehead, but I'm sorry to say it is rented for the summer. It was built so long ago it has pegs instead of nails. It was a seafaring captain's house and has a widow's walk on top where the captain could use his spy glass to observe ships at sea. We will drive by it on our visit to Marblehead."

Then turning to Gini, Mrs. Vose said, "Now for the big news. I was afraid you might become bored in this musty old house, so I have rented a tiny place for you in Ogunquit, Maine. I think you'll enjoy it and find it amusing."

Gini leaped to her feet and threw her arms around her mother. "Oh, thank you, Mother. You know how much I love Maine, and it will be a grand place to paint."

Her mother brushed her aside. "Now I must get to know my new daughter."

My heart jumped with joy. When Mother married Kelley, I felt like I had lost my mother. Mrs. Vose and I talked until midnight. When she saw me yawning, she said goodnight. Gini and I climbed the stairs to our rooms.

Once in bed, I reviewed all that had happened to me since we left Rollins. I was enthralled with Mrs. Vose. She was a handsome, fair skinned blonde woman who gave the appearance of sternness, but she had a loving heart. It was easy to see she was disciplined in her life and in her planning for those she loved. She became a second mother to me—my beloved Mum Vose.

******

Even though Mum Vose said that we would find Ogunquit enjoyable, I still had no idea what was awaiting us. But one thing we could count on was

63

that she would see we were prepared for anything. As we kept loading the car, I thought, "We're going to look like gypsies riding down the road."

Mum Vose said, "It's better to be prepared, to have too much than too little. The two of you will be on your own. I have a busy schedule and will only be able to come occasionally." Then she chuckled, "to check up on you."

As we stuffed the car with an ironing board, iron, a small scrub board, a radio, lamps, sheets, towels, pillows, canned goods, and suitcases, I wondered if there would be room for Gini and me. And then there was Snookie. Mum Vose was a cat person and would not leave him behind.

Snookie roamed the car as we rode to Ogunquit. Thank goodness the trip was fairly short, about sixty miles from Boston. On the drive Mum Vose told us Ogunquit was called "beautiful place by the sea" because of its beautiful sandy beaches, and it had been attracting tourists since the 1920s. It also attracted artists who came to paint scenes of the unspoiled beaches and the fishing village of Perkins Cove.

Once we arrived in the tiny village, we turned down a dirt road which eventually came to a dead end. We were at a point high above the sea. A weather beaten shack stood on the right. It was painted sky blue. Mum Vose unlocked the door and informed us that it had been a fisherman's shack which had been converted into an artist's studio.

As we walked through the door, we could see the whole house. On the left side of the one room shack the entire wall had been replaced with one gigantic window. Double studio beds flanked the window. Opposite the entrance was a door which led to a tiny porch hanging high above the rocks. If you dropped something, it would fall into the sea below. To the right of the porch door were a table and chairs with a brightly painted screen hiding our tiny kitchen. Our primitive bath was like a closet. There was no hot water, but Gini and I thought it was all grand.

After unpacking, we drove to town. I was surprised there were so few people. Mum Vose explained that it was just a small fishing village except when the summer people arrived. Then the huge hotels, shops and restaurants would come to life. That was hard to believe because it looked mighty dead to me. Gini assured me that it would be quite different when the season opened.

Mum Vose stayed with us several days, giving us enough instructions to last a lifetime. Then she and Snookie left, and Gini and I were finally on our own. After a week of idyllic life, Gini and I became bored. We walked the Marginal Way which is a path that goes across the top of the cliff, looking down on the ocean. The surf swirls and crashes on the rocks below, resembling a Winslow Homer painting. Gini and I talked, rested and dreamed as only young women can. The solitude and beauty kept bringing Ollie to my mind. I wished that he was there.

At the end of the week we decided our rest was over, and it was time to get jobs. We had heard that waiting on tables was very lucrative when the summer people arrived. Little did we know that these jobs were spoken for a year or two in advance.

We set out on our job search with high hopes, only to be turned away at every place. As we walked home, we took a shortcut and spotted a striking sight. Perched high on a hill overlooking a colorful garden which sloped down to a glistening blue cove sat a Chinese pagoda. It was a tea room, and its name was *Dan Sing Fan.* We looked at each other and said, "Let's give it one last try."

As we walked up to the *Fan,* the proprietor met us at the door with a questioning look on his face. Mr. Coolidge was a tall aristocratic man. We told him that we would like to apply for jobs as waitresses. Looking us up and down in a snobbish manner he began questioning us. "Do you attend college?"

When we nodded yes, he asked us where.

Rollins seemed to pique his attention. He said, "We cater to a very select clientele. I have hired only male students in the past, but because of the war, I now hire young ladies. We talked for awhile, then abruptly, he said, "I only have an opening for one of you." Gini and I were of one accord and said, "No, but thank you anyway."

That night there was a violent rainstorm. We had just gotten settled in our snug shack when suddenly there was a knock on our door. "Who could that be?" I asked. "We don't know anyone here."

We cracked the door open, and there stood a rain-soaked Mr. Coolidge. We invited him inside, but he refused. Standing there in his yellow rain slicker he said, "I've thought it over, and I like the fact that you are loyal to each other. The jobs are yours, if you want them."

We didn't have to think it over. We said, "Yes."

Mr. Coolidge told us we should report the next morning at ten o'clock for training. With that, he quickly dashed to his Cadillac convertible.

When morning came, the sun was shining as we walked to our first day of work. We learned many new things that day. Our first chore was to go into the garden and cut fresh flowers for table arrangements.

I was surprised at the layout of the *Fan.* To enter the tearoom guests had to pass through a well stocked gift shop filled with exquisite items. From there the hostess led them to their tables. The whole dining room was one long tier-covered porch which overlooked the garden and the water. We were given black skirts, white blouses and white aprons to wear.

The hostess, who also ran the gift shop, seemed to like us. She filled us in on the history and gossip of the *Fan.* She confided, "Mr. Coolidge is quite rich, and his romantic preference runs to men. His partner, Luige, is in the military. The *Dan Sing Fan* is Mr. Coolidge's hobby. It is only open two months out of the year. The rest of the time, he and Luige travel abroad buying gifts for the shop and enjoying life. Mr. Coolidge is very sad without Luige."

Then she gave us instructions on how to set the tables. She told us Mr. Coolidge was very particular about the settings and the clientele. "We only accept reservations for lunch, and they have to be approved by Mr. Coolidge. Tea time at four o'clock is open to the public."

Next we were taken to the kitchen. To our astonishment, the chef was Mr. Coolidge. He was fanatical about his food. It had to be delicious, different and most of all beautiful. He delighted in everything that he cooked. Two of his specialties were puzzle cake and harem cake. The puzzle cake was painstakingly made by baking a white sheet cake, cutting it into precisely cut strips, and then putting the strips into loaf pans. The first layer of strips went in one direction. Next, the specially made rich chocolate icing was poured over them. Then another layer of cake strips was placed crosswise, more chocolate, and the process was repeated until the loaf pans were filled. Finally, the cakes were refrigerated. When it was time to serve them, they were removed from the pans and cut into divine checker board slices of cake. The harem cake was spice cake with tart lemon icing.

We learned a few of Mr. Coolidge's cooking secrets. His jellied consommé was straight out of a Campbell's soup can, but everyone raved about it because of the way it was presented. He put it in a wide mouth stemmed goblet filled with ice. There was a small cup in the center of the goblet filled with consommé and a slice of lemon and a sprig of mint.

Helen was the only other waitress. She came from New York. Her family had been coming to Ogunquit for many years. She was a pretty blonde with large, wide blue eyes who had a passion for the music of the black singer Cab Callaway. She was fun, and by the end of the summer Gini and I adored her.

The opening of the tea room was the next weekend. We were nervous about it, but events went well. After serving the midday crowd, we had our lunch and a rest period before serving high tea at four o'clock.

The tea room was closed on Mondays, and we were off each day after high tea. On the days we worked, we ate Mr. Coolidge's gourmet food, which was quite a change from college beanery food. It was a very satisfying arrangement.

The only person upset with our waiting on tables was my mother. When I called to tell her, she said, "Bettye Lorraine, it just isn't done by well brought-up young ladies."

"Mother you don't understand," I said. "Gini's mother approves, and I know Gini had a good upbringing."

Finally, Mother relented and said, "If you say so, just keep me posted on how you get along."

Gini and I were serious about our jobs, but we still found time for social life, especially after we met two young naval officers. They had been stationed in Sanford, Florida, right out of Orlando. They and several other officers had rented a cottage in Ogunquit and drove back and forth to their Naval Air Station nearby. They were having the time of their lives. There were few eligible bachelors, and the girls went flippy over the flyers. That was old hat to us.

One night the flyers were bragging about some girls they had dated who came in every morning after they left for work. The girls made their beds, emptied their trash, washed their dishes, and thoroughly cleaned their cottage. Gini and I thought this was ridiculous, so we came up with a plan to sabotage their subservient actions. We got up very early one morning, put scarves around our heads, and donned dark glasses. Then we made our way to a secluded spot near their cottage. As soon as we saw the men leave, we rushed to their place. Opening the door, we couldn't believe the mess that we saw. Undaunted, we set to work. First, we short sheeted the beds, dumped the salt shakers and sugar bowls, exchanging salt for sugar and sugar for salt. We howled as we quickly did dishes, hung up clothes, and cleaned. I knew it was immature, but once we started, there was no stopping. I knew Ollie would never be like the men that lived in the cottage. I wondered where Ollie was.

On the way out we took the trash which included beer bottles galore. We couldn't stop laughing on the way home. They never had a clue that we were the guilty parties who scuttled their house.

We continued to date the naval officers occasionally throughout the season, but most of our life revolved around working at the Fan. The owner, Mr. Coolidge, was a somber man who seldom laughed. The first time I saw him laugh was the day I had my big accident. There were two swinging doors going into the kitchen, one for going in and one for coming out. After a bit of practice, I learned to gauge my steps and kick the door open without missing a beat. It was ballet in action. I was very good at it, or so I thought, until one day during a busy lunch hour when I started through the door with a tray full of dirty dishes. Helen had just gone into the kitchen before me and dropped a lettuce leaf coated with oil and vinegar. As I kicked the in door, my other foot hit the lettuce. I let out a scream. The tray and dishes went up in the air and came down all around me as I lay on the floor.

Mr. Coolidge saw me and laughed hysterically, tears running down his face, as he raced to pick me up. "Georgia, are you hurt?" I shook my head no. He picked me up, put his arms around me, and it was then that we became friends.

Often when we had time off, Gini would rest and I would walk the Marginal Way, stopping to sit on a bench high above the sea. I thought about my mother and how I missed her. I looked forward to her letters. I wondered how she was handling Kelley with his drinking and gambling, but she never complained.

I also thought about Ollie. Why didn't I keep up with him? I knew that he loved me, and I was sorry I was too scatterbrained at the time to realize he was all I could ever want. He was my first real, mature, grown-up love. What could I do about it? Then I remembered he had talked about his family in Dover, Ohio. His father ran the S. Toomey Company, a Dodge/Plymouth agency. I decided to write to Mr. Toomey and ask for Ollie's address. Then I turned my attention to my job.

The Dan Sing Fan was an exciting place to work. One day Madame Chiang Kai-Shek and her entourage came for tea. They sat at one of Helen's tables. Madame Chiang gave Helen a small satin bag containing her own special tea. She asked to have it brewed and served with her order. Helen was excited as she raced into the kitchen to give us an eye witness account of Madame Chiang. Without thinking, Helen put the tea down, and the young man washing dishes scraped it into a huge pail of garbage. When Helen realized what had happened, she shrieked, "What am I going to do?" Dear Mr. Coolidge calmed her down and sent her out to tell Madame Chiang the whole story. In the kitchen we held our breath. Helen returned all smiles. "Madame Chiang is the most gracious lady I have ever met," she said.

As if that wasn't enough excitement for one day, Gini went to the post office and returned with a letter for me. I tore into the envelope and the first words I saw were: Dear Georgia, I am surprised and pleased that you wanted my address. I thought our relationship was over. I must confess that I was amused by Mother's letter." Later, I learned his mother had scowled at him and thought he had gotten some poor girl in trouble. He assured her that wasn't the case. This was the beginning of a lengthy period of correspondence. Letters are an excellent way to feel free to express thoughts and to come to know a person's heart and soul.

Mum Vose came up occasionally to check on Gini and me. I treasured the days we spent with her. She was interested in everything we did. She questioned me about Ollie. Finally she said, "I think I would like this young man." That pleased me.

Mum Vose took us exploring. Once we drove to Kennebunkport and had lunch in a tea room. We all agreed that it couldn't hold a candle to the Fan. Mum Vose was always amused by my southern expressions. She teased me when I said, "Wait on me."

She would ask, "Georgia, how much weight do you have on you?"

When the season came to an end, we were amazed at the gifts and huge tips that our regular customers presented to us. Mr. Coolidge gave us a substantial check and a farewell dinner at his home. We kept in touch through the years until his death in 1971.

It was with tears that we packed and said our final goodbyes. I think that during this period of my life I had finally grown up.

Mum Vose took Gini and me to Boston for one final fling. Gini and I spent almost every cent we had earned on clothes. Gini insisted that I purchase a pale pink linen dress, a color I had never been allowed to wear because of my red hair. She assured me that I looked gorgeous. The chains of my youth were being broken.

Chapter Sixteen
The Second Knowing

When I arrived back in Savannah, Mother told me that she and Kelley were both working at the Bull Street drugstore. Business was so good they were considering opening a prescription store at the shipyard. Mother said they could hardly keep enough merchandise in the stores – it seemed to fly off the shelves. She also said they were very pleased with the Abercorn drugstore. Nearby Jones Street was filled with doctors' offices, and they had hired a second pharmacist to help Dr. Caldwell. In addition, they had a motorcycle delivery service. A man had been hired to deliver prescriptions from both stores. Mother seemed quite proud of their accomplishments.

That night Mother and Kelley took me out to Johnny Harris' to celebrate my homecoming. They seemed particularly excited. I learned why when they handed me the keys to my very own car. It was a maroon 1940 two-door Mercury. I was giddy with the joy of unexpected freedom as I drove myself to Rollins for my sophomore year, but as I rode along I started thinking about my father.

I remembered begging Daddy to teach me to drive when I was fifteen years old. Finally, he agreed to give me a driving lesson. He had a 1939 black Packard coupe. It was long, low and polished with a high gloss. The front hood seemed to stretch forever. There was a tall silver ornament at the end of the hood that pointed the way for me. The car had a rumble seat and a small door on the side for newspapers and small objects. The seat in the front was low and deep. When I sat behind the wheel, I couldn't see over the front panel. I had to look through the steering wheel. I never saw the road ahead. I drove, I think, by looking at the telephone poles and the tall Georgia pines.

For my lessons Daddy took me to De Renne Avenue which was dirt and outside the city limits. I had a hard time with the gearshift that was on the floor. Sometimes it sounded like I was tearing up the engine or stripping the gears. After several lessons, though, I got the hang of it, and Daddy said I was ready for traffic.

My first lesson in driving in traffic was a trip to Fort Pulaski. Mother kissed us good-by, and I took my seat in the Packard (sitting on pillows). We proceeded down Waters Avenue to Victory Drive, a beautiful double drive with palm trees and azaleas in the median. The trees were planted to commemorate the Chatham county men who had been killed in war. Victory Drive runs into Tybee Island Road. It was only a short distance before I met the first drawbridge. Oh, how long and narrow it seemed! I clinched my teeth, pulled my shoulders in. Cars were approaching on the other side, but we made it. I couldn't believe it! Since I couldn't get a clear view of the road over the dashboard and long hood, I was certain there wasn't enough room for two cars.

After my successful crossing of the first bridge, my confidence mounted and crossing the bridges became easier. I even ventured a glance at the marsh beside us. I'm one of those rare people who love the smell of the marsh.

As we got closer to Fort Pulaski, I put my left arm out of the window to signal that I was going to make a left turn. As we pulled in front of a small building, a man came out. He directed us down a path to a dock. He told us a boat would be leaving shortly for Cockspur Island. I could hardly wait to see a real Confederate fort.

At last, we boarded the boat and made our way across the water. (Today there is a bridge to the fort.) The first sight of the fort was thrilling. There was a moat that went all around the big brick enclosure. The drawbridge was down. Excitedly, I ran across it, but as I entered the fort, a sense of gloom came over me as I thought about all the brave Confederate men who fought there.

Daddy said, "Let's do some exploring." We went up a brick staircase to the top wall. Standing topside, the soft breeze rumpled my hair. I could see Tybee Island in the distance. It was a clear day with huge, white fluffy clouds in the air. As we stood there, Daddy told me the construction of the fort began in 1829 with my hero, Robert E. Lee, in charge, and Confederate troops occupied the fort during the War Between the States. The Confederates thought the fort with its eleven-foot thick walls was impregnable, but they were wrong. Yankee troops fired new experimental cannons from their position off Tybee Island a mile away, and breached the walls. Faced with defeat, the Confederate leader surrendered the fort in April 1862.

Finally, we climbed down the dark, winding stairs. We found a huge room that had been a barracks. There were several cots and a table full of artifacts. There was more to see, but Daddy said it was time to catch the boat. I agreed with him. I didn't want to spend the night at the fort. The mosquitoes were enjoying our visit too much, and I had visions of rats coming out in the dark.

******

Upon arriving at Rollins, I went to the Alpha Phi house and met our housemother. I got the key to my mailbox. I was eager to go to the student center and check my mail. Opening the box, I found two letters, one from

Danny and one from Ollie. My heart leaped with joy. I immediately sat down under a huge Oak Tree to read my letters. I loved both men. How could that be?

When Gini arrived, I met her at the train station. I said, "Gini, close your eyes and give me your hands." I led her to the curb, then told her to open her eyes so she could see my new car which I had named Dodo.

"Oh, Georgia, we've been liberated!" she said and we had. We cruised all over southern and eastern Florida. Everything seemed perfect, but I had a foreboding feeling, a knowing that something terrible was about to happen. I was actually relieved when the radio issued warnings that a huge hurricane was due to hit our area. Preparations were in progress to batten down when the wind and rain began, a foretaste of what was to come. Classes were canceled, and we were instructed to stay inside.

It was nightfall when the Florida West-Coast Hurricane of 1944 hit in all its fury. The electricity went off, and we found ourselves in soot black darkness. Some of the girls were hysterical. I was trying to reassure them I had been through several hurricanes when we heard a pounding on the front door. Miss Apperson, our house mother, tried to calm the nervous girls. She cracked the door open. There stood a rain-drenched young man. He delivered a telegram. Miss Apperson signed for it, struggling to close the door. She cast her flashlight beam on the telegram. With surprise, she said, "Georgia, it's for you."

I had never received a telegram and took it with shaking hands. I saw the dreaded red dot on the envelope which meant it was from the War Department. I knew it was bad news. I opened the envelope and words seemed to fly off the page: *We regret to inform you that Lt. D. W. McClain is missing in action.*

I stood in the black night filled with disbelief saying, "No, No." With tears streaming down my face, Gini put her arms around me and led me to my room. I kept murmuring, "The hateful *knowing* has happened again, just like with my father."

I never knew when the hurricane hit us full force. My storm was within. Gini stayed with me through that long, sad night. When daybreak came, my tears were spent. I fell into a fitful sleep. Why couldn't men live together in peace?

When the hurricane was over, the campus looked like a battlefield. Huge trees were uprooted and debris was everywhere. We ventured outdoors, shocked with disbelief. As soon as the rain stopped, the student body began cleaning the campus. I worked with a heavy heart but life had to go on.

Amazingly, it was in sharing my grief with Ollie that I received the most comfort about Danny. Ollie's letters revealed his love and understanding.

He knew exactly what to say to me, giving me strength and courage. Slowly, I began the process of healing and was surprised and delighted when just before Christmas a letter arrived from Ollie inviting me to visit Gulfport, Mississippi, for a New Year's celebration. I showed the letter to Billie, bemoaning the fact Mother would never let me go.

Billie said, "Leave that to me, I'll handle it." She told Mother that Ollie and another officer, Andy Sackman, rented rooms from a gracious, patriotic Southern lady, Mrs. Eaton, who was going away for the month of December. Her Christmas gift to them was her whole house for the holiday season. She suggested that perhaps Andy's wife, who lived in Colorado might come and Ollie could invite his girlfriend for a few days. Billie explained to Mother that Andy and his wife, Mary, were older. They had been married for many years, so they would be perfect chaperones. Billie must have had a silver tongue because Mother agreed to let me go.

Gini was just as excited as I was and immediately went to work on my wardrobe. She had more sense of style than I did, so she insisted that I try on everything I owned. She mixed and matched. At last, her critical eye was satisfied. She went to her room and returned with her beautiful gray wool princess fitted coat with a black velveteen collar. On Gini it was a three quarter length coat, but on me it a perfect full length coat. Gini stood back, looked me over and said, "Georgia, you're fixed. You'll look just right for any occasion."

Happily, I packed and headed home for Christmas. As always, I was rejuvenated the moment I drove into Savannah. It was good to be home but somehow strange. There was no loving family, just Kelley and his bawdy friends. Mother was busy trying to make everything seem like Christmas of days past, even though that was impossible. But I was in such a good mood about the New Year I barely noticed Kelley and tried to be pleasant.

One nice surprise was that Sidney was home on furlough. We spent several evenings together reminiscing about our high school days. He even drove me to the train station grumbling all the way that I was going to visit "some soldier." We were only two blocks from the house, right in front of Savannah High, when the car began to sputter and jerk. Then the engine died. We were out of gas. Sidney thought it was an omen. He looked at my crestfallen expression and said, "I can see your heart is set on going. I'll run back and get your car." He did and we made it to the station with only a few seconds to spare.

As I got settled on the train, I noticed there were only a few women. The car was packed with soldiers. I sat there wondering about my fellow travelers. Where were they from and where were they going? Were they sad? Were they afraid? Did they have families far away?

I felt a slight tap on my shoulder. It was a young soldier. He said, "Excuse me, but I saw you get on in Savannah, and I wondered if it was your hometown. I was born and raised there."

I breathed a sigh of relief. I felt like we were practically kinfolk. He moved his luggage over and took the seat next to me. We began the game of, "Do you know?" He was familiar with Clary's Drugstore and said he often stopped there for a chocolate ice cream soda. He also said his father owned a shoe store on Broughton Street, that he was Jewish and was member of Temple Mickve Israel on Monterey Square.

We fell into a comfortable silence, dreaming our own dreams. The train was noisy with continuous commotion, stopping often to let someone on or off. As dark descended and the train rambled on, occasionally sounding a long, mournful whistle, I wondered what in the world I was doing on a train full of soldiers. Then I remembered I was on my way to Ollie. I brightened up and decided it was time to open the box Alma had handed me before I left. She had said, "Now Miss Bet, don't forget to eat."

I shared the fried chicken, red rice, deviled eggs, buttermilk biscuits, and fruit cake with my new friend. It was nice to have a protector, although all the other soldiers were perfect gentlemen when the word got around that I was on the way to visit my beau. Finally, the lights were dimmed and the train car became quiet and the sandman had his way with all of us as we nodded and dreamed of a peaceful world.

At first daylight, I awoke and raced to the ladies' room to make myself presentable. I was excited and nervous. Ollie and I had shared our thoughts and confidences by correspondence, but it had been months since we had seen each other.

At long last, the train pulled into Gulfport, and I nervously got off. It only took me a few minutes to find good, dependable Ollie who had been patiently waiting for me. He joked about me riding a troop train. Then he took me out to breakfast.

Next, we drove to Mrs. Eaton's big, old Southern home that faced the Gulf. Across the street, I saw a seawall, built to protect the homes. Ollie introduced me to Mary, Andy's wife, and showed me to my room. He asked me if I'd mind if he went back to work. He thought I might like to rest and get to know Mary. The bed looked inviting. I stretched out and slipped into a peaceful slumber.

Mary was a beautiful, dark haired woman and as gentle as a dove. She remarked that she was glad I was there because it was lonely while the men were at work. She was preparing dinner. I pitched in and helped. When the men arrived home, we had dinner in Mrs. Eaton's stately dining room. The men graciously offered to do the dishes. Mary and I giggled and accepted.

Andy was anxious for us to play cards. He said, "Georgia, I'm so glad you're here. Now we can play bridge. Mrs. Eaton's favorite game is Rummy. I couldn't take one more night of it."

About midnight Ollie walked me to my room. He put his arms around me, gave me a sweet, lingering kiss and said, "Rest well. Don't hurry to get up. Andy and I leave at daybreak for the base, but we'll be home early. There's a dance at the Officer's Club tomorrow night. I'm glad you're here."

When Ollie arrived home that afternoon, we took a long walk along the sea wall. Everything looked so peaceful it was hard to realize that across the ocean the war was raging. I told Ollie how guilty I felt about Danny. He gently told me not to worry. Things have a way of working out. I believed him.

I enjoyed getting ready for the New Year's Eve party. I took an unhurried, long warm bath. Everything during my visit seemed perfect. Even my leg make-up went on smoothly. I slipped into my lavender strapless short evening gown and stepped into gold high heel sandals that matched the gold threads in my dress. I hooked the catch on my thin gold chain necklace and put on a large pair of gold drop earrings. Then I grabbed my purse and wrap and walked into the living room. Andy and Ollie both rose. Andy gave a low whistle, and Ollie said, "I can't wait to show you off tonight."

At the Officer's Club I met Ollie's boss, Major Fred Burley, and his wife, Marge, as well as all the men Ollie worked with. The party was fun. We had balloons, crazy hats, horns and confetti. The band was good and we danced until the lights flickered and dimmed. The countdown began—nine, eight, seven, six, five, four, three, two, one. Happy New Year everyone! Happy New Year! Ollie kissed me and whispered in my ear, "I'd like to spend a lifetime with you." The band played "Auld Lang Syne" and we danced one last dance.

The next morning we were up early, raring to go. A captain and his wife came by for us in their big Oldsmobile. Three of us climbed into the back seat and three into the front. We didn't mind being slightly crowded. We were young, had gas stamps, and, most important, we had tickets to the January 1, 1945, Sugar Bowl game in New Orleans. Ollie was excited. He was one of Duke's biggest fans. The day was sunny, cold and crisp, but the best part of the day was that Duke defeated Alabama twenty-nine to twenty-six.

Following the game, the six of us made our way to the famous Roosevelt Hotel. We were anxious to find a rest stop. That was no problem for the men, but the ladies' room had a long, winding waiting line. We were desperate. Andy secured the men's room and our men stood guard. They were our heroes!

We had a delicious dinner at the Roosevelt. Then we ventured into the French Quarter. The captain knew a nightspot that had a floor show. The place was packed, but we managed to find a table. The hot sultry blues from the band filled the dim smoky room. At one point during the floor show, I became embarrassed and turned my head to the back of the room, only to be shocked by one of the waiters who had his pants down around his knees, tucking his shirt in. His eyes met mine. He grinned. I quickly turned back to the naughty floor show, accepting the fact: That's the way it is in the French Quarter.

On the second of January, Ollie put me on the train. We wondered when we would ever see each other again.

I rode home on the train thinking what a grand visit we had, and how much fun it was, but as I neared Savannah it all seemed like a dream.

******

On the long drive back to Rollins from Savannah, I had plenty of time to think about all the recent events. The memories of Ollie and Gulfport were sweet; but as I neared Rollins, my thoughts turned to Gini and my concern for her. At the end of last summer Gini dated a young man, Robert McDonald, whom she had known most of her life. At prep school dances they always had eyes for each other. He called Gini when she got home from Ogunquit, and they started seeing each other. He was in the Air Force and after a short time left for flight school.

When he graduated from flight school, he called Gini, "I have a week's leave and I'm coming to Rollins to see you." Gini was ecstatic, but his parents were dismayed, thinking that he should come home because this may be his last leave before going overseas.

What a time Gini and Bob had! Gini was juggling school and being with Bob. She was on a cloud. I remember watching them one evening at Dubstred Country Club. Bob was an accomplished musician. He was seated at a baby grand piano playing "Body and Soul" and looking at Gini with eyes of love. I thought they were the most glamorous couple I had ever seen. Bob was handsome in his officer's uniform, very self assured. Gini was beautiful, standing beside the piano, smiling as she held a cocktail glass in her hand.

On the last night that Bob was there they walked down to Lake Virginia and Bob asked Gini to marry him. That same night Gini ushered me into her room. She closed the door and said, "Georgia, I want you to be the first to know. Bob and I are engaged." I was shocked. I had thought it was just

76

another wartime romance. Gini was only eighteen years old and Bob was twenty. I was heartbroken. They were too young and it all happened too fast.

Of course, when their parents found out, they were dead set against the marriage, but what could they do? Gini and Bob were of age. Mum Vose called me and asked if I would try to talk some sense into Gini. I tried but to no avail.

Over the Christmas holidays the date and place were set, January 25, 1945, in Kansas City. What would life at Rollins be like without Gini?

My new suitemate was Katie Brown from Chattanooga, Tennessee. She was the perfect fit for me. We were both southerners. She was fun-loving and very upbeat. The only thing that disturbed me about her was that she was an incessant smoker. True, I smoked, but not like Katie. Her feet never hit the floor in the morning until she had a cigarette. Years later Katie died of lung cancer.

Gini was married at St. Paul's Episcopal Church in Kansas City with only Bob's parents and Mum Vose attending. How I wanted to be there!

Gini's letters were joyful. She loved being an Air Force wife and life seemed perfect, but three weeks from the day they married Bob crashed in a B29 bomber on a training mission in Salina, Kansas. A broken Gini went home to Mum Vose who tenderly and lovingly walked through months of grief and sorrow with Gini until she was whole again.

Chapter Seventeen
The Death of the President

The war brought tragedy, not only to Gini but to many people. There seemed to be no end to the war. People were war weary, but we had to keep the faith and go on with life. We partied and laughed, trying to block out anxiety. I received a letter from Danny's mother, but was afraid to open it, fearing it was bad news. She wrote that she had heard from the Red Cross that Danny was a prisoner of war in Germany. Danny was alive, but dark shadows invaded my mind. Were his captors torturing him? Was he well? Did he get enough to eat?

I worried about Danny, but thankfully, I had school activities to keep me busy. It was hard to believe that my second year of college was almost over. I had no plans for the summer, other than to go home and get a job. I knew that I could always work at Clary's Drugstore, but I didn't want to be in such close proximity to Kelley. Hopefully, something else would turn up.

On a beautiful spring day as I stretched out on my bed to study I heard a news flash on the radio. I vividly remember the dreadful moment in the late afternoon of April 12, 1945. "President Franklin D. Roosevelt has died in Warm Springs, Georgia." I leaped out of bed and ran through the halls screaming, "The President is dead." All the students were aghast. We gathered together in the living room and listened to the radio. At first, we were too stunned to cry, but slowly the tears and moans came. I heard, "What will we do? Who can lead the country? Will we lose the war?" What will happen to us?" Most of us could remember no other President.

The newspaper gave an account of the slow moving funeral train which carried Roosevelt's body to Washington. Mourners lined the tracks. They stood for hours as the train rumbled by. They bowed their heads to show love and respect for the sixty-three-year-old President.

Our professors tried to help us view this as a time to remember and revere, to know history was being made. They reminded us that Franklin Roosevelt became president in 1932 when the nation was deep in the depression. I didn't need reminding because I remembered Roosevelt's inspiring fireside chats. Men, women and children gathered around the radio to listen to our commander-in-chief. He spoke to the heart of the common man and was loved and admired because he rejuvenated the spirit of the American people. One of his most outstanding endeavors was the enactment of Social Security.

When Roosevelt campaigned for his second term, he came to Savannah. I was twelve years old. As Roosevelt's open car passed Clary's

Drugstore, Daddy said, "Remember this. You have seen a great man." Roosevelt was elected in 1936 by a tremendous majority vote. He gained his third term in 1940 to finish the work he had begun. On December 7, 1941, in a sneak attack Pearl Harbor was bombed by the Japanese. The President went before a joint session of Congress to declare the United States was at war with Japan. The country was locked in fear. The president stated: "We have nothing to fear but fear itself." Through the long years of the war he worked hard with leaders of the allied nations to defeat the axis powers.

President Roosevelt was asked to serve a fourth term. He had stated his desire to retire but felt it was his duty to serve again. In 1944 he was re-elected for an unprecedented fourth term. No one wanted to "change horses in the midstream." The president reminded the nation: "The fate of America cannot depend on any one man. The greatness of America is grounded in principles and not any single personality."

I thought of these words when the President died, but it was still a frightening time. We cried, dried our eyes, and cried some more. The President was buried in a 900 pound, copper-lined casket at his family home in Hyde Park, New York. His final resting place is in the center of a rose garden.

Vice President Harry S. Truman was sworn in as the thirty-third president of the United States. I shuddered. Could he do the job? But our dark night was not over yet. The death of the monster Adolph Hitler was the next big surprise. On April 30, 1945, only twenty days after President Roosevelt's funeral, Hitler was dead. He had killed himself knowing the defeat of Germany was near. A week later Germany unconditionally surrendered to General Eisenhower and the allies in the city of Rheims, France. The European war had ended. Now the War Department could concentrate on Japan.

******

My sophomore year at Rollins ended with jubilation over the end of the war in Europe, but I could not forget the death of the President or the war that was raging in the Pacific. I drove thinking of the war, but as I neared home my thoughts turned to Kelley. What a paradox! I was driving home to spend the summer in my beloved Savannah, but I would be living with a stepfather I despised. As I pulled in front of the house, I gritted my teeth and decided all I could do was stay out of his way as much as possible and make the best of my situation.

When I arrived, I found Mother had taken the day off from the drugstore and was waiting for me. She fixed tall glasses of iced tea, topped with a sprig of mint and a wedge of lemon. We went into the sun parlor and curled up on the settee for a real visit. Kelley arrived home about nine-thirty that night. He made a fuss over me and said it was time for a celebration. I thought to myself: You celebrate every night with Old Overholt (which I sarcastically called Old Overcoat).

It was close to midnight before Mother put dinner on the table. The rye whiskey had loosened Kelley's tongue, but we had a good time in spite of his drinking. Finally Kelley said, "I'd better get to bed. I open the store in the morning." Mother and I soon followed.

After a few days at home, I received a call from my Odum, Georgia, cousins, Kitty and Margie, who were working at Camp Stewart. They invited me to a dance at the Officers' Club the following Saturday night. Kitty said, "I'll ask my boss to make reservations for us at the guest house for Saturday night. The dances are fun, and it's been a long time since we had a visit." I thought that was a great idea.

The dances were reminiscent of the USO dances I attended in high school, but these were for officers only. I was surprised that I could still pinpoint the part of the country a man was from by the way he jitterbugged. One young major seemed to particularly like my dancing. After we danced to "In the Mood," we walked to the bar for a cool drink. He introduced himself and asked, "Where do you work?"

I told him that I had just gotten home from college and was looking for a summer job.

"Oh," he said, "Perhaps I can help you with that. I need another girl in my office."

I laughed. "You don't need me. I can't type, take shorthand, or do much of anything."

"Don't worry," he said. "We can surely find something for you to do. Why don't you come to the dance next week and stay over until Monday. Then I'll see what I can arrange."

I was thrilled that finding a job was so easy.

Sunday night Ollie called me. We had a nice chat. I told him all about my experience at Camp Stewart. He didn't seem at all enthusiastic.

The following Saturday I met my cousins for the dance. There was nothing I liked better than dancing the night away. I never sat out a number, so I was happy when Maggie, Kitty, and I finally got to bed. It seemed like my head had barely hit the pillow when I felt someone gently shaking me. "Dear, wake up. There's a phone call for you. It's your mother," said the chaperone.

I staggered to the phone. Mother told me Ollie had just called. He said he was flying from Gulfport to Savannah and would call me when the plane landed. My sleepy head cleared. Ollie was coming to Savannah! Mother said, "You must come home right away."

I dressed as quickly as I could, gathered my belongings and headed home. Once I got there, I sat by the phone waiting for Ollie's call. Finally, it rang. Ollie asked if I would pick him up at Chatham Air Field.

When I arrived at the base, there was Ollie waiting for me with a big smile on his face. "I have a couple of days leave, and I wanted to spend them with you," he said. That was more than all right with me.

Mother set the dining room table with our best silver and china and fixed a centerpiece of fresh flowers. Then she and Alma prepared a delicious Sunday dinner. Kelley was in a jovial mood and played the perfect host. Ollie was at ease. It was a lovely dinner.

After we ate, I wondered what I could do to entertain my guest. I asked, "Ollie, would you like to see a little of my home town?"

He seemed delighted, so off we went to one of my favorite places, Bonaventure Cemetery. It is situated on a high bluff on the Wilmington River. The whole area is covered with live oaks and huge azaleas. We parked the car at the Clary gravesite where my father and baby brother are buried. We held hands and walked down the narrow, unpaved roads, reading the inscriptions on the markers—some dated back to the 1700's, some were new. We found a bench facing the soft green marsh grass and wide river. We sat enjoying ourselves without saying a word.

The following day Alma packed one of her special picnic lunches, and we leisurely drove to Tybee Island. We spread a large quilt on the sand, half in the sun for Ollie and half in the shade under the pavilion for me. We frolicked in the water, rode the waves, walked the beach, played handball and when exhausted, sat on our quilt to eat our lunch. For entertainment, I sang a Rollins song. We laughed and laughed.

I had never seen Ollie out of uniform. I liked what I saw. He was a small man but perfectly proportioned. He had good looking strong, muscular legs and wide square shoulders. I chuckled to myself. We are a perfect fit.

That night during dinner Ollie got a call from his commanding officer telling him he was sending an AT6 aircraft for him at ten o'clock the next morning. That call brought us back to reality. There was still a war being fought. We listened to records. Then about eleven o'clock Ollie suggested we take a walk. It was a warm, balmy summer night. The moon was visible high in the sky. We walked holding hands, enjoying the beauty of the night until Ollie stopped abruptly. He turned to me and in a husky voice said, "Georgia, will you marry me?"

Without even having to think, I answered, "Yes." I knew it was right. He smiled as he kissed me. "You know I was ordered to ask you."

"You what?" I was startled.

"Major Burley watched me mope around all last week. Finally, he asked what was wrong. Is it that little red headed girl from the New Year's Eve party? I told him yes.

"Then the major said, 'On Sunday morning at eight o'clock there will be a plane to fly you to Savannah. Go over there and don't come back until you ask that girl to marry you. Then I expect you to come back here and get to work.'

"On the phone tonight the major asked if I had popped the question. I said, 'No sir.

"'Well, you better do it tonight,' he said. 'Tomorrow you're coming home.'"

Ollie confessed that he couldn't work at all after I told him I was offered a job at Camp Stewart. He said, "I could see that major chasing you around his desk. I couldn't stand it!"

I laughed. "I won't work there if it worries you."

He broke into a grin, and we had a big laugh. He was on the plane the next morning. He went back happy.

Chapter Eighteen
A Diamond Ring

Since I had promised Ollie I would not work at Camp Stewart, I decided to start going to the Bull Street drugstore. It was here that I found the greatest peace and contentment. Mother asked if I would be willing to clean and rearrange all the cosmetic counters. The showcases were old and beautiful. They were deep mahogany with intricate carving. I cleaned and polished them with oil, letting my hand slide down the satin smooth wood. I could sense the presence of my father and was happy feeling he was pleased. It was fun displaying the Coty's, Evening in Paris Perfume and the Max Factor products. There was plenty of work to do, and I fell into a routine.

Then the unexpected happened. Ollie received a transfer ordering him to go to the University of Virginia with a group of men who were being trained to set up a military government after the invasion of Japan. With the change of stations, Ollie received a leave. He asked me to go to Ohio and meet his family.

My mother was pleased. "Ollie is a fine young man, but you need to meet his parents. You know you marry the whole family."

Ollie met me at the train in Atlanta, and we started the long drive to Dover, Ohio. On the way we had time to talk, but best of all we had time to be alone. We enjoyed the beautiful scenery and our time together.

Once in Dover, we drove up to a large two story brick house. Ollie said, "Darling, this is it." I was nervous. About that time a nice looking gray-haired man rushed out to greet us. "Pop, this is my Georgia."

Mr. Toomey put his arms around me. "Ollie, I'm so glad you brought a little red-head home." My nervousness flew out the window. I knew that I could love this man. Then I saw Ollie's mother standing on the porch, smiling and waving. She was a beautiful, aristocratic woman whose silver hair had a faint touch of blue. She took me in her arms and welcomed me, leading me into a spacious home filled with oriental rugs and antique furniture. The Toomeys were just like Ollie, gentle and kind. I felt right at home.

After freshening up, we had a delightful dinner with Ollie's parents. We talked non stop and got to know each other better. They wanted to know all about Savannah and my college life. They were surprised that I didn't have a thick southern accent. I related to them how hard I had worked in my public speaking classes at Rollins to erase my southern accent. I think they were a little disappointed, but they praised my hard work. Finally, Mrs. Toomey said, "I can see you two are tired, and tomorrow will be a busy day."

Each day, in fact, was busy. While I was there, Ollie tried to show me the whole town and introduce me to all of his relatives.

Ollie's dad had Tennessee and Kentucky walking horses. Ollie and I rode every chance we had. After riding one afternoon, I took a long, warm bath. I had just finished dressing when I heard a knock at the door. I opened it, and there stood Ollie smiling at me. "May I come in? I have something for you." He took my left hand and placed a gold ring with a solitaire diamond on my finger. "Do you like it, Darling? Pop and I have been looking at rings all week."

"I love it," I told him. "It's beautiful."

When we had our last breakfast before leaving, the Toomeys were sad, although they tried not to show it. Wartime was so terrible. Folks always wondered what the future held. The Toomeys had three daughters, but they were saying goodbye to their only son. They tried to keep up the conversation. At last, Ollie's mother said, "Georgia, we're so glad that Ollie brought you home to us. Now, won't you please call us Mom and Pop?"

I was deeply touched. I leaped up and threw my arms around those dear people. "I would love for you to be my mom and pop." With tears we said our goodbyes, and Ollie and I headed to Charlottesville, Virginia. It was a long hard drive through the mountains. We hadn't called ahead for reservations and to our dismay, every place we stopped was filled or there was only one room. We kept driving through the dark, around hairpin curves, stopping anytime we saw a hotel until Ollie found a place he hoped would be suitable. "Georgia," he said, "they have only two rooms left, and they have a connecting bath. Would that be all right?"

I looked at his tired eyes and nodded, "Yes, it will be fine."

We had a late supper and took a long walk before going up to our rooms. I kissed Ollie goodnight. "Why don't you use the bathroom first. I'll probably take longer than you." I closed the door, unpacked my gown and removed the clothes I would need for the next day. Then I propped myself up in bed and started reading Betty Smith's *A Tree Grows in Brooklyn* while I waited for Ollie to finish bathing. The walls in the bathroom were paper thin. I could hear the bath water running and Ollie singing, "I'm a Prisoner of Love." Next, there was a loud crash and a huge splash followed by silence. I closed my book, not knowing what to do. Was he all right? I could just see the headlines in the newspapers: Man Found Dead in Bathtub, Red Headed Woman in Adjoining Room. My mother would kill me! Then I heard a faint little humming and at last a rap on the door. "Honey, I'm through."

The next morning as we went down to breakfast in a crowded elevator, I said, "Ollie, by any chance did you fall in the bathtub last night?" With a sheepish grin he answered, "I hoped you hadn't heard." I guess we were talking too loud because all of the people in the elevator started laughing. They saw a young soldier and his girl away from home. We could feel their understanding and love.

We finally made it to Charlottesville. Ollie took me to a hotel and reported to his military unit. The next day he put me on a train to Savannah. He bought a newspaper, a magazine and candy for me. Then he looked me straight in the eye and said, "Please don't leave the station. I don't want you to miss your train." He was so serious and sweet I was deeply touched. After a kiss and hug, I was on my way. It felt good to have someone who cared so much for me.

Chapter Nineteen
The Dreaded Call

When I arrived home in Savannah, I showed my engagement ring to Mother. She hugged me and we celebrated like two school girls. She liked Ollie and was very happy for me. I walked around in a state of euphoria until I received a phone call that brought me back to reality. The phone call was from Danny. I had been dreading it since I had begun a serious relationship with Ollie.

Danny was home from the war and wanted to see me. He had been awarded a Distinguished Flying Cross. I prayed to the Lord to help me not hurt him. When Danny arrived, I had tears in my eyes as I told him about my relationship with Ollie. To my relief, he understood my mixed emotions and reached out to embrace me. He said, "I guess you and I were just not meant to be."

At that moment I thought he was the most chivalrous man I knew. He thanked me for being his inspiration to live while in the prison camp and explained the events that led to his imprisonment. He said when his plane was hit by enemy artillery he parachuted to the ground and landed in a wooded area. Italian peasants carried him to their house, hid him and treated his badly sprained ankle until the German soldiers finally found him. They transported him to Germany where he was put in a prison camp.

"Do you know what saved my sanity?" Danny asked.

"I can't imagine," I said.

"It was a deck of cards. We played bridge morning, noon, and night. And oh yes, I got a tattoo on my chest. Do you want to see it?"

He pulled his shirt out, opened it, and looked down, "Oh gosh, the ship must have sunk!"

That was his sweet way of trying to make me laugh, but it only made me cry. He cried too. We cried for what might have been.

After our crying jag was over, he said he was going to the University of North Carolina on the G.I. Bill. I was thankful that he was alive, and I wanted nothing more than for him to have a life filled with all that was good. He left early the next morning. As badly as I felt, I knew it was right. Ollie was the man for me. He was my soul mate.

On August 6, 1945, the nation was in shock. President Truman gave the order to drop an atomic bomb on Hiroshima, Japan. We didn't know what an atomic bomb was, but it sounded ominous. The following day we read in the newspapers about the deadliness and horror of the bomb which sent a huge mushroom shaped cloud into the air and wiped out sixty per cent of Hiroshima, a city of over three hundred thousand people. On August 9, 1945, a second bomb was dropped on Nagasaki. On August 19, 1945, the Japanese surrendered.

The United States went wild, celebrating with abandon. People flooded the streets, laughing, crying, cheering, embracing and kissing. Never was there such a celebration. The long nightmare was over.

******

Now that I was an engaged woman, I knew my social life would change. Ollie was the only man in my life and my life revolved around news from him. Shortly before I returned to Rollins, Ollie called and told me he was being shipped to California to practice the invasion of Japan. Of course, there wasn't going to be an invasion of Japan because the atom bomb had taken care of that. The military just didn't know what to do with Ollie's unit.

When I returned to Rollins to begin my junior year, I was glad to see all my sorority sisters. They were eager to hear all about the proposal, as they eyed my diamond ring.

In our sorority house living room, there seemed to be a constant bridge game. Finally succumbing, I agreed to play. Bridge had never been on my agenda. I was always on the go, never wanting to sit around. The girls were patient with me, and I began enjoying the game, plus it helped pass the time.

Mail was my lifeline, and Ollie was a faithful correspondent. Opening my mailbox one morning, I found the usual letter plus a small package. I tore into it and found a beautiful jeweled Phi Gamma Delta fraternity pin. The note inside said, "Georgia, will you wear my pin?" I chuckled to myself. Ollie had told me how he hated that my college years were not normal because of the war. He didn't want me to miss a thing.

I spent many weekends at Aunt Billie's. It was like old times. I adored her. Once, as I drove to Billie's, I passed the road where Ollie and I had impulsively stopped the car one night, jumped out and danced under the Florida stars to one of our favorite songs, Glenn Miller's "Moonlight Serenade." And so it was that the days sped by with visits to Billie's and thoughts of Ollie. Then, as the fall term was ending, I received a telegram. I shuddered remembering the sad telegram from Danny, but this one was happy news. The message read:

WONDERFUL NEWS DARLING WILL BE DISCHARGED IN
CALIFORNIA SOON AFTER DECEMBER 1ST DATE UNKNOWN
DREAMS WHITE CHRISTMAS AND YOU REAL AT LAST
I LOVE YOU
      OLLIE

When Christmas vacation arrived, I drove home to Savannah with a happy heart. Mother and I prepared for a gala Christmas, made especially grand because there was no more rationing and because of Ollie's telegram. Aunt Claudia, Uncle Louie, Aunt Billie and Uncle Stanley were all coming, and most important, I was looking forward to seeing Ollie. But days went by and I didn't hear a word from him. My excitement turned to anxiety. Finally, on Christmas Eve morning the phone rang. Ollie said, "Honey, I'm home. I got in last night at three o'clock in the morning. Merry Christmas, Darling. I'll be in Savannah as soon as I'm rested." Then he laughed. "I'll bring you a Christmas present."

Ollie arrived just before New Year's Eve. We dressed up and went out on the town. There was great jubilation everywhere. Savannah was ready to party now that our troops were coming home from the war. I was thankful my man was already home.

The night was cold for Savannah. When we returned home, we sat in front of a roaring fire catching up on all our news. I wanted to hear everything about Ollie's separation from the service. He explained that an order was issued stating that anyone who had served sixty months was eligible for a discharge. He said, "I had sixty-two months. They tried to talk me into staying in the service and keeping my commission. No way! I'm going to go home and get married."

He held my hand a few minutes then continued. "After all the paperwork was done, the next thing was to find quick transportation home which wasn't easy. Two other officers and I put in seventy-five dollars each and bought an old used car. It was a piece of junk." He laughed, "But what the heck? We didn't care as long as it would get us across the country. It burned oil like a thirsty alcoholic. The tires were threadbare. We had a few flats, but we were excited and happy to be free."

"How long did it take you to get home?" I asked.

"We spelled each other off driving, and we made it to Columbus, Ohio, in five days. The other officers dropped me off, and I wished them well on their way to Philadelphia and New York City. The last man got the car. I took a Greyhound Bus to Dover. My folks went wild with joy, but all I wanted to do was sleep."

"That is quite a story!" I said.

"It was all worth it to be here with you," Ollie said as we snuggled up together in front of the fire. We sat enjoying the warmth of the fire and the glow of the moment as we made plans for our future. We didn't want to wait to get married. We discussed several dates and finally compromised on Valentine's Day, Thursday, February fourteenth.

Ollie teased me. "You're picking a date I'll never be able to forget."

"I'm picking the most romantic date I can think of." I teased back.

Ollie took me in his arms. Rollins and everything else went out the window. Soon I would be Bettye Clary Toomey.

We asked Mother and Kelley to join us, telling them that we had set a date. Mother exclaimed, "Oh dear, that's not enough time to prepare for a wedding!" But Ollie and I wouldn't budge. The date was set.

Kelley shook Ollie's hand and with a big smile said, "I'll fix us a drink. This calls for a celebration."

For once, I agreed with him.

Luther M. Clary - 1930s.   Clara and Luther Clary - 1930s.

Clara Carter Clary
photo given to Bettye Lorraine.

Bettye Lorraine Clary
High School photo - 1940s.

Aunt Claudia
as a young woman about 1918.

Aunt Billie and husband Stanley.

Bettye Lorraine Clary - 1926.

Luther Martin Clary
as a young man circa 1900.

Bettye Lorraine and curb boy
at Clary's Drugstore - late 1920s.

Bettye Lorraine and Luther Clary
at Clary's Drugstore on Bull Street.

Tuba and Bettye Lorraine - circa 1926.

Tuba, Bettye Lorraine and Velma Carter.

Clara, Bettye Lorraine and Luther Clary
at Forsyth Park Fountain - Easter 1930s

Luther, Bettye Lorraine and Clara Clary
at house on 49th Street in Ardsley Park, Savannah.

Cousins in Odum, Georgia
Kitty Hires and Margie Hires
about 1926.

Clara Clary and
her sister Claudia
Christmas 1930s.

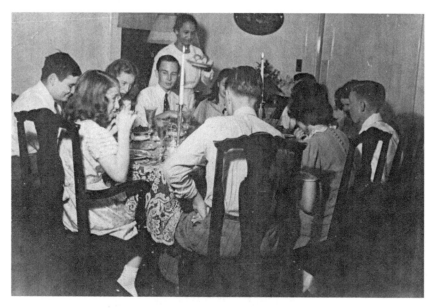

Bettye Lorraine - 13th Birthday Party
Lulline Standing.

Benson B. Kelley

Benson B. Kelley and Clara Kelley ("Bella")
February 14, 1946 - Wedding of Bettye
Lorraine ("Betsy") and Ollie Toomey.

Oliver and Bettye Clary Toomey
Wedding in Savannah - February 14, 1946.

Sidney Boone 1943   Danny McClain 1944

Oliver Toomey 1945   Roy Hussey - The boy upstairs
at Ardsley Park.

Dan Sing Fan - Ogunquit, Maine
Teahouse where Bettye Lorraine worked during summer of 1944.

Fisherman's shack in Ogunquit, Maine - where Bettye Lorraine
("Georgia") and Gini lived during the summer of 1944.

Bettye Lorraine ("Georgia") and
Gini - Rollins College Winter
Park, Florida,
on Lake Virginia.

Gini Vose
Bettye Lorraine's Roommate
at Rollin's College.

Rollins College - 1944 - Alpha Phi Sorority Sisters
Bettye Lorraine ("Georgia") wearing pearls in center
Gini Vose (behind Betsy on right).

Soda jerks at Clary's of yesteryear smile for the birdie.

Clary's -Soda Jerks of yesteryear.
Courtesy *Savannah Morning News* - November 1, 1980.

Pictured above is the Enlarged Store of the **CLARY DRUG CO.**, at Abercorn and Jones Sts. We have closed our store on Bull St. and enlarged this one sufficiently to handle our entire business.

Our Fountain and Luncheonette is serving the finest meals in Savannah at a price that will amaze you.

Our Drug Department is second to none, using only the Purest Drugs and utmost care in filling your prescription the way "The Doctor Ordered."

B. B. KELLEY,
P. H. G. Manager

Clary's - Courtesy *Savannah Evening Press* - October 1, 1952.

Letters to the Editor

The Way It Was: Clary's Drugstore Remembered

Editor:

It was with regret that I read in the Sept. 17 *Savannah Morning News* of the demise of Clary's drugstore at 402 Abercorn.

When I returned to live here three years ago, after living in many elsewheres since 1939, I discovered Clary's was no longer at the corner of Bull and Perry Lane.

My feeling of nostalgia goes back to the late 1920s and early 1930s when Clary's was a principal hangout for Savannah High School students across the square.

Our main interest, aside from social mingling, was to stop by the soda fountain for a "dope," an euphemistic term for a Coke. Strangers in the city thought they'd wandered into a modern opium den.

"Dopes" were a nickel and could be jazzed up by the soda jerk to suit your taste at no extra charge. Some of the more popular flavors were fresh lime and cherry, making it taste like Dr. Pepper, and chocolate.

It paid to stay on the good side of the soda jerk against the time when you were stricken by an ailment calling for a shot of castor oil. If the soda jerk was your friend, he'd make up a smoothy, being careful to leave out all your favorite flavors so you wouldn't forever associate them with castor oil.

He must have used some exotic flavor nobody in Savannah had ever seen in a store or tried before. At any rate, it must have been highly detergent because the oil didn't stick to your lips and everything quite as much as if you'd taken the oil neat.

Clary's had a good marketing tool, too. The soda jerk made up a scoop of ice cream stuck on the end of a tongue-depressor. then dipped in chocolate and placed in the freezer.

The ice cream was vanilla and cost a nickel, but if you got a strawberry one, you received another free. Conventional wisdom held that Clary's used more tongue depressors than all the doctors in the city.

I've been wanting to renew my indulgence in these favorites, but apparently that wish has been overtaken by events and Revco.

JOHN B. HOLST

Letters to the Editor - Courtesy *Savannah Morning News* - September 29, 1992.

Clary's -Scratching Post - Courtesy *Savannah Morning News* - November 19, 1980.

(In the early 1960s, News/Press photography chief Buddy Rich caught this waitress clowning with the Scratching Post in Clary's.)

Sale of Clary Drug Company - 1977
Clara Clary Kelley sold the drug company to John Drinkard
(far left). John Ranitz is on the far right of Clara Kelley.

Clary's 2008

Survival of the Sweetest:
A Few Savannah Soda Fountains Still Have Fizz

By TRUDY STEIN
Staff Writer

Stop the clock. Relax and remember those by-gone days when the corner soda shop served marvelous frothy sweets in surroundings almost as familiar as your mother's kitchen.

Life moved a little slower before the dawn of modern-day mobility afforded us by the automobile. Neighborhoods congealed into close-knit blocks of familiar faces. People didn't travel far from home for entertainment.

Recollections of sweet, drippy treats served in such neighborhood establishments richly flavor Savannah's history. Most local soda shops have been washed away by waves of progress that have made fast foods king.

This week the World's Fare dishes up the scoop on three survivors of the good old days — Solomons Pharmacy Inc., Clary Drug Company, and Basil Leopold's Restaurant — all of which still serve soda-fountain treats and each of which has an atmosphere that you just don't find in fast-food establishments.

CLARY DRUG COMPANY at 402 Abercorn St. retains a soda fountain that propably most closely resembles the old-fashioned notion of a community gathering place and sweet shop. Their sinfully thick milk shakes still win great local acclaim and surrender from even hard-nosed calorie counters. Downtown residents often meet friends for coffee and a chat at Clary's.

"Most of the people over there," said owner and pharmacist John Drinkard pointing to the lunch crowd at the soda fountain, "are the same ones that come in here every day. This really is a popular neighborhood gathering spot."

Half a dozen swivel counter stools fronting the fountain, plain wooden chairs surrounding a handful of equally modest tables, and a pole support in the middle of the room that bears the sign "scratching post" create a homey atmosphere that is reminiscent of the '50s.

"The reason most drugstores don't have soda fountains anymore is that it is virtually impossible to serve ice cream and sodas for a profit. You have to serve sandwiches and other foods, too," said Drinkard, who purchased the drugstore in 1977.

When the Clary family bought the business in the 1930s there was already a fountain in the store, Drinkard recalled. A cosmetic display case now stands where the soda fountain was located prior to

> '*There is a whole generation of kids that are hardly aware there was something better.*'
> — *Archie Whitfield on the obsolescence of neighborhood soda fountains.*

remodeling in 1957, he added.

Although Clary's milk shakes still sell well, Drinkard says the soda fountain serves more club sandwiches than anything else — except coffee.

"The coffee pot goes steadily from 7 a.m. to 5 p.m. The waitresses pour it as fast as they can make it, especially in the winter, but in the summer, too, even as hot as it is in Savannah," Drinkard said.

Clary's no longer serves banana splits. Customers didn't order them enough to warrant keeping bananas on hand, Drinkard explained.

"People are just too diet- and weight-conscious now," he suggested.

Mary Gallagher, who has been working at the Clary soda fountain for 18 years, recalls mountainous banana splits made with three scoops of ice cream, assorted toppings, real whipped cream and a cherry. They sold for 69 cents in her early days at the fountain.

"When I first started, ice cream cones were 10 cents. Now they are a quarter a scoop," she said, bemoaning inflation.

"The people who come in now are pretty much the same as those that came in the old days — maybe a little older and not as patient as they used to be," Mrs. Gallagher said. Most of the customers she serves now are familiar faces.

"I've got 'em learnt so well, I usually know what they want before they sit down," she said.

The unpretentious, yellowed menu does not spotlight fountain foods. Rather, they appear in conspicuously on its corner. Milk shakes (regular 75 cents; thick, 85 cents; and extra thick, 95 cents) sodas and sundaes, plain or with nuts are listed.

The thick chocolate shake, sampled by this reporter, was served in a paper cup which collected a residue at the bottom, giving evidence to the real chocolate syurp used in making the frosty treat. It

Continued on Page 2

Article November 19, 1980 - Courtesy *Savannah Morning News*.

Katherine Yoder and Georgia Toomey
in Dover, Ohio - 1952.

Katherine Yoder and husband
in later years.

Ollie Toomey and Georgia Ann Toomey
Dover, Ohio - 1950.

House in Dover, Ohio.

Gold Stocking Review - 1970 - Goldsboro, NC
Betsy Toomey and Howard Caudill (in center).

Gold Stocking Review - 1970 - Goldsboro, NC
Ollie Toomey and Carolyn Russell.

Georgia Ann Toomey   Mary Claire Toomey

Bettye Lorraine ("Betsy") and Ollie at Mary Toomey's Wedding
March 28, 1981.

Bettye Lorraine ("Betsy") and
Ollie at Betsy's 50th Savannah
High School reunion.

Feeding the pigeons - Forsyth Park
Mary Toomey Johnson with
Georgia Toomey Wieler
and her son Scott.

Feeding the pigeons - Forsyth Park
Left to Right - Ollie, Mary with her son Mark, Scott (Georgia's son),
Georgia and her son Tuck.

Chapter Twenty
A Savannah Wedding

A few days later Ollie left for Ohio saying, "I have to get to work. I need to start making a living for us." He was going to work in his father's automobile agency, so this was not a sad goodbye. It held the promise of all our tomorrows.

Mother and I started making wedding plans, but there was a question that was hanging between us. Who would give me away when I marched down the aisle? I longed for my father. Mother wouldn't ask, but I could see the questioning look in her eyes. I knew what I must do for her. I gritted my teeth and asked Kelley if he would give me away. He seemed surprised and pleased. I told him that there was one stipulation. "You must promise me that you won't have a drink the day of the wedding until the reception."

Kelley crossed his heart and said, "I promise." With that major hurdle over, Mother and I went to work preparing for my big day.

Trinity Methodist Church is a beautiful, downtown church where my daddy's brother was the minister. The church was available on February 14, and Uncle George said he would be delighted to perform the ceremony. His wife, Lucy Quin, immediately came to visit us and insisted on having the rehearsal dinner at the lovely, spacious rectory. Without hesitation, I said, "I'd like that very much. Thank you."

Lucy Quin was one of the most charming ladies I have ever known, a true southern jewel. She was a capable, elegant woman, the perfect minister's wife. She loved to entertain, and her cook, Lillie Mae, made rolls that were as light as a fairy's touch, a morsel of pure delight. I don't think there was a better cook in all of Savannah.

Lucy Quin also said, "Bettye Lorraine, as our gift to you, your Uncle George and I would like to provide the decorations for the church. I've seen every wedding in the Methodist Church for the last ten years. I know just what to do." Mother and I were delighted with their generous gift.

Next, I had to select my bridesmaids. I chose Katie Brown and Grace Warren, Rollins classmates, and Betty Hubert, a Savannah friend. Of course, I asked Gini to be my matron of honor. To my joy, they all accepted. The ushers presented somewhat of a problem, but we took it in stride. All of Ollie's friends were scattered, many still in the service. Ollie said, "Pop will be my best man, and anyone you pick for ushers will be fine with me. Just make sure it's you who walks down the aisle."

I gave him a big hug and assured him. "You can count on me. I'll be the one wearing the white dress and walking toward you."

A Savannah Wedding

When Mother and I started shopping for a wedding dress, we found that the selection was slim because of wartime shortages. We ended up at Fine's on Broughton Street where I bought one of two wedding dresses that were available in my size and ordered bridesmaids' dresses.

I didn't realize how many details had to be taken care of to complete wedding preparations. Mother and I compiled the wedding guest list and ordered invitations. Then I picked out silver, china, and crystal. This was an easy process because there were so few choices. Only two silver patterns were available. I quickly chose Edward VII by Frank Smith Sterling Silver. My china pattern was Caselton Rose. I was easy to please.

At last, Mother told me my work was done, and I could leave the rest to her. That was great news because true to Savannah tradition, the parties began. There were bridal showers, teas, a supper party and several luncheons held at the Pink House, a Georgian style home built in the late 1700's that had become one of Savannah's favorite restaurants because of its lovely décor and good food. It was known as the Pink House because of the light pink color of its stucco exterior. The parties kept me in a mad whirl. Then, suddenly the enormity of the major change my life would soon be taking began to creep into my mind. Savannah would no longer be my home. I would be living in a northern city hundreds of miles away with no family close by. I had a close friend who wouldn't date a serviceman for fear she might fall in love and have to leave Savannah. True to her word, she waited patiently until our boys came home and married a Savannahian. Even though I loved my hometown as much as my friend, I couldn't follow in her footsteps. I was too much in love. But the thought of leaving Savannah was like a nightmare.

The day before the wedding I went downtown to do some last minute shopping. As I drove home down Whitaker Street along the boundaries of Forsyth Park, I was suddenly overcome with grief. How could I leave my beloved city? By the time I reached home I was hysterical. Mother was frightened when she saw me. She thought I had been in an automobile accident. As my words tumbled out, she took me in her arms and soothed my fears saying, "You can always come home. You'll have two homes."

The next morning, however, I was awakened by a crying mother. "Bettye Lorraine, it's raining and the bride that the rain falls on will weep all her married life." But the rain didn't fall on me. The wedding wasn't until five o'clock. By noon the sun was shining, and it was a beautiful warm February day.

Ollie, his mother, father and an aunt were staying at the DeSoto Hotel. He called saying how nervous he was. In fact, he was plain scared! Poor dear

Ollie, I'm sure he felt like a man in a foreign country. None of his friends were there, and the only support he had was from his parents and one aunt.

I was in high spirits, but I tried to stay out of the way. Everyone in the house was busy, rushing about. Lulline, Alma, Rosa and even Thelma came home to help with the reception. Thelma said, "I just have to see my baby married." Aunt Claudia and Aunt Billie arrived and Mother was bubbling with enthusiasm. All the women I adored were with me. My nervousness had disappeared and I was enjoying myself. I slipped into my wedding gown, adjusted my headpiece and remembered what Kelley had said that morning at breakfast, "Bet, are you sure you want to go through with this? I hear that Yankee women even scrub floors." I laughed; I thought he was joking. Kelley looked quite handsome when I saw him in his tux, and hallelujah, he hadn't touched a drop of whiskey all day.

Mother was like a top sergeant in charge of everything, and things were going just as she had planned. The house was decorated with white carnations, snap dragons, smilax and white candles. Most of the furniture had been moved out to make room for guests at the reception. The food was ready and the champagne was on ice.

Mother tapped on my door, "It's time for you and Kelley to leave. The limousine is waiting." Next, she hustled all the relatives out and handed her car keys to Thelma, urging the maids to leave for the church. She was pleased with the way everyone followed orders. She gave one last look at the decorations in the house. Then suddenly she realized she was all alone. Panic struck, she scrambled to find Kelley's car keys, but they were nowhere to be found. Rushing outside, she saw the photographer loading his equipment into a ramshackle old Ford coupe. She ran across the lawn, long dress held high, and yelling, "Will you drive me to the church?"

At the church, Aubrey, my cousin, was outside pacing up and down wondering where Mother was. When she arrived, Aubrey escorted a breathless, flushed Mother-of-the-bride down the aisle. Mother later related all she could think about was, "I missed my daughter's high school graduation and to think, I almost missed her wedding, too!"

I was calm and at peace as Kelley and I stepped out of the ante room. I was struck by the beauty of the church. Lucy Quin had performed magic. I heard the organist softly playing, "Always," a song Ollie and I had requested.

The wedding procession began. On the circular altar rail there were candles and smilax. I walked down a path of soft light to the altar where Ollie was standing. In my heart I knew that he would always be there for me. When Uncle George pronounced us man and wife, I became a very happy Mrs. Oliver Ralph Toomey.

At the reception, Mom Toomey asked Lulline if there was any rice. Lulline replied, "There sure is, honey, but it ain't cooked." Rice had been too dear to Savannahians to waste on any bride and groom. Lulline, however, relented and gave Mrs. Toomey a five pound bag of rice. Ollie and I left amid laughter, best wishes and a shower of rice.

The first night of our honeymoon we stayed at the Francis Marion Hotel in Charleston, South Carolina. We went to a famous restaurant where suddenly I was so nervous and tired that I couldn't eat a bite of the seafood we ordered. Ollie was forgiving and understanding. We agreed weddings can be exhausting.

The only regret Ollie and I had was that we left the wedding celebration so early because after the reception the bridal party went to Remler's Club Royale, a swanky nightspot, and partied into the wee hours. We made the mistake of telling Mother where we would be staying, and she and Kelley called us every half hour all night long. My tipsy mother kept asking, "Are you all right?"

Ollie said, "I guess we missed the best party in Savannah."

Chapter Twenty One
Honeymoon in New York

Because Mum Vose had been unable to attend the wedding, I promised we would put Lowell, Massachusetts, on our honeymoon itinerary. Ollie agreed, although it was out of the way. Thus, we started our slow trek from Charleston. We stopped whenever we liked, and that was often. It was good to love and be loved in return. Once in Lowell, Mum Vose and Ollie became like two old cronies, giving Gini and me time to be together.

After a short visit in Lowell, we proceeded on to New York City. Upon arrival, we checked into our hotel, the New Yorker. Looking out of the window in our room, I could see snow beginning to fall, not just flurries with flakes that melted before they hit the ground as in Savannah. It stuck to the sidewalks and streets and turned everything white. I was excited and begged, "Ollie, let's go outside. I want to see the snow."

I donned my fur coat and hat which had been a present from Mother and Kelley. They had said, "We don't want you cold up north."

Ollie looked at my new high heel alligator pumps, "You can't walk in the snow in high heels. You need overshoes."

"I'll be all right," I convinced him, so off we went. We actually walked the sidewalks of New York in a blizzard, laughing like two kids.

Finally, Ollie said, "Brr...it's really cold! Let's duck into a hotel and find a bar."

Once we were seated, I visited the ladies room to dry my shoes. The attendant watched me. Then she said, "How can you walk in this storm without boots?"

"I don't have any. You see, I'm from the South," and blushing, I went on, "I'm on my honeymoon."

'Well, you won't find any overshoes in all of New York, thanks to the war. What size do you wear?"

I told her and incredibly she said, "Come back tomorrow afternoon around five o'clock. I have an extra pair you can have."

I rushed to the table to tell Ollie. He was doubtful, but the next day we returned. The attendant was waiting for me. Smiling, she handed me a paper bag. Inside was a pair of brown galoshes. I pulled them over my shoes. They fit perfectly. I snapped them up, thinking how ugly they were and how they made me feel like an old lady, but they would keep my feet dry. "How much do I owe you?" I asked.

She broke into a big smile. "Not a penny. They're my wedding gift to you."

Ollie was amazed the woman showed up. He thought she would forget or have some excuse for not having the overshoes. We both learned a major lesson that day. People are basically good and kind no matter where you go.

Our friends had considered us daffy to go to New York in February, but I found it exciting. I enjoyed dressing up, catching a cab and going to the theater. I loved that breathtaking moment when there was a crescendo in the overture and the curtain went up. I squeezed Ollie's hand to let him know how much I appreciated his efforts to get us tickets for *Oklahoma, Anna Lucasta,* and my favorite, *I Remember Mama.* We also saw the Rockettes, the high kicking chorus girls, and we caught a matinee starring the great comedian, Danny Kaye. What a perfect honeymoon!

Ollie's last surprise was that we were going to drive to Hamilton, New York. He wanted me to see his Alma Mater, Colgate University. That trip was one I shall never forget. The roads had been cleared, but there was snow half way up the telephone poles. No one was on the highway. It felt like we were the only two people in the state. As we rode along, Ollie told me tales about his life at Colgate. Arriving in Hamilton, New York, we stayed at a quaint inn. As we sat by an open fire that night, Ollie recounted the story of Mike the dog that was expelled from Colgate.

Mike was an all white Pit Bull owned by one of my Phi Gam fraternity brothers. He was our mascot. He ate, slept, and went to class with us. His daily recreation was walking around a lake in the middle of the campus. He was fascinated by the swans that glided across the lake. Dr. Cutten, president of the college, had an office overlooking Lake Taylor. He also found the swans fascinating. Watching them was one of the president's favorite pastimes.

One day a swan came out of the water and attacked Mike. Several days later he took his revenge and killed the swan. Unfortunately for Mike, Dr. Cutter witnessed the event from his office window and expelled Mike from the campus.

When Mike's owner, Robbie, went home for Christmas vacation he took Mike with him. They boarded a train to Detroit. Somehow, Mike got loose and jumped off the train in Buffalo, New York. Robbie was told and immediately started looking for his dog. He searched for several days, but Mike had disappeared.

Months later an emaciated dog covered with cuts and scars appeared at the Phi Gam House. It was Mike. We never knew how he survived and found his way back. He had walked over two hundred miles. The Phi Gams celebrated that a dog is truly man's best friend. Mike was reinstated and allowed to stay on campus. He graduated with us.

I was in tears when Ollie finished. "That was some story!" I told him.

After showing me around the campus the next day, we started our drive to Dover, Ohio, my new hometown. I rode along sitting close to Ollie thinking about honeymoons. They can take place anywhere, on islands, in the mountains, in the city or wherever. The important thing is to be alone, to start from the beginning exploring your mate, body, soul and mind. I snuggled closer. Ollie was my man.

As we drove into Dover, I was struck by how cold and dreary everything looked. I asked Ollie why all the houses looked vacant. There were no curtains or drapes at the windows. Through the windows I could see furniture piled up and step ladders. Ollie laughed and said, "Sweetheart, this is March, spring house cleaning season. The whole town goes into a frenzy."

I had never seen anything like this. He continued, "Most of the people here are of German or Swiss descent. To them cleanliness is next to godliness or maybe it's the other way around."

The Toomey household was in a state of disarray, but that didn't stop Ollie's mother from welcoming us warmly. A man was seated on a tall ladder, patiently washing the intricate dentel molding in the living room. Women were scurrying around. One man was cleaning wallpaper with great wads of a sticky green substance. I couldn't believe what I was seeing. Cleaning was never mentioned in Savannah. It was just done. That was part of the Savannah charm.

The first week in Dover we stayed with Mom and Pop because the house they had rented for us wasn't available yet. Housing during the war years was scarce—there was no construction. Sometimes it took a death for a house to become available, which was the case with us. We rented from the family of a woman who had passed away.

The first night with the Toomeys, they said they had a wedding gift for us. Then they led us down into a dark basement. This was strange to me because in Savannah there were few basements. The city is just above sea level. They pulled sheets off of a beautiful antique dining room table and chest that glowed under the dim light with a soft patina. The third piece of furniture was a handsome corner cupboard. We were dumbfounded. A look of shock passed between Ollie and me. We had agreed we wanted the crisp, clean lines of modern furniture, Florida style. Without a word our plans changed. We simply couldn't refuse their gift and spoil their joy. In the years that came later, I was glad because we have grown to love and appreciate their gift of love.

Within a few days the spring cleaning was finished and the house was back to normal. The following Sunday afternoon Ollie's two sisters, Marj and

Mary Jane, and their families came to call. As we sat visiting, I casually pulled out a cigarette. Dear Pop almost broke his neck jumping up to light it. Marj and Mary Jane must have hated me because they never smoked in front of their parents—in fact, they always went to the upstairs bathroom and stuck their heads out the window to smoke. Later Ollie told me how much Pop hated smoking. I wailed, "Why didn't you tell me?"

"Because I wanted you to be yourself," Ollie answered.

Chapter Twenty-Two
A Yankee Home

In Dover things didn't go quite as we had planned. It was a month before we could move into our little furnished house, but that was just fine. The Toomeys were gracious and Mom taught me the Dover ways. She said things like, "Betsy, let's red up the house before we go shopping." I didn't know what she was talking about. Another odd saying was, "You know, your house has three clothes presses." I didn't want to seem ignorant, so I cornered Ollie in the bathroom before he left for work and asked him to translate.

He grinned. "Betsy," (that was his new name for me because he said I didn't look like a Lorraine) "red up simply means to ready the house and clothes presses are closets. You'll get the hang of it."

I nodded. "I guess so, but it's all like a foreign language."

We were busy with parties and people coming to call. It seemed as though most of the town wanted to meet Ollie's Southern wife, but the parties that I dreaded were the huge bridge luncheons at the country club. Ollie's sisters informed me that the ladies played serious bridge. I rode to the club with my nose in a bridge book.

At last we moved into our little house. It had a porch across the front, a living room, dining room, bath and two tiny bedrooms. If I sat on the bed in our bedroom and leaned over to pick up my shoes, I hit my head on the dressing table.

The first morning we were in our new house, I got up early to fix a hardy breakfast for Ollie: grits, bacon, eggs, coffee and even homemade biscuits. As I surveyed the table, I felt proud. When I served Ollie a glass of orange juice, he squirmed in his chair and finally said, "Honey, could I just have some cereal?" I broke into tears. Ollie jumped up and put his arms around me. "I'm sorry, sweetheart, I'm just not a breakfast man."

I said, "Well, I'll never cook breakfast again." And that has worked out well. I never have.

We spent the weekend unpacking our beautiful wedding gifts. On Sunday afternoon Ollie said, "I'm going to clean this dirty wallpaper." We pulled off our shoes and slipped into our shorts and old shirts. I said, "I'll help you."

"Oh, no, Betsy, you just watch."

"Okay, I'll fix us a rum and Coke."

We were having a grand time when we heard the door bell. "Oh, my gosh," I told Ollie as I looked through our glass paned door. "There's a man on the porch."

"Well, let him in," Ollie said.

I opened the door and there stood the Lutheran Pastor, Mr. Nicely. We invited him in and asked him to have a seat. He sat on one of the big, overstuffed chairs. Ollie and I sat side by side on the sofa like two naughty children. Mr. Nicely was a tall, big man with ruddy cheeks and an overly joyous disposition. His name fit him perfectly.

We were making small talk when out of the corner of my eye I saw a mouse running across the dining room floor. I screamed and without thinking, jumped up on the back of the sofa. Ol saw it too and ran into the kitchen and came out swinging a broom. Poor Mr. Nicely looked undone and said a hasty goodbye. Ollie and I collapsed in laughter. Mr. Nicely never returned.

While Ollie was at work, my days were spent poring over cookbooks, running to the grocery and trying to brighten our house. Ollie came home every day for lunch and often left the car for me. He rode his bike back to work. Ol's dad insisted that all his customers get cars before any of the family. Cars had not been built during the war, and everyone was clamoring for a new car.

I was busy and happy thinking myself the perfect housewife until my sister-in-law, Marj, came by one afternoon. I fixed tea for us. Then Marj said, "May I use your bathroom?"

When she returned, I noticed a strange look on her face. I said, "Marj, what is it?"

"Betsy, don't you ever clean your toilet?"

I smiled brightly. "Oh yes, we flush it every time we use it."

Marj laughed and laughed. Then she finally said, "I'm going home and get a few cleaning supplies. I'll be right back."

I had never seen anyone clean a toilet in my whole life. In my house they were just always clean. Then I remembered how *Thelma* or *Alma*, our maids, closed the door when they went into the bathroom and that sometimes they stayed a long time. They must have been cleaning.

Marj returned armed with Clorox, Old Dutch Cleanser, a bucket, an old tea cup, and rubber gloves which she pulled on. I couldn't believe what I was seeing. She dipped all of the water out of the toilet bowl with the cup, sprinkled the Dutch Cleanser inside and scrubbed with vigor. Then, with a flourish, she flushed. Next, she poured in Clorox and stood back admiring her work. I thanked her profusely.

After Marj left, I sat down on the sofa feeling like an ignorant child. I must be the laughing stock of Dover. The next day I went to the library and checked out a book *Efficiency House Cleaning* which became my bible. I worked hard. I wanted Ollie to be proud of me.

All the Toomeys were kind to us, and we enjoyed wonderful meals at their homes. From my Southern upbringing, I knew we should return the hospitality. Ollie thought it would be too much for me, but I assured him that I could do it. I had met a young high school student who agreed to help me on Saturdays. All I wanted her to do was serve and clean up. I took great pains to show her what to do, serve from the left, remove from the right and be careful with my crystal and china. I invited ten of Ollie's immediate family in addition to us which made a total of twelve. By crowding three card tables into the living room, I could use the dining room table for the food. I agonized over the menu, finally deciding on baked ham dressed with cloves, pineapple, brown sugar, and cherries, scalloped potatoes, tomato aspic, green beans, biscuits, and a fresh peach chiffon pie.

I worked like a Trojan, and the night of the party I was ready. Ollie and I stood in the dining room surveying my handiwork—candles, flowers, and all of the food that would be placed in our new silver serving pieces. We were ready for our first dinner party. Ollie served wine, and everything was fine until it was time for my helper to remove the dinner plates. I was proud as I saw her remove a plate from the right and go to the next person. Then to my horror, she scraped the first person's food into the next person's plate, carefully removing it from the right. She scraped and stacked all twelve plates. Oh well, so go the best laid plans. What could I do but smile? The one redeeming highlight of the evening was that everyone raved about the chiffon pie, and Ollie told me he loved me. What more could I want?

Ollie's best friend was Gene Spence. They had not been together in years because Ollie had been in the military and Gene had not passed the physical for the service. He became a licensed funeral director, married his childhood sweetheart, Libby, and had two little boys. Luckily, I liked Libby, and she became my best buddy. Libby was full of life and ready for whatever devilment I proposed. I think sometimes I shocked her, but Libby and Gene introduced Ollie and me to the young set who embraced us. Soon we had a busy social life.

In the south, I had never fully appreciated spring. It was just a continuation of scattered, beautiful warm days during the winter months. In Savannah you could actually miss spring altogether as overnight the hot, lazy days of summer suddenly enveloped you. This was not the case in Ohio. Spring crept in and made herself at home awhile. Dover perked up and came alive. People scrubbed their porches and planted flower boxes. They sat on their porches visiting with their neighbors and laughing, glad to finally shed their boots, winter coats and scarves.

Chapter Twenty-Three
Homesick in Ohio

Spring finally turned into summer. I was happy but with the warm weather my thoughts turned to Savannah. I think Ollie could read my mind because one day he asked if I would like to go home for a visit. I said, "Go home! Oh, Honey, I would love it. Can you go, too?"

He shook his head and in a mournful voice said, "I'll try to survive without you for a couple of weeks."

I hugged him. "When should I leave?"

"Well, you need to go before winter sets in."

As the plane took off, I felt like I was leaving part of me behind. Then the excitement of seeing Mother and my cherished Savannah took over. I was even glad to see Kelley. I cried as we drove home from the airport. My eyes took in all the old familiar places. What joy!

I was energized. I wanted to do it all and I did—lunch and shopping with friends, lengthy chats with Mother, trips to the beach where I took long walks drinking in the beauty of the white sand, the blue sea and the waves as they crashed against the shore. Kelley even arranged for a man to take Mother and me fishing for a whole day. I tried to permanently sear the beauty of coastal Georgia into my mind.

Some things had changed. Kelley had started closing the drugstores at nine-thirty at night instead of eleven-thirty. So, we often went to Johnny Harris' for our dinner or Alma prepared my favorite food and left it for us to eat at home. Also, Kelley had started teasing Mother by calling her Clara Belle. She hated it, so he changed it to Bella.

One night a long shrill sound pierced the two o'clock silence. I heard Kelley get out of bed and make his way to the front door muttering in a sleepy voice, "Who can that be at this hour?"

Mother called to me. I went into her bedroom and crawled under the covers with her. We waited fearfully. We could hear Kelley talking and finally we heard footsteps on the stairway. Kelley told us, "That's the damnedest thing I ever heard. Bella, your nephew is in a bit of trouble and wants to hide here. He was paying a visit to a lady friend up in the country when her husband returned and found them together. He was quick enough to escape through the back door. He jumped into his car and headed for Savannah. The husband followed him. There was a high-speed chase, and your nephew lost him. Then he came to our neighborhood, parked his car several blocks away and walked here. He begged, "Please let me stay here until daylight. Then I'll get up early and head for the North Carolina mountains. I'll stay there until this blows over."

Mother shook her head in disbelief, "What in the world is wrong with him?"

After Mother's nephew got settled in his room upstairs, the three of us plotted to give him a scare. I tiptoed to the door, opened it and laid my hand on the doorbell and pounded on the door. On cue, Kelley stomped to the door, and in a loud voice said, "I tell you we haven't seen him. No, he's not here and I don't appreciate you disturbing us." With that, he slammed the door.

After several minutes our guest crept down the steps. He was white-faced and trembling, "Kelley, what did the man say?"

We started laughing and he realized we had played a joke on him. Mother said, "I can't believe you did such a shameful thing."

He said, "Aunt Clara, believe me I've learned my lesson."

I guess he did because he lived an exemplary life the rest of his days, and he lived past ninety years of age.

As the days marched by, I began to compare my Ohio family to my Savannah family. In Ohio everything was in order and scheduled like a day in school. I realized my Georgia family would be considered unorthodox in Ohio. In Savannah in our free time there were no schedules for eating, sleeping, or going places, but there was always time for a joke and fun. I enjoyed the carefree days, but I missed Ollie and loved both families even though they were entirely different.

Ollie's letters were a continual source of joy. A letter arrived near the end of my visit. It read, "Darling, I miss you so much and damn these letters. They can't show you how much I adore you. Yours, Ollie." I was ready to go home to Ohio.

Chapter Twenty-Four
Georgia – Our Bundle of Joy

Home is where the heart is; and after my visit to Savannah, I knew my heart was definitely in Ohio. Ollie met me at the plane. It was a sweet reunion. Even our little house looked like a castle. After the war the great desire of young couples was to get on with life. We wanted it all, a home, security and a family.

On our first anniversary, February 14, 1947, Ollie had a big treat for me. We drove to Canton, Ohio, about twenty-five miles away. Our destination was Bender's, a restaurant which specialized in Maine Lobster. I licked my lips as the waitress tied a bright red bib around my neck and placed lobsters before us. Ollie sat back and laughed at the way I attacked the lobster. I reminded him my summer in Maine had taught me a few tricks. As I finished the last morsel, I began to feel strange. Ollie said it was because it was so warm in there.

Just as we got outside, I gave a gasp and lost my dinner on the beautiful white snow. I was so embarrassed I wanted to become invisible. People were lining up, waiting to go in, and they witnessed my dilemma. I'm sure they thought I had had too much to drink.

Later, I discovered I was pregnant. My nausea was morning sickness, but for me it turned out to be morning, noon, and night sickness and the beginning of nine months of hell. In addition to the sickness that lasted until the week our baby was born, it was the hottest summer in Ohio in over a hundred years.

In spite of my discomfort, Mom and Pop were thrilled. They were so thrilled they bought us our first home. It was red brick with a living room, dining room, small sunroom, and kitchen. On the second floor there were two bedrooms and a bath. The basement was an added bonus, and it had a commode. I was always trying to guess which john I could reach to throw up. Sometimes I didn't make it. Ugh!

It was a difficult delivery, but on Labor Day, September 1, 1947, our little bundle of joy arrived. Ollie named her Georgia Ann. We were told that seventy million babies were born in the post-war era. I was in the hospital two weeks and could go home only if Ollie got a hospital bed for our bedroom. I was confined to bed rest for two weeks, then two more weeks of not being able to use the stairs. Ollie informed me this would be our only child. He said he could not watch me endure this again. I only smiled as I held my baby. I knew she was worth it.

Thank goodness we had hired a woman for six weeks. Her name was Emma and she was better than any doctor. She knew just what to do to get me on the road to recovery, and little Georgia thrived under Emma's care.

Everything seemed perfect. And then Mother, Kelley, and Billie unexpectedly arrived. Mother said, "We just had to see our baby." They were ready to celebrate Savannah style. Emma was not happy. Her schedule was shot. The Toomeys were all amazed by the jubilant confusion at our house. Kelley was delighted Dover had a state liquor store, and he was ready to toast the new arrival morning, noon, and night. It was party time and confusion reigned. Mother and Billie shared the double bed in my bedroom. I, of course, used the hospital bed. Emma and Georgia were in the nursery and Kelley slept on the sofa in the sunroom. Ollie went home to Mom and Pop.

I hate to admit it, but I was glad when Kelley announced they had to go home. I was just too weak to enjoy the pandemonium, though I still cried when they left. Emma went into high gear and quickly put everything into order and made sure that I followed her instructions. I was in good shape by the time we said a tearful goodbye to Emma.

After that, Ollie and I were on our own. At lunch time every day Ollie came home to check on his girls and do the laundry. (I was not allowed to go to the basement.) He was fascinated by our new automatic front-load Bendix which had a round window in the door. Ol liked to watch the diapers tumble by. When the tumbling was completed, he hung diapers in the basement. He felt very important.

As the days went by, I became very quiet. I seemed to have lost my joy. The cold grey days made me feel blue. I couldn't help it. I was constantly finding fault with Dover and felt particularly blue when I thought about being away from Savannah at Christmas. However, Christmas in Ohio turned out to be picture book perfect with parties, snow and on Christmas Day, a gathering of all the Toomey clan at Mom's beautiful large dining room table. Everyone loved Georgia. She was such a happy baby.

Our Valentine anniversary rolled around again, February 14, 1948, and Ollie had the perfect gift for me, the gift of all gifts, an airplane ticket to Savannah. It was little Georgia's first airplane ride, and I was nervous and excited. Mother and Kelley met us at the airport with a huge blanket which Mother wrapped around the baby saying, "We're having a cold snap."

I laughed. It was fifty-four degrees, and I thanked God it was sunny.

Seeing family and friends was just what I needed. Lulline came one day and said, "Miss Bet, who's nursing your baby?"

I smiled and said, "Me."

Lulline just shook her head. She couldn't believe it. Savannah babies always had nurses.

104

Uncle George and Lucy Quin came to see the baby. Uncle George said, "Lorraine, are you going to let me baptize the baby?"

I replied, "Uncle George, let me talk with Ollie."

I called Ollie that night. And of course, Ollie said, "Go ahead."

I thought that was great, so Little Georgia was baptized while we were there by her great uncle, Dr. George Clary at Trinity Methodist Church where Ollie and I had been married.

Kelley truly fell in love with Georgia Ann. He had never been around a baby. He would get up early in order to have time to play with her. Then he would rush home at night and beg to wake her up. I saw an entirely new side of Kelley and I liked it.

The weather had warmed enabling me to take the baby to the park in her carriage almost every day. It was there that I searched my soul, and I didn't like what I saw. I had been mean and critical about Dover even though everyone had been good to me. And it was Ollie's home. It was just as special to him as my Savannah home was to me. I had been unkind to the man I loved. Right then and there I promised myself that things would be different. After all, Dover would be my home for the rest of my life. I was ready to return and apologize.

As always, Ollie was there waiting for us and welcomed us home. Perhaps little separations are good for married couples because we were like honeymooners all over again.

Shortly after I arrived home, Ollie told me, "Betsy, I've arranged several things since you've been gone. I've ordered one of those new televisions for us, but in order to get reception from Cleveland we have to build a tower beside our house. Is that all right with you?"

I was flabbergasted. "That's wonderful! Now, what else?"

"I found a young woman who can come once a week to help with the housework if you like her. What do you think of that?"

I threw my arms around him and said, "Honey, you are too good to me."

Amy came and she was perfect. She was tall and slender with light blond curly hair and blue eyes. The two of us were about the same age. In Ohio you had a helper, not a maid. Amy almost worked me to death. I was her helper. She sized up my situation and at once took charge of me, Georgia and my house. As we toiled together, I learned a bit about her background. Amy's father had been a junk man and her family had lived in squalor. As soon as she was old enough, she got a job and moved into her own sparkling clean, little place. Psychologically Amy had been marked. Dirt was her enemy and she attacked it with vigor. She offered to bathe Georgia, but I was afraid she'd rub off her skin.

One morning Amy walked in all squeaky clean saying, "Well Bets, today we're going to wash down the kitchen: the walls, woodwork, and clean the cupboards." That evening Ollie found a half dead but happy wife on the sofa.

Amy had one fault. She took the Lord's name in vain. She'd say something like, "G. D. Betsy, I told you not to put the salt in the cupboard without wiping off the box."

As the months passed by, the house was in such perfect order I said to Amy. "I think I'll have a bridge luncheon."

Amy smiled and answered, "Bets, don't count on me for bridge. I'll keep Georgia."

I never had the party. I'd have died before hurting Amy's feelings.

The TV tower was finally erected and Ollie brought home a large wooden floor model TV with a ten-inch round screen in the middle. We were excited. Imagine, being able to have entertainment in your own living room. We got it all hooked up, put Georgia to bed, and got comfy to watch the *Milton Berle Texaco Theater.* It was thrilling.

Then the family got the word that we had a TV. Every night at eight o'clock I had chairs lined up in the living room for the Sid Caesar-Imogene Coca show or whatever was on. We all agreed that it was a miracle, even though the picture on the black and white screen was often covered by what looked like snow. Eventually, each of the Toomeys bought a TV and stayed home. We weren't lonely at all.

True to my word, I stopped being critical of Dover and started putting my best foot forward. I found a lovely elderly neighbor who would gladly babysit. Ollie got involved in the Dover Chamber of Commerce and later became its president. The Junior Woman's Club welcomed me into its ranks. A gutsy little group of eight girls played bridge every Monday morning, ignoring the age old custom in Dover of Monday morning laundry day.

It was hard to believe that our baby girl was talking and toddling. She was our doll baby. One night we were watching news on TV when Georgia, who was sitting in her little rocking chair, stuck her foot out and said, "Dorda's shoes dirty, dod damn."

Ollie laughed and said, "Betsy, you've got to do something about Amy's cursing."

Our crowd enjoyed going to the Country Club dances, but our favorite affair was the Halloween Ball. We spent months getting together to plan our theme. One year we went as a child's birthday party. We all dressed up like children complete with the cake and all-day suckers. I remember wearing black paten leather Mary Jane shoes and little white socks. Ollie wore navy short pants, a white shirt with a Peter Pan collar and a Bolla hat with a navy ribbon streaming down the back.

Another year each couple chose their own costume. Ollie and I dressed up as the absent minded professor and Mae West. Ollie wore tails, a formal white shirt, black tie, and long underwear without trousers. He walked around reading a book. I padded myself, hips and bust, rented a wig with long white curls, and wore a long, blue, sequin dress and a huge floppy hat with a blue plume. Ollie and I won a prize for our costume.

I often wondered why I had been so critical and ugly. Dover was a perfect place to live if it couldn't be Savannah. But Ollie never forgot my time of depression because he insisted that I return to Savannah with Georgia sometime during the winter months. And then the three of us would go for two glorious weeks in the summer. What a wonderful vacation that was! We were footloose and fancy free as Mother and Alma doted on keeping Georgia.

Ollie met Irving Metz who was the executive director of the Savannah Chamber of Commerce. And they often had lunch together, enjoying discussing community service. We had such good times, but we were always ready to head back to Dover.

Chapter Twenty-Five
The Deadly Punch

Life in Dover just couldn't have been any better, or so we thought, until one day I visited Mom and learned everyone (Mom, Pop, Mary Jane, and Marj) was all stirred up,   Floss and her husband Dale were coming from California for a visit. I hadn't met Floss, Ollie's sister, yet, but I had heard some wild tales. She had been the baby girl in the family, and when Ollie arrived seven years later, Floss wasn't happy. Tales were that she tried to drown him in the bathtub and when that failed she pushed his carriage down a long hill. Ollie must have had nine lives because he survived.

But what made the family nervous was that she had gone to Billy Graham's first crusade in Los Angeles. It was scheduled for three weeks but lasted for eight weeks. Floss was carried away, claiming that she had been born again and that no one else in the family was "saved" even though they all attended church regularly. We knew that she was coming to Dover with a mission, and we were more than a little afraid. To my surprise, I thought she was funny and very stylish.

Ollie and I invited Floss and Dale for dinner to give Mom and Pop a night off. I had been informed that they were teetotalers and that I was to serve them nothing stronger than tomato juice. Dinner went well, but then that frightful, fateful moment happened. Floss smiled brightly and said, "Well kids, are you born again?"

We said in unison, "I hope so."

That did it. Floss became very stern.

"Well you aren't. If you were, you wouldn't say you hope so. You'd know."

That turned my even tempered husband into a maniac. Floss and Ollie went at it like two small children. It made my head hurt, and I was glad when Floss said they had to leave.

No one cried when Floss and Dale returned to California. In fact, we all gave a sigh of relief.

******

As fall approached and the trees turned brilliant flaming colors, I shuddered, thinking of the grey sunless days that were ahead. But I had learned a new trick. If I couldn't have the sun, I would at least have light, so first thing in the morning I turned on all the lights in the house. I was as happy as a clam.

The Deadly Punch

We were invited to a large Thanksgiving Eve cocktail party given by a local banker and his wife. Two other couples, Ann and George, Libby and Gene, went with us. George picked us up and we all crowded into his car. The night was cold and snow was falling, but that didn't dull our spirits. As we approached the large house ablaze with lights, we were all in a holiday mood. The house was beautifully decorated. In the huge dining room a large table was laden with food and a handsome silver punch bowl was filled to the brim. We noticed a steady stream of guests filling and refilling their cups at the punch bowl. Ollie and I joined the group and filled our cups.

I took one sip of punch, and I couldn't believe my taste buds. It was the deadly Chatham County Artillery Punch. I grew up knowing about this drink. The recipe was kept secret by Savannahians for years. It originated with the Chatham County Artillery and had been widely served in Savannah since the late 1800's. It is delightfully delicious but dangerously powerful. It can knock you out if you are not very careful. Then I thought it can't be, so I took another sip. I knew I was right. I whispered into Ollie's ear, "I can't believe it, but this is Chatham County Artillery punch. Be very, very careful."

It was at that party we met Dr. Ray Crawley and his wife. He was the new doctor in town and Dover's first obstetrician and gynecologist. They were delightful people. I wished he had been there when Georgia arrived. As the six of us drove home, we all agreed that it was a swell party. Ollie and I invited our friends to come in for awhile.

Ollie took our babysitter home and when he got back, he fixed drinks for everyone. We were laughing and joking when suddenly we realized that George was missing. "Oh he must be in the bathroom," I said. But he wasn't. We looked everywhere.

We called, "George, where are you? Come join the party." We searched the house. No George. The men put on their coats, boots, and hats and went outdoors to see if they could find him. They didn't. We were beginning to get frightened. Finally, Ollie looked in George's car and there he was, curled up on the backseat, out like a light. Chatham County Artillery Punch had claimed one more victim.

Chatham Artillery Punch Recipe from Clara Clary's Files

> 1 ½ gallons Catawba Wine
> ½ gallon rum
> 1 quart gin
> 1 quart brandy
> ½ pint Benedictine

1 ½ quarts rye whiskey
1 ½ gallons strong tea
2 ½ pounds brown sugar
Juice 1 ½ dozen oranges
Juice 1 ½ dozen lemons
1 bottle maraschino cherries

Mix ingredients two days before time to use. Add a case of champagne when ready to serve.

The Chatham Artillery, organized in 1786, is the oldest military organization in Georgia. No one is sure how this strong punch recipe originated, but Savannahians know that it is a powerful brew, and you have to know how to handle this devilish concoction. Some say that gentle ladies made up the first recipe, and one by one, officers of the Artillery added this and that until they created the most famous concoction in Savannah history.

Chapter Twenty-Six
Make Mine Schlitz

January 1950 came and Ollie's Christmas gift had been a ticket to Savannah. As always, Georgia and I stayed a month. That set the Dover gossips on fire. I could just hear them. "Well, she's finally left him. He should have married a good Dover girl." I bet they were surprised when I always came home.

Georgia loved to visit Bella and her KK. She and Kelley were fast friends. He spoiled her terribly. They took rides in the car before breakfast. He said he wanted to show her Savannah. But when the weather was warm, he put her in the red wagon he had bought for her and pulled her all over the neighborhood. Kelley called Georgia his boy.

One night as Alma was fixing dinner, Georgia wanted to help. Alma tied a big towel around her, placed her on a stool and said, "Miss Georgia, you can wash these beans for me." Georgia worked very hard and finally informed Alma they were all done. When we ate dinner that night and bit into the beans they were just as soapy as they could be. After all, little Georgia thought when you wash something it takes soap.

Georgia and I always said goodbye with tears, but we arrived in Dover with smiling faces. Ollie was there welcoming us home with hugs and kisses. I knew without a shadow of a doubt that home was where he was.

Dr. Ray Crawley and his wife Dorothy had joined our crowd, and it seemed we were seeing more and more of them. There was nothing shy about Ray. He asked how many children we had. When we said one, he asked "Why?" He kept at us until Ollie took him aside and told him about my whole horrible experience.

After that, Ray's new conversation went like this: "Having one child is a terrible risk. What if something happened to Georgia?" Then with a smile and the most sincere look, he said, "If Betsy gets pregnant, I will personally take care of her. She would be fine. Just think about it."

We did think about what Ray said, but I had been asked to interview for a teaching position at the new Fred Astaire Studio. I explained to them I only wanted to work two evenings a week. Miracle of miracles, they wanted me, and my schedule could be just as flexible as I wanted. Ollie was all for it saying, "I'll keep Georgia. You'll really enjoy that."

It was fun for me, but as the weeks rolled by, Ollie and I kept thinking about what Ray had said. I quit teaching and immediately became pregnant. What a difference this time! For the first three months or so Ray gave me shots and I was never sick. I felt wonderful and everybody said I looked great. As my due date approached, Ollie and I made plans.

******

Sugarcreek, Ohio, is a small town which has a large population of Amish people. It is just twelve miles from Dover. We had heard that you could hire an Amish girl to come live and work for you. We wanted someone who would take care of Georgia, the new baby, and me. We made contact with an Amish family, the Yoders, whose daughter wanted to work. There were just a few stipulations. The family must come to your home and look you over. The Amish are wonderful, God-fearing people who live by very strict rules including no electricity or cars. They drive horses and buggies. Unmarried men drive open wagons, but once married they are allowed to have a covered buggy. Marriage seems to have its privileges. Unmarried men are clean shaven. Once married, men can have beards.

The Yoders hired a driver and came to inspect our house and look us over. They are very clean people. Amy and I scrubbed and cleaned our house until it sparkled. Ollie and I did not know what to expect.

The day of the inspection arrived. Mr. and Mrs. Yoder were dressed in black. She had on a very long cape and a hood. Their daughter Katherine had a little white cap on top of her head. And over that was a black hood. She had on a green cotton dress, a white apron, and a huge black shawl. The Yoders were pleasant people, but when they walked around my house, they spoke in Dutch to each other. (Pennsylvania Dutch is a form of German.) They looked inside closets and kitchen cupboards. Finally, Mr. Yoder said, "Yah, our daughter can work for you."

With a sigh of relief, we all sat down to make plans. It was agreed that Katherine would come two weeks before my due date. We hired her for six weeks.

After the Yoders left, Ollie and I collapsed and wondered what was in store for us. Amy called and wanted to know if we had passed the test. She was happy for us. We had agreed that she would help Mom on my day until I needed her again.

Katherine arrived late one afternoon in mid-January, 1952. She took her meager possessions upstairs to the room that she would share with Georgia Ann. I left Georgia and Katherine to get acquainted and went to the kitchen to put the finishing touches on dinner. Ollie came in from work and headed to the refrigerator for a cold beer. I shook my head. As Katherine and a happy little Georgia walked into the kitchen, Ollie looked up and welcomed Katherine. Then jokingly he said, "Katherine, would you like a beer?"

She smiled. "Make mine a Schlitz."

You could have knocked us over with a feather.   She was going to fit into this family just fine.

******

Dr. Crawley's words came true.   He said I would get along just fine if I had a second baby, and I did.   I was never sick during my nine months of pregnancy, and there were no complications with my baby's delivery.   It all seemed too good to be true.

Mary Claire Toomey was born January 30, 1952, and within a week Katherine, Ollie, and Georgia welcomed us home.   Georgia was four and a half years old.   She loved her new baby sister and stroked Mary Claire's hands saying, "Oh Mommy, softie hands, softie hands."   I kept admiring my baby's perfectly round head and remembering how Georgia's poor little head had been shaped like an ice cream cone because of the forceps used in delivery.

I was glad to have Katherine with us. Even though the delivery had gone well, it still took some time to regain my full strength, and Katherine was just the right person to look after the children and me.

Chapter Twenty-Seven
The Third Knowing

With Katherine's help the days passed quickly, but one day stands out above all the others. It's the day Mary Claire was six weeks old.

A frown creased my forehead as I recalled the awful dream I had the night before. A shiver went down my spine as I made my way to the kitchen. I poured a cup of coffee and sat down at the dining room table. Katherine and Georgia were eating oatmeal and Ollie had his head in the morning paper. He didn't pay any attention when I said I had a bad dream. I persisted in a whisper, "Ollie," I said, "I had a frightful dream. I dreamed Billie died. It was so real. I saw her lying in her casket. She had on a white formal gown and her dark hair framed her face. She looked like an angel."

Ollie patted my hand and said, "Betsy, you're just remembering Bella, Kelley, and Billie being here when Georgia was born, and you are missing them."

I glared at Ollie. He didn't understand. It was the horrible *knowing*. I pulled myself together and asked, "Is this the day you're going to Cleveland on business?"

"Yes, and it looks like the roads might be slippery. I probably won't get back until dinnertime."

Ollie left and I went upstairs to check on the baby. Try as I might, I just couldn't forget the dream. I picked little Mary Claire up and settled down to rock her. I began to sing a song my mother had made up. It was sung to me and I had sung it to Georgia. It went something like this:
This is Mother's baby. This is Mother's baby. Yes, it's Mother's baby. You could name everyone in the family, like this is Daddy's baby and so on. I was just singing, *This is Billie's baby* when the phone rang. I put Mary Claire in her crib and answered the phone.

There was a hesitation and then Kelley in a hoarse voice said, "It's Billie."

I replied, "I know she's dead."

I could hear Kelley speaking to Mother in a shaken voice. "Bella, she knows."

I must have been in shock. I didn't cry. Somehow, someway I listened and heard about the sudden death of my precious aunt, my buddy. She had influenced my life and I loved her so.

Kelley related the details of her death to me: Billie and Stanley had gone out for dinner. Returning home, Billie had undressed and gotten into bed to read a while. Stanley was in the bathroom when he heard a gurgling sound. Fearing that she was in trouble, he went to her and called an ambulance. Billie died on the way to the hospital. She had suffered a cerebral hemorrhage.

It was all such a shock to me. Billie was only forty-six years old. In a daze I went downstairs. I collapsed on the loveseat. I whispered to Katherine, "My aunt died." A tear rolled down my cheek. Georgia said, "Mommy, Mommy!" And I turned to Georgia and said, "Georgie, Porgy puddin' and pie. Mommy's all right. I bet Katherine will read you one of your favorite Golden Books. How about, *The Happy Family?*"

Left alone all I could think about was that I wanted Ollie, and he would be late getting home. I don't know how long I sat there. Then I heard the doorbell ringing. I opened the door and there stood our best friends, Libby and Gene. They took one look at me and gently led me back to the loveseat. I began weeping and saying, "Oh, Libby, it was the knowing." She and Gene looked puzzled. I explained how the day my father died I had an unshakable feeling that something terrible was about to happen, and it did.

I told them, "The only way I can explain it is that it is a knowing deep inside. Last night I dreamed that Billie died. And this morning I received a call that it was true. It frightens me." They stayed all day until Ollie got home. When he heard, he held me tight. I cried. He cried. He felt and shared my pain. I don't know how we got through the following days. We decided it wasn't feasible for me and the baby to attend the funeral, and that made me feel worse.

Later, as Mother and I talked on the phone, I told her about my dream and the knowing. "Mother, I saw Billie lying in her casket. She had on a beautiful white dress." There was a long silence on the phone. Then Mother said, "Bettye Lorraine, Billie was buried in a white dress."

******

As much as I loved my Aunt Billie, I knew I couldn't let my grief overtake my life. After my father's death, my mother threw herself into running the Clary Drugstores. It filled her days with new activity, a reason to get out and go on with her life.

"That's what I need," I thought, "new activity, a change. Billie would want me to keep moving on." With the addition of a new baby, I realized our house seemed too small. Ollie agreed, so my days became filled with looking for a new home.

We found a perfect house. It was a two-story, white colonial with a living room, dining room, den, kitchen, and powder room downstairs and three bedrooms and a bath upstairs. But it was the basement that thrilled us most. It was divided into a recreation room, a laundry room, a playroom for the children and even a room for a work bench. We made an offer and it was accepted. We had some painting and remodeling done and suddenly we were moving. Katherine's parents agreed for her to stay, and what a help she was. Mom and Pop were in the process of building a smaller retirement home just three blocks away from us, and they gave us all the furniture they couldn't use. Our house was furnished overnight.

Ollie was so excited with his shop in the basement he bought a complete set of tools, even down to a leveler. He bought every size nail and screw and put them in glass jars neatly arranged on shelves above his work bench. Of course, he had never built anything or fixed anything in his life, but that didn't seem to matter. Every night after dinner he ran down to the basement to sit and admire his new shop, but he never actually used a single tool, nail or screw.

Katherine and I spent hours putting the house in order. As we worked, she told me bits and pieces about her life. I was fascinated as I learned the Amish way and about growing up on the Yoder farm. Her family raised chickens, milked cows, and canned summer vegetables from their garden. They had no electricity and no cars, so all the work on the farm had to be done manually. Her father was very strict, and she and her sister had to tow the line. Their weekends were spent worshipping with the Amish community.

Katherine told me about a strange custom. She said, "When girls are of a marriageable age, the father paints the front door blue. If a couple fancies each other, after a reasonable time, they bundle."

I asked Katherine, "What in the world is bundling?"

She laughed and replied, "The suitor comes to your house and spends the night with you." My eyebrows shot up.

She explained, "A bed is put in the living room. At bedtime the young couple retires. A board is placed down the center of the bed. There is no hanky-panky as the mother and father are awake listening all night."

"Wow, that seems like a strange custom, Katherine."

She smiled and said, "It is our way."

"Have you ever bundled?"

"No, but I'm close to it."

I knew she had a boyfriend because he called her sometimes. When he called, they spoke in Dutch. I couldn't understand a word, except occasionally when Katherine giggled and I heard *Betsy* which she pronounced Bet-ceee.

Now that we were all settled, we began to plan our Savannah vacation. I came up with a brilliant idea, providing it was agreeable with

Mother, Kelley and Katherine's family. We would take Katherine to Savannah with us. Everyone agreed and in late June the five of us set out for Savannah. It was a long, hot ride. We had to ride with the windows open which added to our misery. There was no air conditioning. In the end, however, it was all worth it.

Katherine had never been out of Tuscarawas County, Ohio. This was an adventure for her. The children were good. We sang songs, read books, and were grateful when they slept.

Mother had plenty of room. Bella, as Georgia was now calling Mother, always made everyone feel welcome, and she and Kelley doted on our girls. We took Katherine on sight seeing trips around Savannah, and she cheerfully helped Alma with the cooking and household chores.

One day while Georgia, Ollie and I were at the beach, we decided we must take Katherine to see the ocean. So the next day I asked, "Katherine, would you like to see the ocean?"

"Oh yes, Betsy."

I gave her one of my bathing suits. She went into the bathroom to put it on. She didn't come out, and she didn't come out. Finally, I asked, "Would you like one of Ollie's shirts as a cover up?"

"Oh yes, Betsy. Thank you."

When Katherine saw the vast expanse of the Atlantic Ocean, her eyes opened wide in disbelief and wonder. She uttered a soft prolonged oh-h. After some prodding, she ventured ankle deep into the shimmering foam as the waves rolled onto the shore. Then Ollie and I simply couldn't get her out of the water. I will always remember her standing in the waves, Ollie's white shirt flipping in the breeze and a constant, incredible smile on her face.

Chapter Twenty-Eight
Consolidating Clary's Drugstores

Just before we left, Mother told me she and Kelley had come to a momentous decision. They were going to close Clary's Drugstore on Bull Street and consolidate the Abercorn and Bull Street Stores. This made me sad. The Bull Street store held so many memories of my father.

Kelley told me that many of the beautiful old row houses on Jones Street were being bought by physicians. They were restoring them and moving their offices there. That neighborhood was going to produce a steady flow of prescriptions.

As we talked Kelley said, "Bet, I know how badly you feel, but business is business. The consolidation will give us less overhead."

They were going to completely remodel the exterior of the Abercorn store even to the point of tearing down several connecting row houses on Abercorn Street to make room for a parking lot.

They were also planning to perform the major feat of removing the top floors over the store. I hated seeing historic buildings changed, but all was in the name of progress, according to them. And to my amazement they planned to have it all finished by the fall of 1952.

Mother said she would keep me informed of the progress, which she did. The Abercorn store became a one-story building with a large parking lot. Kelley was thrilled with the new exterior. They sent me pictures. I thought the store looked horrible. It had a flat top and looked too modern for my taste.

To my surprise, all the remodeling was done without closing the store except for one full day.

When we returned to Ohio, Katherine's parents said it was time for her to come back home to Sugarcreek. With tears we said our goodbyes. She had come to stay six weeks with us and had stayed eight months.

******

After Katherine left, there was a big void in our lives. But as the days passed, we found we enjoyed having just our family in the house. Amy came back to help me one day a week, and that was enough to keep me on my toes with my housekeeping.

Sunday mornings became a special time for Ollie and me. Ollie would pull his clothes on over his pajamas and drive little Georgia to the Lutheran Church for Sunday school. He would drop her off and Mom would bring her home. I'd get Mary settled for her morning nap, and when Ollie returned we would enjoy our time together.

One Sunday morning as I was giving Georgia her breakfast, she looked up at me with her big blue eyes and said, "Say, why do I have to go to church and you guys don't?"

That gave me a start. The next Sunday we all went to church, and we've been there regularly ever since.

We had settled into a good life in Dover, but I still found that my thoughts kept returning to Savannah and to Kelley in particular. I had begun to see something good in him. It was his love for my children. It was evident that he had experienced hurt in his life, but I could also see the love that kept shining through each time he looked at Georgia and baby Mary Claire. I began to feel the lump of bitterness dissolving in my heart. It wasn't his fault that my father had died or that my mother fell in love with him. I began the journey of forgiveness and acceptance of my stepfather. I felt free, but best of all I felt love.

As autumn came upon us, Dover went into its annual frenzy. Halloween was coming and the celebration wasn't just one night of tricks and treating. It lasted a whole week. There was never a peaceful dinnertime because goblins were ringing our doorbell. Little Mary was frightened by the spooks. Georgia picked up on this and took great delight in scaring her sister. I finally took a horrible rubber skeleton mask away from her and hid it in my closet.

One night as I pulled off my clothes to get ready for bed, I reached for my gown and spied the mask. In a moment of devilment I pulled the mask over my head. I walked into the bathroom where Ollie was busy brushing his teeth. I just quietly stood there.

Ollie glanced up and saw the skeleton lady. He almost slammed his toothbrush through his jaw. Laughing, he said, "Betsy, you're a nut."

Chapter Twenty-Nine
Let's Sell

I bemoaned the fact that my precious little girls were growing up so fast. Georgia was six on September 1, 1953. Because Dover's cut-off date for school entry was August 31, I had Georgia at home for an extra year.

When Georgia started school in the fall of 1954, I found it was very different from Savannah's Charles Ellis that I attended. The children in Dover came home for lunch. Then they went back to school until mid afternoon. In Savannah we had lunch at school. I went to the cafeteria and got my favorite pineapple sandwich and a bottle of milk for ten cents. School was dismissed at two o'clock p.m. When children got home, family dinner was on the table. Most businessmen came home for dinner and forty winks. My father ate at his drugstore, so it was just Mother, me, and whoever else she invited for our two o'clock dinner.

Georgia liked school, and Mary Claire was thriving. Everyone in the family was happy but Ollie. Something strange was going on with him. I noticed that he was very quiet and less jovial. I finally asked him what was wrong. His answer shocked me.

He said, "Betsy, I hate my work and it saddens me to think I'll be doing this for the rest of my life."

Ollie had such high expectations for his job when he came home from the war. He had been raised with the knowledge that one day the S. Toomey Company would be his. All his life he had heard how his great-grandfather, Samuel Toomey, had come to America from Cork County, Ireland and settled in Canal Dover, Ohio.

Samuel was a blacksmith by trade. In the 1850s he built buggies, training carts, and some of the finest racing sulkies in America. He manufactured a lightweight double axle racing sulky which bettered racing time. They were shipped to customers all over the world.

The Toomeys phased in the new horseless carriage in 1910. The first car they ever sold was an Everett Metzgar Flanders. They also sold the Hudson Super Six and Apperson Jack Rabbit. With the purchase of a car, the Toomeys offered driving lessons. They also had the distinction of becoming one of Dodge Brothers first dealerships in the country.

In 1940 Henry Ford placed a Toomey Sulky in the Ford Museum in Dearborn, Michigan, a fitting tribute to Samuel Toomey, a master craftsman. I could understand Ollie's turmoil. He felt an obligation to continue the S. Toomey Company's fine tradition, but he was miserable running the business.

120

What could I do to help my husband? I was glad when I answered the telephone one day and heard our friend Libby saying, "We ain't got no body." She and her husband had bought a funeral home in the small town of Gnadenhutten, just outside of Dover. Someone always had to be on duty, so Libby often asked us to come to their place for supper.

I said, "Fine." I thought maybe this would cheer Ollie up. Gene was his best friend.

When we arrived we walked into Libby's big country kitchen. Pots were bubbling on the stove. I walked over to the door that led to the staircase and their family living quarters. I yoo-hooed, "Libby, Gene, we're here."

Libby answered, "We'll be down in a jiffy. Just don't get nosey."

With that, Ollie and I went into the sitting room of the funeral home. I sat down and began to play the piano. Ollie opened a door and went up a ramp.

"I'm going to look at Gene's new casket and preparation room." He was groping around looking for a light when he saw a hanging cord. He reached over a casket and pulled it.

I was just going up the ramp to take a look also when Ollie came down full force and knocked me over. About that time Libby and Gene came into the living room. Looking at the two of us on the floor, Gene said, "I see you got nosey. We had a call after we talked to you."

We all had a good laugh, and believe me, we never wandered around the funeral home again. Ollie had almost gone nose to nose with a cadaver.

While visiting Gene and Libby, Ollie relaxed and had a good time, but when we returned home he became tense and quiet again. He couldn't shake the guilt he felt, the guilt of letting his father down if he left the business. His solace was found in volunteer work.

At last, he went to his father and told him his feelings. To his surprise, his father said, "Let's sell. I always wanted to live in Kentucky, and I never lived my dream." The S. Toomey Company was sold in 1955. The business was over a hundred years old.

Now what? It took considerable time to get everything settled. And then we were in a state of limbo, not knowing which way to go. Ollie started looking for jobs and got an interview with the Petroleum Trade Association in Jacksonville, Florida. They were looking for an Executive Director. Ollie kissed his three girls goodbye and drove to Savannah to stay a day or two with Mother before his interview.

Upon his arrival in Savannah, he called his friend Irv Metz, the Chamber of Commerce executive, to tell him what was going on in his life.

Irv said, "Ollie, why would you go to Jacksonville? This is Betsy's hometown and it's a wonderful place to live."

Ollie replied, "Yes, Irv, but I need a job."

"Ollie, I know just the perfect job for you. The Home Builders of Chatham County are looking for an Executive Director to organize a trade association. You'll be perfect and when I have an opening, I want you at the chamber."

Ollie had the interview, took the job and never went to Jacksonville. He called to tell me the news. When I picked up the phone, I heard an excited, happy hubby. I said, "You got the job."

"I sure did, and it's in Savannah. You're going home."

I couldn't believe my ears. It just wouldn't sink in. When the news got out in Dover, the word was that I had won and poor Ollie was being forced to take his wife back south.

Things moved quickly. Our house was sold overnight. We packed and suddenly in the fall of 1956 we were saying goodbye to dear friends and a wonderful family. Leaving Mom and Pop was the hardest of all.

The morning we left all the neighbors congregated around our car to say goodbye. I started to weep. When the little girls saw me crying, they cried too. Ollie drove for miles with three weeping females.

Finally, he said, "Betsy, you're the damdest woman I ever saw. If you don't stop crying by the time we reach the Ohio River, I'm going to turn this car around and I promise we'll go back to Dover and never leave."

I quickly stopped crying and so did the children. We dried our eyes and soon we were all laughing. We were heading toward a new adventure.

Chapter Thirty
Returning to Paradise

My face was flushed and my heart was pounding as we drove across the big bridge which takes you into Savannah. I said, "Georgia, Mary, look, that's the Savannah River." Although we had all seen it dozens of times before, this was different. Even the children sensed the excitement. I was coming home.

Mother and Alma were waiting for us as we pulled into Bella's drive. There was hugging, kissing and a little crying. What a relief to be here. Mother quickly told us that Kelley was coming home for dinner. He didn't want to miss the fun.

Our plan was to stay with Bella and Kelley until we found a house. Then our furniture would be shipped from Ohio.

Monday morning we all were up bright and early to see Ollie off for his first day at his new job. After he left, I started making a list of all the things I needed to do to get us settled. It was important to get Georgia enrolled in school. She was shy and didn't want to go, but I told her she would like Charles Ellis and said, "Just think, that was where Mommy went when she was a little girl." That made her smile and off we went.

I was amazed at how little the school had changed and delighted that everyone was so nice. I felt fine leaving Georgia.

My next project was taking Mary to a preschool and that, too, worked well. Mary was a happy-go-lucky child, and she was laughing and at home as soon as we walked in.

On the weekends Ollie and I did our house searching. We were surprised at how the city had grown. There were new subdivisions everywhere. At long last, we zeroed in on the location we liked.

Meanwhile, Mary had made a new friend. He was one of the cutest little boys I had ever seen. His name was Kirk Victor. He had a sister Andrea who was Georgia's age. Soon our girls were at the Victor's house or they were at ours. When I met their mother, Terry, we became friends overnight. She immediately joined us in our house search. Her husband was Dr. Irving Victor, a urologist, whom I remembered from Charles Ellis.

Savannah is such a friendly city. We didn't let too many weeks roll by before we started church shopping. We finally fell in love with the Lutheran Church of the Ascension. The church is beautiful and historic. The original church dates back to 1771.

The Church of the Ascension is across from Wright Square where there is a monument to Tomochichi, the brave Indian who was a friend to General Charles Oglethorpe the founder of Savannah. The monument is a large granite rock that's placed there in Tomochichi's honor. I asked Georgia and Mary the same question Savannahians have been asking for years. "Girls, do you want Tomochichi to talk to you?"

They nodded yes.

"Well, you must walk around the monument three times and then ask, 'What are you doing Tomochichi?' And he'll answer you."

The girls eagerly walked around three times and waited patiently. "Mommy he didn't answer."

"Oh, yes, he did. You asked him what he was doing and what did he say?"

"Nothing."

"That's what he always says." I laughed.

"Oh, Mommy, you tricked us," they answered in unison. And I remembered the story of my mother being so gullible when she first came to Savannah and walked around the stone. That was back in 1917, and here were her grandchildren doing the same thing in 1957, forty years later.

We finally found a house in Kensington Park. It was a brand new ranch style with almost the same amount of room we had in Dover except there was no basement. Savannah has few basements because the town is at sea level. We moved in and I worked hard getting us straight. How I longed for Katherine!

Georgia's new school, Virginia Lord Heard, was within walking distance and Mary had a neighbor friend, Lennie Shore. One day while Lennie and Mary were playing in Mary's room I peaked my head around the door and caught a glimpse of Mary in conversation. Mary said, "Lennie, we're going to play school and I'm the teacher."

Lennie nodded her head and smiled.

Mary said. I'm going to read you the Twenty-Third Psalm. She cleared her throat and began.

The Lord is my shepherd I shall not want.
He makes me to lie down in green pastures.
He roasteth my soul...

Then she went on and finished the Psalm.

I called out to Mary, "That's wonderful! Would you read it to me once more?"

And Mary "roasteth" her soul again. Of course, I knew she couldn't read a word.

I've always heard it said that you can't go home. I don't agree with that but I will say that it isn't an easy task. It's hard to leave one culture and enter into another. Part of my heart was in Ohio. I missed my friends, yet I loved being in Savannah. In some ways it all seemed like a fairy tale. Many nights I slipped out of bed and tiptoed into the living room. Standing at the picture window, I looked out at the southern moon shining on the long silvery Spanish moss swaying in the trees. I had to pinch myself to make sure it was real.

But it didn't take long for us to settle in. I rekindled old friendships every day. And Ollie was so happy he said, "I'd work for free if I didn't have to support my family."

Our joy seemed to know no end. Then one day Mother called, "I have a surprise for you."

I couldn't imagine what she was talking about. Bella, the unpredictable, I thought.

"Kelley and I have been looking at houses, and we've found one in Kensington Park. Would you like to see it?"

She took me to see it.

"Well, how do you like it?" she asked.

Of course, I said it was wonderful. It was similar to ours, and it would be grand for them to be just around the corner. Mother's eyes twinkled and she smiled, "I knew you'd like it. We bought it today."

When I told Ollie, he was not quite as enthusiastic as I was. I said "Don't worry, I will have a little talk with Bella." And I did.

I said, "I am thrilled we can be so close, but Mother, we need a few ground rules. We can be together all day. But when five o'clock comes, I don't want you to be at my house, and I'm not going to be at yours."

To my relief Mother smiled. "That's fine with me." And it was. She kept her part of the bargain and never complained.

Chapter Thirty-one
St. Patrick's Day (in Savannah)

Savannah is always ready to party, and St. Patrick's Day is the perfect excuse. The holiday has been celebrated since the 1800s. And it seems to gather more momentum each year. Ollie tried to explain to Mary and Georgia the phenomenon that was to take place on the seventeenth of March. "Girls, you are about to get a holiday. Every school in Savannah will close on the March 17. In fact, all of Savannah becomes Irish on that day, black and white alike."

The idea of a holiday caught Georgia's attention, and both girls became excited.

Their first St. Patrick's Day in Savannah arrived, and Bella, the girls and I went to Clary's on Abercorn Street. It was a prime location from which to watch the parade. Kelley was ready for us. He had a big, broad smile on his face and wore a green bow tie. His white pharmaceutical coat sported a shamrock. He told the girls St. Patrick was a priest in Ireland who used the three-leaf shamrock to explain the trinity. He said, "The three pronged green leaf represents God the father, God the son, and God the Holy Spirit, three in one."

I smiled to myself remembering that eons ago Kelley had been a preacher.

The streets were jammed with a noisy, happy crowd. And beer, much of it green, was flowing. In the distance we could hear the boom, boom sound of a big drum. The excitement was mounting as the parade came into view. Never had I seen so many bands. They came from neighboring towns.

All branches of the military were represented, even a Marine band from Parris Island, South Carolina. Savannah High School's marching band and the Catholic Military School, St. Benedict, were also proudly marching. But the bands that received the most applause were the black bands. Their music was lively, and the drum majors and the majorettes strutted their stuff. We had to hold Mary down. She wanted to strut with them.

There were floats and men on horses as well as the men of the Hibernian Society, marching, smiling and tipping their green bowlers. The parade went on and on. Everyone sang "When Irish Eyes Are Smiling" and shouts went up: *Erin Go Bragh,* which means "Ireland forever."

That evening Ollie fixed us a martini, which he delighted in calling a Mar-Toomey. The two of us sat in the living room to discuss the events of the day while corn beef and cabbage simmered on the stove. Ol said, "I'm glad

126

we're home tonight. I hear that Savannah is one wet town on Saint Paddy's Day."

I answered, "The whole day has been fun and I learned something new--Savannah's parade is only second to New York's."

Ollie laughed. "I heard Savannah is second largest and New York's is second best."

Smiling I said, "Ollie, I believe you're under the spell. We call it the Savannah enchantment. Once you have it—it never leaves you."

******

One day while I was visiting Mother a phone call from New York came out of the clear blue. It was Thelma saying "I'm coming home and I want my job back."

Mother was worried about how Alma, who was working for her then, would take the news. But when Mother talked with Alma, she was amazed at how she responded. "Lordy, Mrs. Kelley, I'm glad that girl is coming back to us. Of course, she can have her job back. I think I'll just stay home and take care of my husband."

Thelma returned to Savannah and was happy to be home and at Mother's. However, Thelma was a bit different. She put on airs and reminded us that she had lived in with rich Northern folks, and they did things different, more sophisticated-like. "Mrs. Kelley, you wouldn't believe how much silver I put on the table for every meal—butter knives, silver plates under the regular plates, forks galore. And I wore a headpiece with lace and black ribbons that matched my black uniform with a white lace-trimmed apron." Mother and I listened and just smiled.

Summertime had arrived and the living was easy except that I had forgotten about Savannah's hot, humid weather and the little gnats that can drive you crazy. We called them no-see-ums because they're so small. They are tiny two-winged insects that appear late in the afternoon and bite. If you're wise, you'll dab a little insect repellent on. And whatever you do, don't use any perfume or hairspray. They simply love it. I guess even Paradise can have a few little annoyances.

Across the street from our house was a lovely, natural wooded area. Behind that was the Kensington Park Swimming Pool. We thought we had died and gone to heaven. We had all the advantages of a pool without the headache of maintaining it.

I quickly fell into the pattern of getting dinner ready early and putting it into my warming oven. Then when Ollie got home from work, we'd don our bathing suits and head for the pool. Neighbors gathered bringing coolers. We sat about having a drink and visiting while the children paddled in the water. When we were all tired and hungry, we'd go home, get quick showers, put on nightclothes, and have a late supper.

Sometimes on the weekends we went crabbing, a favorite pastime in Savannah. Ollie bought a small Johnson outboard motor which we took to one of the rivers. We rented a bateau (a lightweight, flat bottomed boat) and as Savannahians say "got in the river." Ollie made great fun of my attire, but I didn't care. I had learned my lesson as a child. I blister, so I dressed accordingly: slacks, a long sleeved shirt, a huge sun hat, and gloves with the fingers cut out so I could bait my hook if we decided to fish. He teased me and said, "Please walk ahead of us. We don't want anyone to know you're with us." The girls thought their daddy was funny.

How we loved gliding along the river and exploring the creeks with green marsh grass embracing us on either side. Some people used crab pots, but not us. We enjoyed the sport of catching crabs with a hand line. First, we tied a chicken neck or a smelly piece of meat on a line with a sinker. I instructed Ollie and the girls to throw their lines overboard and have patience until they felt the sinker moving. Then they would know the crab on the bottom was trying to walk away with the meat. That's when the fun began. They slowly pulled their line up, and when the crab was in sight, they scooped it up with a net.

Once at home we dumped the live crabs into a pot of boiling water. Georgia and Mary didn't like this. Next, we had to clean the crabs. Thelma had taught me years ago to clean crab or, as she would say, pick crab. She warned me to be careful to get all the dead man's hand out. "You know it's poison," she would say shaking her finger at me.

******

I was happy to learn my first cousin, Dr. Upton Clary, a neurosurgeon, and his wife Ruth, had moved back to Savannah. They invited Ollie and me to a dinner party at their home. I was thrilled that Irv and Terry Victor and Freda and John Ranitz, childhood friends, were guests also. We found that the eight of us enjoyed each other and had much in common. We had children the very same ages and they enjoyed playing together. That night was the beginning of a long and staunch friendship. The eight of us formed a supper club. The girls liked to cook, but the best cook was Irving Victor or "Vic" as we called him. He was a gourmet cook and he kept us all on our toes. (Today (2008) he has a restaurant on the waterfront in Savannah—Vic's on the River.)

St. Patrick's Day (in Savannah)

Vic and Terry had a little summer house on Shad River. Often we met there on Sundays after church. The children would swim and dive off the dock.

It was at the summer house that the men introduced my Yankee husband to a true Savannah game, Half Rubber. As far as I know this game is unique to Savannah, though Charleston also claims to have originated it. To play the game, you must have a sponge ball, which you cut in half and a broomstick--broom part is cut off. Teams can have any number of players, but the most popular is the two-person team, a pitcher and catcher. You can have as many teams as you want.

The pitcher has to learn the technique of sending that little half rubber ball spinning through the air so that the batter will swing at it but not hit it. Savannah boys learn this game at a young age and they are masters by the time they're older. My poor husband took a lot of ribbing that first afternoon that they played. But he was a good sport. The men and boys gave him the honorary title, Southern Yankee. Believe me, that's quite a compliment.

******

One day when I was visiting Mother, Thelma said, "Miss, Bet, I think it's time you had some household help. I have a good friend looking for a job. She's kinda old, but she sure can work."

I said, "I'll have to talk it over with Ollie."

Ollie said, "I think that's a good idea."

Shortly after that Thelma's friend, Rena, came to work for us. She was a short, old lady with kinky white hair and tiny gold rimmed eye glasses which she wore on the tip of her nose. In spite of her age, her step was lively and she really could work. She turned out to be a wonder woman with the housework, cooking, and the children.

Once Mary defied her, and as Mary later said, Rena lifted the skirt of her white uniform, grabbed a frying pan and waving the iron skillet chased her for half a block. From then on Rena and Mary had an understanding and grew to love each another.

Sometimes when I was gone all afternoon, I'd come home and say, "Rena, did anyone call?"

If my friend, Terry Victor, had called Rena would say, "Yes'um, Mrs. Wictor called." Or I'd inquire, "Rena, what did you do this afternoon?"

She might reply, "I dusted and ran the waccum."

Rena was a true Geechee. Her ancestry went back to an Indian tribe who had lived along the Ogeechee River. They intermarried with the blacks, and they had a dialect all their own, referred to as Gullah. But the term

Geechee was also adopted by other Savannahians. I remember that my Savannah High School football team was called the Geechees.

******

We enjoyed the summer Rena came to work for us. It was 1957. Dwight Eisenhower was President. The phrase, "I like Ike" had been a popular campaign slogan and people still remembered it. We enjoyed going to the movies to see Fred Astaire and Cyd Charisse in *Silk Stockings* and Doris Day in *Pajama Game.* At home *Father Knows Best* was our favorite TV program. But all too soon, our perfect summer ended, and it was time for school to start. Georgia would be attending Virginia Lord Heard Elementary School and Mary, and her cousin, Patsy Clary, would go to St Paul's Lutheran Church kindergarten. As the children headed off to school, the weather was still warm and beautiful. I shuddered when I remembered the cold, gray autumn days in Ohio. I was thankful to be in Savannah.

Mother and I grocery shopped together each week and also took sewing classes two days a week. It was wonderful to be home. I was invited to join the Savannah Junior Women's Club and a bridge club. With Rena to care for the girls, I felt footloose and fancy free.

Often I drove downtown and met Ollie for lunch at the Pink House. I never had to look at the menu. I always ordered their homemade vegetable soup and delicious featherbed light homemade rolls. Dessert was always a Carolina trifle which is made with bits of pound cake and a thick creamy pudding laced with plenty of sherry, whipped cream and toasted almonds. There was only one word for it, *yummy.*

After lunch Ollie and I sat on a park bench in one of the squares and watched the people walking by. Sometimes you have to go away and come home again to appreciate such simple pleasures. Once as Ollie left me to go back to work, I smiled as I watched his retreating back. How quickly my Yankee husband had adopted the style of Savannah executives. He had on a blue and white seersucker suit, and he never went anywhere without his big black umbrella. He jauntily used it as a walking cane which was the Savannah custom.

Just before Christmas Ollie's dream came true. Irv Metz, the director of the Chamber of Commerce, called and told Ollie some exciting news. There would be an opening at the chamber, and Irv wanted Ollie to come to work for him. Without even having to think, Ollie said, "Yes." This was the work he had dreamed of.

St. Patrick's Day (in Savannah)

Christmas was a gala celebration. Thelma and Aunt Claudia were with us, and Mother's next door neighbors, George and Eleanor Blood, and their two sons joined us. They became dear friends of ours. With great pride, Thelma handed out the Christmas gifts, just as she had done when I was a little girl.

******

Thelma was an important part of our family. She had been with us off and on since the 1920s, but Mother must have forgotten the telltale signs that Thelma was ready to go on one of her sabbaticals. After the holidays Thelma went into a frenzy, cleaning all the silver and brass plus putting the house in apple pie order. Then it happened. Thelma just didn't show up. Mother finally called her sister who said, "Miz Kelley, this is a bad one. She's taken to her bed and she just keeps drinking. You know she never wants anyone to see her like this."

But later we learned Thelma finally did leave her bed. She ran out of alcohol and in a drunken stupor, clad only in a long pink nylon nightgown and barefooted, she stumbled down the road to a house that sold white lightning. In my mind's eye I could see my wonderful, neat, prissy Thelma, hair on end, staggering with determination to find whiskey. Locals produced white lightning made by long-held secret recipes with the primary ingredients being fermented corn and sugar. Mother was always warning Thelma that a bad batch could be deadly, and furthermore, it was against the law.

On her quest for liquor Thelma was picked up by the police and taken to jail. Kelley was called and he went down to the police station to put up bail. Mother and Kelley took a remorseful Thelma home and gave her strict orders to get herself straightened out. Her trial would be in ten days.

Ollie found out that the judge would be holding court that day. The judge was a friend of Ollie's, and he went to see him pleading for mercy for Thelma. Mother called Thelma each day, checking on her and encouraging her. We thought that everything was fine.

The day of the trial arrived. It was cold, damp and dreary and a chilling northeast wind was blowing. Mother called Thelma and said, "We're coming out early to pick you up. We want to go over a few things with you."

When we arrived at Thelma's, she wobbled out to the car. Our hearts sank. She was tight. I was so angry with Thelma I wanted to wring her neck, "How could she do this?" I helped her into the back seat and rolled down the windows. Thelma was talking a blue streak and kept saying, "Miz Bet, I'm cold. Can I roll up the windows?" I turned a deaf ear. I was determined to sober her up.

131

At Mother's we brewed strong black coffee and made Thelma, who had never consumed coffee, drink a whole pot. At last, it was time to go meet Ollie. We instructed Thelma to be very quiet.

We walked into the crowded courtroom. I sat next to Thelma and thought, "Oh my goodness she smells like a whiskey barrel." But I kept patting her hand whispering, "Now, now, it's going to be all right. Be quiet." Demon liquor seemed to loosen her tongue. But fate was kind to us that day. We sat there all afternoon, and Thelma was the very last case.

When Judge Oliver instructed Thelma to come forward, I cringed as Thelma started on a long tirade of what had happened. The judge snapped, "Be quiet and get rid of that chewing gum." Thelma obediently took a big gulp and swallowed the gum.

Mother, Ollie and I were worn out but grateful to a kind judge who dismissed Thelma's case since it was a first offense and he knew we would take care of her all of her days. Thelma left with her head held high, a smile on her face and a light step.

Chapter Thirty-Two
N.S. Savannah

Happy Times

Now that we were all settled in Savannah we had a constant stream of company. We loved it. We delighted in playing tour guides for all our friends from Ohio. We always took them to the riverfront to explore the old and the new.

We told them the story of the "Waving Girl" just as I remembered my daddy telling me about her. He told me that Florence Martus stood on her porch on Elba Island and waved to every ship that came up the Savannah River. The legend was that she waved so she could be the first one to greet her fiancé when he returned from sea. Unfortunately, he went out one day and never returned, but she still kept standing on her porch and waving. It was a romantic story even though she may have been waving only because she was lonely. At any rate, she was faithful and her story (whether legend or truth) was spread by sailors and known all over the world.

We never tired of showing our friends all the historic spots. We took them to the Pirate's House Restaurant and devoured black-bottom pie. And of course, we took them to Clary's drugstore on Abercorn Street for one of their famous sodas with whipped cream and cherries. I delighted in telling them about the drugstore and my father who had bought it in the 1930s and how by the 1950's the Abercorn Street store had become a community gathering place where people could get their prescriptions filled as well as have lunch, meet friends and socialize. Our friends liked the scratching post near the soda fountain and the swivel counter stools. Kelley would come out from behind the prescription counter, and pour on his charm to give them a special welcome to the drugstore and Savannah. I was sorry I couldn't take them to the Bull Street store which had closed in 1952.

Ollie went to work each day with a song in his heart. He was the manager of the chamber's Membership and Trade and Affairs Division. He was dealing with people, and his gentle sincere manner was appreciated by all. The Chamber of Commerce was housed in the historic Cotton Exchange Building erected in 1886 and located on Bay Street. It was one of two places in the world that quoted the price of cotton daily (Liverpool, England, being the other). Ollie was able to sit at his desk and watch the big freighters make their way up the Savannah River.

One day at Mary's school the teacher asked each child to stand up and tell the class what work their father's performed. When little Mary stood up, she said, "My daddy doesn't work. He just talks on the telephone. Mother's the only one in our family who works." Out of the mouths of babes!

******

On May 22, 1958, the keel was laid in Camden, New Jersey, for the first atomic merchant ship, the *N.S. Savannah*. A large delegation from Savannah attended the ceremony.

This caused much excitement in Savannah as this ship was to be named in honor of the first steam-propelled vessel, the *S.S. Savannah*, which crossed the Atlantic Ocean in 1819. The nuclear ship was launched July 21, 1959 and christened by first lady Mamie Eisenhower. After a final test, the *N.S. Savannah*'s first port of call would be Savannah. Then she would sail to Liverpool to duplicate that first history-making voyage in 1819. When the beautiful sleek nuclear ship sailed into the Savannah port, it was a day to remember. The whole town turned out to welcome her.

Mary, Georgia, Ollie, and I viewed the festivities from a narrow balcony with a wrought-iron banister at the Cotton Exchange Building. Almost every boat in the city of Savannah was on the river to welcome the ship. Horns were blown. Streams of water sprayed into the air from the fire boats. The bossy little tug boats escorted the proud nuclear ship into port. Once docked, the *N.S. Savannah* was host to thousands who toured the ship.

It seemed that something thrilling was always going on in Savannah. The next St. Patrick's Day the Chamber of Commerce made arrangements to dye the Savannah River green. Barrels and barrels of chemical dye were dumped into the river upstream. As the tide changed, the dye tinted the muddy, yellow river green as it flowed twenty miles out to sea. And true to tradition, St. Patrick's Day was joyous, fun and beloved. It was a huge celebration for one and all.

Chapter Thirty-Three
A Close Call

1960 was a miracle year for me, just as 1929 had been when my mother sat up all night caring for me after a double mastoid operation, patiently spooning life saving nutrients into my mouth. In 1960 Ollie was my guardian angel.

It all started late one Sunday afternoon when Dr. Victor stopped by the house to pick up his daughter, Andrea, who had spent the weekend with Georgia. Ollie greeted Vic at the front door. "Hi, where's Bets?"

Ollie answered, "She isn't feeling well. Do you want to speak to her?"

"I sure do." As the men walked into the bedroom, Dr. Victor took one look at me and called my doctor. He came right away and told me I was going to the hospital.

"I'll get up and get ready."

"Oh, no you don't. I'm calling an ambulance."

As I was being transported to the hospital, I thought, "This is silly. I feel just fine." Little did I know my blood pressure was so low it was almost like I was on a cheap drunk. I ended up having a hysterectomy, which went just fine. In fact, I was doing so well that over my mother's objection I insisted that she and Kelley go to Atlanta for the state pharmaceutical convention.

Then my doctor walked into my hospital room and asked, "How's my star patient?"

"Fine," I replied.

"Do you mind if I drive my daughter to Athens? She's entering the University of Georgia as a freshman and she's just a bit nervous."

"Oh, please go," I said.

"I have a new associate, and he will look in on you."

That evening the new doctor came into my room. He raised his eyebrows in disdain and asked the nurse, "Why does she have a catheter?"

I tried to explain that I had a bit of a problem with my waterworks and my doctor wanted me to have it for a few more days.

The associate doctor looked at me like I had no business telling him anything. In his eyes, I must have crossed over the line of patient-doctor relationship.

He told the nurse, "Remove the catheter at once." He ordered shots, declaring that I was tense and they would relax me. Then he hastily left the room.

I received the shots every six hours.

The next morning Ollie appeared before going to work. "How's my best girl?"

I giggled, "I'm fine."

He said, "I have a meeting at noon so I won't be here to see you."

"That's fine, Ol," and "please don't come back tonight. Spend the evening with the girls. And for goodness sakes, don't worry about me."

That afternoon my friend Nita came to sit with me. As she sat there chattering, I could hardly keep my eyes open.

At last I said, "Nita, do you mind if I close my eyes?'

Later, Nita told Ollie that as she sat there, it was almost like watching a person leaving this world.

I couldn't move nor could I take my eyes off the ceiling, but I knew what was going on. The nurses came and went not disturbing me, just giving me the shots.

That night there was a creaking sound, the sound of my door opening and I heard a beloved voice. It was Ollie. He took one look at me and in a panic rang for the nurses. They called the young doctor. The nurses could hardly get my blood pressure; it was so low. The weird thing was I could hear everything, but I couldn't respond in any way.

The doctor appeared. He seemed angry and annoyed with me, but he stopped the shots and left. Ollie finally had to go home. He had left the girls with a neighbor.

I lay there all night, eyes wide open, fixed on the ceiling. I wasn't able to move. The nurses came in constantly checking on me.

As I lay there, I thought, "I'm going to die." I wasn't a bit afraid, only sad. I would not be there to raise my children. I began to think about what I should be buried in. I had bought a beautiful blue dress at Fine's. It would be perfect; however, it was at the store being altered, so sadly no one would know about it.

Very early in the morning Ollie entered my room. He had been busy after he left me. In tow, he had my doctor, Dr. Irving Victor, Dr. Jules Victor, and my cousin Dr. Upton Clary.

My doctor said, "It's obvious. She's lost her mind."

Vic said, "I'll be damned if that's so." Upton, who is a neurosurgeon walked to my bed and said, "Lorraine, if you can hear me, squeeze my hand."

I strained and with all that was in me, I managed to lightly squeeze his hand.

Upton said, "She can hear us."

Jules, who was an internist, said, "Lorraine, don't worry, we'll get you out of this. You'll be all right."

Tears rolled down my cheeks. I was going to live and raise my children.

Later, I learned that I had been given massive shots of a tranquilizer. They said if I had received one more I would have just slipped away, and no one would have been the wiser.

It took several days for me to recover from the shots. I was too small for the huge doses.

I was still in the hospital recovering on September 17, 1960, my thirty-sixth birthday. That day Ollie appeared with a big, gaily wrapped box. When the nurse opened it, I saw a beautiful mink stole. He was so pleased with himself. He said, "I thought if anything could make you well, this would."

The nurses hung it on my IV rack, so I could look at it.

He was right. I got well.

Chapter Thirty-Four
Bella, My Bella

When I got home from the hospital, all I could hear from Mother was talk about the presidential election. Vice President Nixon was running for the presidency on the Republican ticket, and John F. Kennedy was the Democratic contender. The campaign was fiercely fought and tempers were running high. Bella was so embroiled in politics that she made a mighty decision. She left her Democratic roots. I couldn't believe my mother. She didn't have one good word to say about John Kennedy. Richard Nixon in her eyes, could do no wrong.

Finally, Election Day arrived. Mother was in high spirits. She was sure her man would win in spite of the poor showing Nixon had made in the first presidential debate on September 26, 1960. Nixon looked like he needed a shave and was perspiring profusely. His appearance was a sharp contrast to the youthful John F. Kennedy who was perfectly groomed by make-up artists and at ease. Alas, Nixon was soundly beaten in the November election. John Fitzgerald Kennedy was sworn in as the 35th president of the United States. Bella was downright sick. In fact, she took to her bed. She would see no one.

After a couple of days, Mother emerged from her room looking no worse for the ordeal. She seemed happy and in good spirits. She said, "Bettye Lorraine, you must remember to always honor the man who is your President." And with that, she went about her business. She was true to her word. We never heard an unkind word about the new President, and as Bella would say, "That's that!"

******

I wasn't completely sure how it would work out to have Mother and Kelley living so close to us, but one morning I was particularly happy they were nearby.

Sleepily, I rubbed my eyes and looked at the clock on the bedside table. It was three o'clock in the morning. But what was that horrible ringing? Then I knew. It was the telephone. Who could be calling at this ungodly hour?

I shook Ollie and whispered, "Answer the phone." In a stupor he picked the phone up and said, "Hello."

Kelley said in a frightened voice, "It's Bella. She's sick and she wants Betsy right away."

I threw on some clothes and drove around the corner to Mother's house. I found her writhing in pain saying that her right side hurt and she was sure she was going to die. My first thought was, "It's her appendix." Then I remembered it had been removed years ago.

Kelley said, "I'm going to call the doctor."

Thankfully, the doctor came quickly. When Dr. Robert Gottschalk got there, he examined mother carefully and said, "Clara, I'm pretty sure it's your gall bladder, but we'll have to run some tests, so you'll be in the hospital several days."

In the final analysis, it was necessary to operate. When Bella received the reports of the tests, Kelley gave her a letter expressing his concern and love for her. She kept the letter until the day she died.

January 4, 1962

Dear Bella,

I know that I have been the world's greatest procrastinator. Many times I have thought I would write you and just put it off. I have always known you were a wonderful person; however, Saturday night I realized that without you I would be the most miserable person alive.

I know that you have been the most patient, longsuffering and tolerant wife in the world. I appreciate the love, devotion and understanding that you have always shown me.

I am sorry that you are ill and that the report yesterday was not all favorable, but I am thankful that you are much better and maybe you will respond to the treatment and can come home tomorrow.

When I walk into the house, I am overcome with loneliness and the bedroom gets smaller and smaller. Of course, I miss you, miss you, miss you.

The most important thing is for you to get well, so please don't worry and keep your chin up.

I love you (not just sometime), but all the time.

Love,
Kelley

The doctor was absolutely correct and surgery was scheduled a few days later.

The morning of the operation Kelley, Ollie and I got up early and went to the Candler Hospital to see Mother. We wanted to be there before her surgery. We were happy to find her in good spirits. We were all laughing and joking with her when a nurse came into the room. She said, "I'm sorry, you'll have to step outside. I need to get Mrs. Kelley prepared." We dutifully filed out and stood in the hall waiting for what seemed like hours.

Finally, the door opened and the nurse informed us we could go in. The nurse had given Mother a shot, and that shot had put Bella into outer space. She was wearing a hospital gown and sitting straight up in the middle of the bed. Her long red hair had been unpinned, and it was hanging down around her shoulders. She looked a little wild. She opened her eyes wide. They were bulging out of her head and looking straight at us, she said, " I've got my going-to-meet Jesus dress on."

Just then the orderlies came. We quickly kissed her and then waited for what seemed like forever. I was frightened. Her going to meeting Jesus remark scared me terribly. "Oh Lord, please don't take my precious mother from me," I prayed.

Finally, it was over. They brought a deathly pale Bella back to the room. I was so thankful.

One day while Mother was recuperating, the doctor came into the room and handed her a jar with ugly jagged stones. "Clara, I thought you might like your gall stones. I hear that a jeweler can polish them and make an unusual necklace."

Mother took one look at the gall stones and said, "No, thank you. I never want to see those damn things again."

I looked at Kelley and we nodded in agreement. We were thankful that our feisty, lovable Bella was back with us and that she hadn't gone to meet Jesus.

******

In the spring of 1962, a very important event occurred in our family. Georgia was confirmed as a member of the Lutheran Church of the Ascension. Savannah was in full bloom. It was gorgeous with azaleas of many colors, white dogwood blossoms and graceful purple wisteria swaying in the breeze. I was sure that heaven could not be more beautiful. From the largest elaborate homes to the tiniest shacks, lawns and yards had an abundance of flowers.

Georgia's confirmation was on Palm Sunday. It was a milestone in her life. Pastor Derrick had instructed a group of confirmands for three years, and they were well prepared.

Bella, My Bella

The Lutheran Church of the Ascension is a beautiful church but never more so than on that morning with the sunlight streaming in the stained glass windows and the brass and silver polished so brightly it made you blink. The church was filled with friends, proud parents and grandparents, but no one was happier than Kelley. He truly loved Georgia. My hate was slowly slipping away, and love for Kelley was filling my being.

After the service, we all went to Bella's where Thelma had a delicious dinner prepared. The confirmation must have touched Kelley deeply because several days later Georgia received the following letter from him. Kelley's letter really surprised me, but then I remembered he had been a Methodist preacher in his early years.

April 16, 1962

Dear Georgia,

I remember the first time I saw you, how cute you were, how you smiled, laughed and were the center of attraction at the airport. Bella and I were so proud of you. As you grew older how smart you were. You could sing the Ohio song and many others. You could say, "I am my daddy's sweetheart, my mother's girl and K.K.'s boy."

I also remember how you always carried your KEEN cover and always sat in my lap, how early you awoke, the early morning walks we took, or I would pull you in your wagon, or we would take a ride in the car, whichever, you chose, the time the car ran in front of us and I had to stop suddenly. I caught you before you hit the dash. After I stopped I was afraid you were hurt real bad; however, you did not cry but remarked "K.K." I couldn't hold the tiger," and the time we, the two of us, went to the picture show in either Canton or Akron and you thought we were going to see Annie Get Your Gun. Everyone in the lobby was admiring you and talking about how cute you were.

I never could understand how you could select the Chattanooga Choo Choo record from all the rest before you learned to read. Then I remember the afternoon you asked if there was a ballgame that night and would I take you. You said when you got to be a big girl you would be a pretty strawberry blonde and you would take me to the ballgame remember? You were disappointed because the Savannah Indians were not dressed as Indians; however; when one of the players hit a homerun you asked me what his name was. When we arrived home you jumped from the car and ran into the house saying, "Mike Cisco hit a homerun."

I have always been proud of you; however, yesterday you far surpassed any of the previous experiences. During the confirmation service I was able to see the expression on your mother's, father's, sister's and grandmother's face and the radiance of pride and happiness that glowed from them was felt by me.

You are indeed lucky to have been born and reared in a Christian home. I am sure that with the love and understanding you receive at home and with Christ as your co-pilot that the experiences of John Glenn will be small in comparison to the joy and exultation you will come to realize while living a Christian life and belonging to the Lutheran Church. (There is a vast difference in being a member and belonging to a church).

Someone has said,

"If you write upon marble, time will efface it,
If you write upon brass it will vanish away, but
If you write upon the tablet of the human heart
It will brighten throughout eternity."

"So teach us to number our days that we may apply our heart unto wisdom."

So in conclusion, my prayer for you.

MAY THE GRACE OF OUR LORD JESUS CHRIST BE AND ABIDE WITH YOU NOW AND FOREVER.

YOUR DEVOTED GRANDFATHER

K.K.

Chapter Thirty-Five
Hollywood Comes to Savannah

In the summer of 1962 The Chamber of Commerce was instrumental in bringing a movie company to Savannah to film *Cape Fear* with Gregory Peck, Robert Mitchum, Polly Bergen, Telly Savalas and Lori Martin. The whole town was excited and Ollie became good friends with Ernie Wehmeyer, the production manager.

One Sunday morning after our family attended church, Ollie said, "I need to go by the De Soto Hotel and give Ernie some information."

The girls and I sat in the car waiting for Ollie to take care of some business. Finally, he came out and said, "Betsy, I've invited Ernie and his assistant to come out to our house and have lunch with us. You go on ahead and I'll come with Ernie."

I thought, "Has Ollie lost his mind?" We had left the house in a Sunday morning mess. I gave him a strained smile and drove off. My mind was going fifty miles an hour. What could I prepare? I stopped at Gottliebs Delicatessen and ordered corn beef and rye bread. I was going to get other things, but I realized I only had five dollars in my purse.

To add to my misery, once at home, I found we were locked out. I didn't have my house key. We spotted one window that was unlocked. By juggling the screen, we got it open and Georgia and I hoisted Mary up. She pushed the window up, crawled through and opened the door for us.

Once inside, I barked orders like a top sergeant. Make up the beds, pick up the newspapers, and check the bathrooms. I surveyed the contents of the refrigerator, and, thank the Lord, I had plenty of ingredients for a huge toss salad. Good old Rena had left us a chocolate layer cake for the weekend and a plate of deviled eggs. I quickly made sweet ice tea and set the dining room table, but something was missing. Flowers, I thought. I dashed outside and cut zinnias and quickly arranged them for the table. I breathed a sigh of relief. I could do it.

As it turned out, we had a wonderful time. Ernie was glad to be in a home. We loved hearing him tell stories about Hollywood and the stars. Then, to our surprise and delight, he suggested that Georgia, Mary and I sign up to work as extras for the movie. We did, and it was a fascinating experience although it could be pretty boring. Hurry up and wait—that's what we were constantly doing. We were with the company for about two weeks. A school was provided for all the children.

When the movie made its debut in Savannah, we eagerly looked for ourselves. What a disappointment! I was the only one visible, and it was just the rear end of me as Robert Mitchum bumped into me in Wright Square. Oh well, we all laughed and said it was an experience to remember.

******

Earlier in the year, Aunt Claudia's husband, Louie, had passed away and my poor aunt was struggling with loneliness and sadness. She had no children. Bella with her big heart just couldn't stand it. She asked Kelley if it would be all right to invite Aunt Claudia to live with them. Kelley enthusiastically said, "Yes." And Claudia gratefully accepted the invitation.

Once more the sisters were together. Mother was beside herself with joy. After Claudia was settled in, Kelley said, "How would you like to work at Clary's? I could certainly use the help."

Aunt Claudia laughed and quickly said, "Yes, and now I really feel like I'm home." She remembered how she had helped Daddy at the store years ago in the 1930s.

Kelley later told Mother that Claudia was a godsend. Everyone warmed to her happy, sweet personality. Mother, Claudia and Kelley became inseparable, often going to Johnny Harris' after the drugstore closed. Aunt Claudia liked her bourbon and branch water, and that pleased Kelley.

Chapter Thirty-Six
A New Beginning – Goldsboro, NC

When you're happy the days and years race by, but eventually, all good things come to an end. Ollie had a burning desire to have a Chamber of Commerce all his own.

He had several interviews. One was in Vero Beach, Florida, and he was offered the position. Another interview was in Goldsboro, North Carolina. I didn't even know where Goldsboro was. It was in eastern North Carolina, about an hour and a half from the coast. Ollie mulled over the decision. Finally, he told me he was going to accept the Goldsboro offer.

It was a hard decision. Vero Beach seemed sunny and bright, but Vero would be mainly tourism; whereas, Goldsboro would be the key to a well rounded chamber program: industry, agriculture, and it had a big Air Force base. Best of all, it would be a wonderful place to raise our girls because it also had the charm of a small southern town.

When we told Mary and Georgia that we would be leaving Savannah, they dashed into the bathroom, locked the door, and filled the bathtub with hot water. Hysterically crying and screaming, they climbed into the tub sobbing, "We're not going."

We hated this interruption in their lives, but we knew they would adjust. My worry was for my mother. But as usual, Bella took it all in stride. Perhaps having Aunt Claudia with her softened the blow of our leaving. I was relieved to hear her say, "At least, you won't be so far away like Ohio, and you can come home often."

We put our house on the market in hopes that we could sell it and move before school started in the fall, and we did.

Ollie went to work in Goldsboro the first day of July 1963. He had an apartment in the Goldsboro Motor Hotel until the girls and I could make the move. It was with sorrow and a heavy heart that I thought about leaving my birthplace again, but I never doubted that one day I would return. I packed and said goodbye to friends.

Georgia and I drove to Goldsboro to spend a few days with Ollie and house hunt. I had met all the men who had interviewed Ollie, but I had not met one single woman. Ollie knew this, so he arranged for me to spend the afternoon with the wife of a board member. She had a daughter Georgia's age. At three o'clock we parked in front of a large lovely two story brick house. We rang the bell. A pleasant woman and her daughter opened the door and asked us to come in. We settled down in a charming living room for a visit with

145

Cokes and cookies. And then I asked my hostess what she did for excitement in Goldsboro.

I was stunned by her reply. "There's no excitement here."

"Well, then, how do you keep busy," I asked.

"I watch the soaps, like *As the World Turns*."

Still searching, I said, "Do you play bridge?"

With a cynical laugh, she replied, "You'd better not play bridge in this town. They're sharks. They'll eat you alive."

My heart sank, and I was speechless. Georgia tried to fill the silence. She asked the daughter about the high school activities.

The reply was a carbon copy of her mother's, "Nothing's going on." Georgia and I took our leave, and we decided not to burden Ollie with this account of our afternoon.

The next day we continued house hunting with a realtor. This was every bit as depressing as our visit the day before.

As for Ollie, he was having the time of his life and loved his work in this vibrant town. That night I lay in bed beside a peacefully sleeping Ollie. I couldn't sleep and the hours crawled by. Finally, I couldn't stand it one more minute. It was 3 a.m. I shook Ollie. Sleepily he stammered, "What's wrong?"

I said, "I'm not moving to Goldsboro." Then I started to cry telling him about our experience. I sobbed. "I can't come. I would die here. Please call Vero Beach and tell them you've reconsidered."

He took me in his arms and said, "Honey, I can't do that. I gave my word."

It was a long night. Finally at daylight, I fell asleep and Ollie got up and slipped out, heading for his office.

Later I found out what happened that morning. Ollie called in several of the men who had hired him and confessed to them that he had a huge problem. He said, "My wife says she's not coming, and when she says something, she means it."

The committee was stunned. Finally someone said, "What changed her mind?"

Ollie told them that she had spent the afternoon with a certain lady. They rolled their eyes, looking at one another. "Ollie, that's a shame. The woman she visited is a lovely woman, but very negative."

I'll never know how it all happened, but Ollie called me and said the two of us were going to a party at the home of the Hal Tanner's that night. He was the publisher of the local newspaper. I agreed to go although my heart really wasn't in it.

Hal and his wife, Georgia, greeted us warmly at the front door and introduced us to a nice gathering of attractive, charming people. The conversation was jovial. They were interesting and gregarious. I had been like a fish out of water, but now I was in my element happily swimming in the ocean blue. Ollie had been right. This was the town for us.

The next day we rented a house and Georgia and I returned to Savannah to continue packing. Ollie drove home every weekend to help, and we were all in good spirits. There were goodbye parties and so much to do.

In late August a moving van from Goldsboro arrived. The driver and his helper walked around our house muttering and shaking their heads. The driver asked "What block on Oleander did you say you're moving to?"

I told him and he said, "There ain't no house in that block that can hold all this furniture."

I replied, "It was the largest we could find, and we took it because it has a walkup stairs to a full attic." The house actually worked out fine, although it was a bit of an adjustment. We only had one bathroom, something we had not had for a long, long time. We had so much stored in the attic that we hoped the ceiling wouldn't cave in, and it didn't.

******

Once we moved, our life in Goldsboro settled into a routine. We were up early each morning, Ollie eagerly setting out for work and the girls heading off to school. Georgia was a sophomore at Goldsboro High School, and Mary, a sixth grader, attended Walnut Street Elementary School. As for me, I was lonely. I missed Mother, my friends and Savannah.

My salvation was my next-door neighbor, Eva Samia. It wasn't long before I fell into the habit of walking across the lawn and tapping on Eva's door. I was always welcomed warmly. Eva was a Lebanese widow and a gifted seamstress. I sat with her while she sewed and found it amazing that we could find so much to talk about.

One morning Eva said, "Betsy, why don't you make your girls new dresses? I'll show you a few quick tricks."

I thought it was a grand idea and soon we were sewing and chatting several mornings a week, just like Mother and I used to do. I'll never forget one of the things she told me. She said, "You can cheat a dress or you can give it the full treatment." By cheating a dress she meant you can stitch it up without doing the fine finishing work that makes it special.

We stopped sewing in mid-morning and had coffee which she always made in an old-fashioned percolator. She told me about the old country, how she came to America and about her wonderful family. I loved her stories and being with her. She had much wisdom and was the most selfless person I have ever known. Eva called me her red-headed Lebanese daughter and adopted me as part of her family.

One morning she said, "Betsy, lock the door so no one else can come in. I'm going to let you see me do something that I only do in front of my family."

I was baffled, but pleased to be considered family. We went into the kitchen. Eva put on the coffee pot and next she put a charcoal tablet on a hot electric burner. When it was smoldering, she put it into a strange, exotic water pipe like the ones you would see in an Arabian movie. I was fascinated. The pipe held Prince Albert tobacco mixed with a little sugar. This had been wrapped in a piece of wet white linen and placed into the pipe. We sat drinking our coffee while Eva peacefully smoked her pipe.

I had known for some time that something secretive was going on at Eva's because occasionally when I went over her door was locked and there was the strong odor of sweet smelling smoke. I would go home, wait for a little while, and then go back. The door would be unlocked and a relaxed Eva would say, "Come on in." It felt good to now be in on the secret. I even tried smoking the pipe—ugh!

I met another neighbor, Norma King, one Saturday morning when Ollie and I took a walk. She had a soft, smooth southern accent and looked like the movie star Esther Williams. Norma's husband, Clyde, was a professional baseball player of renown. They had three daughters. One was my Georgia's age and referred to as "Little Norma." The other two, Princie and Janet, were close to Mary's age. Norma proved to be a close friend, one who would be my friend forever.

We often had dinner together, and at one of her dinner parties, she introduced Ollie and me to the Bill Kemps and the Jim Zealys. They had daughters, Betsy and Carol, who were Georgia's age. These girls became close buddies.

Mary has always picked up friends like a black suit picks up lint. A Girl Scout troop welcomed her and she was always bringing home new friends. Once she brought home Trista Shirley. Her father was Wilber Shirley who owned the nationally famous Wilber's Barbecue. I smiled to myself when I thought about my first visit to Wilber's.

Ollie thought I needed a night out, so he asked someone for the name of the best restaurant in town. The reply was Wilber's. I got all gussied up, thinking about Johnny Harris' and their barbecue. Ollie and I were in for a surprise! Wilber's turned out to be a down-home casual North Carolina restaurant complete with dinners on paper plates and iced tea in paper cups. We were shocked but decided to make the best of it. However, when my order arrived, I looked at my plate and saw what looked to me like dog food. I had never seen chopped barbecue in my life, only sliced. I wasn't sure what to do. After a few moments, I smiled at Ollie and dug in. To my amazement, the chopped barbecue was delicious. No wonder Wilber's was famous.

******

We liked our rented house on Oleander but wanted a larger house of our own. The day I went to a friend's to look at a house plan is one I will never forget. When I walked into her den where the TV was on, I heard these words: The President has been shot. The President has been shot. It was November 22, 1963. Jack Kennedy and his beautiful wife, Jackie, were riding in a welcoming parade in Dallas, Texas. According to the TV announcers, shots were fired shortly after noon. The cheering crowds were stunned as the forty-six year old President Kennedy slumped down in the back of his open limousine. Jackie tried to cradle him in her arms. The President had been shot in the head. Immediately, the limousine was driven at high speed to Dallas' Parkland Hospital where the President died thirty minutes later without regaining consciousness.

Tears filled our eyes. We were in shock as all the nation was. I could not begin to think about house plans. We said a tearful goodbye.

At home, I listened to news accounts of the President's death on TV, grieving with others in our country. I watched pictures of Jackie Kennedy in her blood-spattered pink suit standing beside Lyndon Johnson as he was sworn in as our new President and watched Jackie Kennedy rest her hand lightly on her husband's coffin as it was taken from the hospital to Air Force One to be returned to Washington for burial in Arlington Cemetery. It was a sad time for our country.

******

We truly liked our life in Goldsboro and felt we would be building a house to live in for many years. We found Goldsboro the friendliest town we had ever been in.

Then one day we received a phone call from Georgia Tanner which helped us form a circle of lifelong friends. I remember Georgia saying, "This is Georgia Tanner. We want you to be our guest at our gourmet supper club."

I was happy to hear her cheerful voice, and of course, I said, "Yes, we'd like to come."

Georgia said, "You'll know everyone, as these are the people you met at our house when you first came to visit Goldsboro. Our host and hostess will be Eleanor and Charlie Powell." She gave me their address.

We went to the party. There were six couples including us. I can't remember when I've enjoyed myself more, and the food was delicious.

About a week later Georgia called and asked, "Will you be home this afternoon? I'd like to stop by."

I replied that I would be happy to see her.

When Georgia arrived, I invited her into the living room where I had placed a tray with fresh brewed coffee and slices of banana nut bread on the coffee table in front of the couch. We drank coffee and exchanged small talk. Abruptly Georgia put her coffee cup on the tray and said, "I was selected to ask you and Ollie to join our supper club."

I was surprised because I felt we barely knew them, but I thanked her for thinking of us.

Georgia continued, "I'll give you a little of the background of the club."

I kept drinking my coffee and just nodded.

"The club was organized about five years ago by six couples. We felt that twelve was the perfect number. We selected the name the International Supper Club because we like to prepare the food of foreign countries. Does this sound interesting to you?"

"I'm always up for something new and different," I answered.

With that, she continued, "We write to embassies to get information and recipes and something of the history as well as customs of the countries. We meet once a month, so you're only a hostess twice a year. All the hostess does is plan the menu and give out the recipes. Of course, she has to get her house ready, set the table and do any decorating she likes. The host provides the bar and orders the appropriate wine."

I laughed, "Ollie would enjoy selecting the wine."

Georgia took a few sips of coffee and went on, "The girls do all the cooking and bring the food already prepared. Each cook is responsible for serving her own dish. I know it sounds like a lot of work, but it's fun."

"I believe you, but why do you want us?"

Georgia shook her head and laughed, "We need a little new blood. One of our original couples has just been transferred out of state, and it was a unanimous decision to invite the Toomeys to replace them."

"Thank you, but I'll need to talk this over with Ollie.'

She answered, "Of course you will. We'll be waiting to hear from you."

When Ollie arrived home, he took one look at me and said, "What's up?"

I related all that Georgia had said.

Ollie replied, "Betsy, I like all these people and the men are active in the chamber. It's fine with me."

We accepted Georgia's invitation and became friends with the supper club members for life. Only death has parted us.

Chapter Thirty-Seven
We'll Never Stop Dancing

The first year in Goldsboro seemed to rush by. We adjusted our lifestyle to the one-bathroom house on Oleander, but we kept dreaming of a larger house. Our dreams came true a year later when a man who was a chamber member called Ollie and said, "Mr. Toomey, I'm building a house that I think you and your wife will like. It is a spacious tri-level with two-and-a-half baths."

That sounded like heaven to me. Ollie told the builder we would like to see it. The house was in the last phase of completion. We entered through double doors into an entrance hall. I knew at once without even looking that this was our home.

That evening we drove the children to see the house. They were so excited they even picked out their rooms. Ollie laughed and said, "I guess I'll have to see if the builder and I can come to terms." They did.

We had been in Goldsboro just a little over a year when we moved. It was wonderful to get our furniture out of the attic. It was uncanny how all our things just seemed to fit this house. I worked so hard getting us settled that ever so often I'd have to sit down and rest. It was then that I recalled Thelma's famous words, "Miss Bet, I have to sit down and blow."

The hot humid days of eastern North Carolina were upon us, but we didn't mind. We were busy with trips to Ohio and Savannah plus we had found the beauty of the North Carolina beaches. Mary even went to Camp Seafarer at Arapahoe, North Carolina, and loved it. She learned to sail, and it was the joy of her life.

How different our two girls were. While we were in Savannah, we sent Georgia to a camp in the North Carolina mountains. She was in tears when we left her, and we learned later that she silently wept into her pillow every night. I'll never forget her first actions when she came home. She walked into the house and said, "My house." She patted her bed saying, "My bed." She even went into the bathroom and said, "My own potty." Ollie and I swore that we would never make her go away to camp again. Funny how different sisters can be.

In late summer I had a terrific idea for a party in our new house. I decided that since Ollie and Georgia have birthdays so close together I would have two birthday parties at one time—two surprise parties. (Ollie's birthday is August 28 and Georgia's birthday is September 1). I told Ollie we were having a surprise party for Georgia, and I told Georgia that I was throwing a party for Daddy. I warned both of them to keep it a secret. I even had them doing things for the party and neither one of them thought it odd that I was so busy cooking and freezing.

Imagine their surprise when all at once a bunch of teenagers arrived plus a nice group of Ol's friends. Drinks and a buffet supper were served from the breakfast room table. The kids ate and partied in the den on the first level of the house. The adults ate and celebrated in the living and dining room on the second level. Later, we all gathered together to cut the extra large birthday cake and sing "Happy Birthday." The party was a huge success. My fibbing ways worked.

******

One Sunday some friends invited us to go to church and lunch afterwards at their home. We had been attending a Lutheran church, but when we walked into St. Stephen's Episcopal Church, it was like we were at home. It felt like a smaller version of the Lutheran Church of the Ascension in Savannah.

The following week I was headed to Savannah for a ten-day visit. Bella had called and said she had a little project she needed help with--draperies for her living room. I almost hated to leave Goldsboro. It was early fall. The weather was so beautiful – warm during the daytime but with cool nights – and the trees had the first hint of red, yellow and orange.

While I was in Savannah, I made an appointment with our pastor at the Lutheran Church of the Ascension. I told him how guilty I felt about thinking of changing churches. "But Pastor Derrick," I said, "St. Stephen's Episcopal Church just feels like home to all four of us."

In a soft, gentle voice he said, "Betsy, you and your family must be happy in your church life. How else can you worship God?"

How I did love this man! He would always be my pastor and friend.

I drove back to Kensington Park where Mother was eagerly waiting for me. I walked into the living room, and it seemed that she had a ton of fabric in the middle of the floor. I thought to myself, when Bella has a project, she goes full steam ahead.

Just as we settled down on the floor, the phone rang and Mother sang out, "I'll get it, Thelma." When she pushed herself up, a pair of sharp scissors was leaning upright against a wad of fabric. Mother let out a yelp! The scissors had gone into her wrist. Blood started spurting up into the air. I yelled for Thelma and grabbed Mother's arm and applied pressure.

Mother was concerned only about one thing. She shouted, "Don't worry about me. Just don't let the blood get on my white carpet."

153

I couldn't stop the bleeding, and I was scared. Thelma and I hustled Mother into the car. Thelma held a huge towel around Mother's arm and I drove like the wind to Memorial Hospital on Waters Avenue. Thankfully, it was only a short distance. All the while Mother kept muttering, "I hope I didn't stain the carpet."

The doctor in the emergency room quickly stopped the bleeding, gave Bella a tetanus shot and asked her if she was all right. She smiled at him sweetly, "I'm fine. I just hope I didn't get blood all over my white carpet." Honestly, there never was anyone quite like my mother!

By the time I was ready to leave for Goldsboro, the drapes were all finished. They were beautiful, and we did get the stains out of the carpet.

******

I had always heard that absence makes the heart grow fonder, and it's true. Ollie and the girls seemed so glad to see me when I returned from Savannah they treated me like a queen. But Ol might have had an ulterior motive. He had been invited to go on a fishing trip with a group of men to Topsail Island.

I said, "Of course, you should go. I hear that the fishing is really good in the fall." The men left Friday shortly after work. It was only a short drive to the coast.

The girls and I looked forward to a nice weekend. They each invited a friend to spend the night. On Saturday we went upstairs early, about ten o'clock. Suddenly, the doorbell rang. I thought, who in the world could that be at this time of night? I went downstairs, opened the door, and there stood Ellen and Milton Clark. He was our physician. What could they want? Could something be wrong with Ollie?

Ellen smiled, "Betsy, we've just come from a Croda Club meeting, and you and Ollie have been invited to join. We just had to stop by on our way home and tell you."

I thought what is the Croda Club? Milton must have noticed the funny look on my face because he looked up and said, "Betsy, the Croda Club is simply a big dance club. It has over a hundred members."

My ears perked up, "Please come in and sit down," I said. "Ollie is not here. He's down on the coast for the weekend."

Then Ellen explained, "It's a dance club that meets twice a year, once in the fall and once in the spring. There's dinner at the country club, and after dinner there's an orchestra and dancing. We dress up, the men in tux or dinner jackets and the women in formal gowns."

154

My eyes began to sparkle. I loved dancing and I had some evening dresses stacked away. I asked, "What does Croda mean?"

Milton said, "I'm not real sure, but I think it means dance in Greek."

I couldn't wait for Ollie to come home. I thought, I've got a big surprise for him.

When I told him, he smiled and said, "I know. One of the men went to that meeting and came down to the coast afterwards."

News travels fast in a small town! We joined the club and happily danced in it for thirty-five years. We resigned to make room for younger couples, but we'll never stop dancing.

******

Our first two years in Goldsboro passed quickly. By 1966 Georgia had finished her last two years of high school and was graduating from Goldsboro High School. She had adjusted well to her new life in Goldsboro and was in love and going steady. She always had definite ideas about what she wanted and college was no exception. She informed us she wanted to attend Marjorie Webster, an all girls school in Washington, D.C.

I asked, "Georgia, why did you pick that school?"

"I want to be in the nation's capital," she answered.

There was no arguing with her. We spent the summer shopping, sewing and getting her ready.

Chapter Thirty-Eight
Nobody Like Bella

In the late summer of 1966, the girls and I decided to go to Savannah for one last fling before Georgia left for college and Mary's school started. They loved Aunt Claudia, their Bella, and they adored Kelley. He spoiled them shamelessly. We all had a good time together and the girls waited patiently at night for Claudia and Kelley to come home from Clary's.

Of course, Kelley had to have a drink or two, but I didn't complain. Bad Boy Kelley was no more. It was easy to see Mother, Kelley and Aunt Claudia were living a happy life. How thankful I was that predictions that she and Kelley wouldn't live together long didn't come true. Many of Mother's friends had thought it was an impossible marriage. I think it was Mother's pride and pure guts that made it all happen. That fall was their twenty-third wedding anniversary,

Some mornings while we were in Savannah, the girls and I packed a picnic lunch and drove down to the beach for the day, never forgetting our beach umbrella and big sun hats. We swam, played in the rolling surf, ate, walked the beach and departed for home happy.

Other days Mother, the girls, and I proceeded downtown to bum around and later amble over to Clary's for lunch. Kelley had hired Birdie as the chief cook, and people flocked to the store for her fried chicken, turnip greens, macaroni, biscuits and corn bread, to name a few items. Business was so good that Mother sent Thelma to the store three days a week to help Birdie. This presented somewhat of a problem because Thelma wanted to take over, but Birdie knew just how to handle Thelma. Good-natured Birdie ignored Thelma's prissy ways and kept on doing her job the way she always had.

Georgia and Mary always had a good time at the drugstore. They enjoyed Birdie's hamburgers and French fries, and Kelley insisted that they have sundaes with Clary's special chocolate sauce that my father had created so many years ago.

That weekend Georgia and Mary were invited to visit their cousins, Patsy and Carolyn Clary, at Halycon Bluff out on the water. Their mother, Ruth, said, "Lorraine, when you bring the girls, stay for lunch." I did, and Ruth caught me up on all the Savannah news.

After lunch, I said, "Thanks for the nice visit and for having the girls, but I must get back to Mother's. She's alone. Claudia and Kelley are at the store."

Even before I opened the door at Mother's, I could hear the TV blaring. I pushed the door open and walked into the den. Bella motioned for me to be quiet and sit down. She had become a big baseball fan ever since the Braves had settled in Atlanta. The game was in the final inning, and she was pulling for her team. I smiled at the gusto of my mother.

She was sitting on the sofa with a TV table in front of her holding the remains of her lunch. She motioned to me to have a seat, but I walked around the room trying to determine where the heavy, smoky odor was coming from.

Finally, the game was over and a flushed Mother said, "You'll never guess what I did?"

I sat quietly waiting for her to divulge her secret. She said, "I had a little accident." She pointed to a big black hole in the sofa cushion. "I was sitting here having a cigarette after my lunch and the game was so exciting. I put my cigarette in an ashtray beside me on the sofa." She gave a little laugh. "I must have knocked the cigarette out of the ashtray when I jumped up to cheer for Hank Aaron. The next thing I knew, I smelled smoke and there was a big black hole beside me. My cigarette went down through the padding of the sofa and dropped through the springs."

In alarm, I said, "Bella, how did you put it out?"

With a shrug of her shoulders and a laugh she replied, "The game was so exciting I didn't want to miss a thing, so I just dumped my glass of ice tea down the hole and kept watching the game. The Braves won and Hank Aaron and Phil Niekro were outstanding! Don't worry." She patted my hand. "The sofa needed covering anyway."

I laughed with affection, "Mother, I know there is nobody in the world like you."

******

When we arrived back home in Goldsboro, we were busy with school opening and taking Georgia to Washington to get her settled in college.

When Georgia came home for Christmas, the girls wanted to spend Christmas vacation in Goldsboro instead of going to Savannah. For the holiday we had smoked turkey and all the trimmings on Christmas Eve and attended the midnight Christmas candlelight service at St. Stephen's. That was the highlight of the holidays. But there were also parties and friends.

In the new year the word was out; "There's no business like show business." Goldsboro was getting ready to produce their show. The Arts Council of Goldsboro was making plans for a production in 1968. The purpose of the musical review was two-fold. First, it was to raise money for a blue ribbon committee to initiate studies to build a civic center for Goldsboro. The other reason was to have fun and to bring the people of Seymour Johnson Air Force Base and the town together.

The next step was to contact Jerome Cargill Incorporated in New York City to find a director. To the delight of the committee, they learned that Jerome Cargill furnished everything, costumes, scripts, dance numbers, and music. "Just supply me with warm bodies, a place to practice," and I will teach them the routines," said our professional director from the Big Apple.

Ollie and Colonel Walter Couser from Seymour Johnson Air Force Base were the co-chairmen. The auditions were open to one and all. It wasn't difficult to get a cast of over one hundred, but it was hard to keep them. Little did we know what poor physical shape we all were in. The doctors in town reported an increase in business for the two and a half weeks of intense rehearsals. People had sprained ankles, aching joints, pulled muscles, and sleepless nights.

At one point, I had my doubts that we would actually make it, but on September 25 and 26, 1968, the curtain went up on the *Gold Stocking Revue*. Tickets were priced at $2.50 in advance or $3.00 at the door. It was a sellout. The show was a great success. The town enjoyed watching friends and neighbors strut their stuff.

As the final curtain came down, plans were already under way for the next production. The date was set for January 30 and 31, 1970. Quin Boyette and I were co-chairmen. Never in my life have I worked so hard. I danced in the chorus line and even had a solo routine. The number was entitled "Under the Sea," and I danced in a shimmering costume to the music of "The Age of Aquarius." There were mermaids, and I came out from behind a huge seashell and seduced a deep sea diver.

But what I will always remember most about the show is that it ran in January. What terrible scheduling that was! Almost the entire cast caught the flu. It spread like wildfire, but they were troopers. They just kept on. Ollie and I were no exception.

The day of the show Ollie and I lay in our bed, side by side too sick to even speak to each other. Silently, in the late in the afternoon we got up, dressed and went to the auditorium for our make-up. In between numbers, I bundled myself in a big heavy bathrobe. I was hot one minute and freezing the next. When we did our "Under the Sea" number, my deep sea diver, Howard Caudill, later told me, "Betsy, as I put my hand on you for the lifts, your skin was as hot as a candle flame." But we made it, and after all, the show must go on!

Production of *The Gold Stocking Revue* continued for many years. Finally, the production was put into the hands of the very talented Lee Brown. And with the help of local dance teachers, tradition was carried on.

Chapter Thirty-Nine
The Awning

In May 1968, it was good having Georgia home after her graduation from Marjorie Webster. She had received a Medical Secretarial Degree and was immediately hired at Cherry Hospital, a state mental hospital in Goldsboro. She liked the job.

Ollie and I enjoyed having both girls together again, but it didn't last long. After working a short time in Goldsboro, Georgia and three of her girl friends thought it would be an adventure to live and work in Atlanta, so they made it happen. They got jobs and rented an apartment. Georgia went to work at Emory University. I was impressed. Atlanta was a bustling town. She and her friends had the time of their lives.

All too soon it was 1970 and time for Mary to graduate from high school. I've said it before and I'll say it again. Georgia and Mary are as different as a straight unbending pine tree and a weeping willow fluttering in the breeze. Georgia was a good student, exact, dependable, quiet and lady-like. Mary was a will-of-the-wisp, never studied but always got by, a scatter-brain, loveable and fun. But she drove us crazy.

Mary's generation was just different. It was a trying time: race riots, desegregation, hippies and drugs, Jesus freaks, communes, not to mention, the horror of the Vietnam War and the protests. I wonder how we lived through it. Years later Mary said to me, "Mother, I wish I had been born in your generation and had been your friend."

At the end of the school year when Mary was taking her final exams, I kept my fingers crossed that she would graduate.

******

Meanwhile, in Savannah, Mother smiled as she walked over to her desk and crossed off the day, Thursday, May 7, 1970. Tomorrow, she and Kelley would be leaving for the pharmaceutical convention in Atlanta. She thought it was fun getting ready to be away for a few days. Humming a little tune, she finished laying out their clothes in the guest room: Kelley's tux, bow tie, cuff links, and the frilly white shirt he liked. She ran her hand over her new sea foam green evening dress. It was just right. And then on the spur of the moment she decided to drive down to the drugstore and have lunch. That way she could have a little visit with Claudia.

The store was crowded and she was greeted by many of the regular customers. Bella ate lunch and motioned to Kelley to come over to the table. "Kelley, when I came in, I noticed the front awning seems to be hanging on one side. Maybe you'd better get the porter to tighten it. If it falls and someone gets hurt, we could be sued."

Kelley patted her hand and said, "Don't worry, Bella, I'll get Fred to take care of it."

Bella kissed him good-bye and said, "I'll see you and Claudia at home tonight." She talked with Claudia for a few moments and leisurely walked to the parking lot. Just as she was backing out, Fred came running shouting, "Miz Kelley, Miz Kelley, come quick. Come quick. Doctor Kelley's been hurt real bad."

Bella jumped out of the car and ran to the store. There, lying on the brick sidewalk, was Kelley. He was crying, "Oh, my God help me!" Blood was pouring from his head. It was three-thirty in the afternoon when the freak accident occurred. Kelley was a big man and not agile. He had climbed about four feet up the ladder when he fell backward, striking the base of his skull on a loose brick that was slightly angled up. An ambulance was called, and they rushed him to Candler Hospital.

Dr. Upton Clary, my cousin a neurosurgeon, took care of an unconscious Kelley. About 10 p.m., Upton said, "Aunt Clara, I'm sending you home. I'll be with Kelley, and if there's any change, I'll call you."

Upton knew that the end was in sight, and he didn't want Bella to be in the room. It was only after Bella and Claudia left the hospital that Mother called me. When I answered the phone, a sobbing mother tried to relay the awful details of Kelley's accident to me.

"Mother, we'll come as quickly as we can get packed."

Kelley died a little after midnight. It was 1 a.m. when Claudia called us with the news that Kelley had died. We left for Savannah before daybreak.

When we arrived at Mother's, we found a houseful of people. Lulline, Thelma, Alma and Birdie were there in their white uniforms, quietly taking care of things. Lulline gave me a quick hug and said, "I'm glad you're here. Miz Kelley needs you."

Mother was in her room lying down with a cold cloth over her swollen eyes. My cousin John Lassiter had taken her to the funeral home early that morning, and all of the final plans had been made. The funeral would take place on Saturday afternoon.

I walked into Mother's room and took her in my arms. She cried hysterically, and her words flowed like a waterfall. "I killed him. It's my fault. I wish I hadn't mentioned that old awning," she moaned. "I never thought I would have to go through this again. It should be me. I'm so much older than Kelley." The very mention of his name sent shivers through her body and a fresh flood of tears. I held her tightly and whispered consoling words into her ear and kissed her wet cheeks.

The funeral service was held at Henderson Brothers Funeral Home on Whitaker Street facing Forsyth Park. It was housed in an old southern mansion with white columns gracing the porch. We buried Kelley at Bonaventure in the Clary family plot with my daddy and baby brother. I stayed on with Mother for several weeks. Those were sad days. Bella was tormented with grief and guilt. She blamed herself. Tears flowed, "It should have been me. Oh, but it should have been me." Then she would collapse into a pity party and sob, "My life is over." But it wasn't.

One day Mother finally said, "It's time I go to work and look after things. The store is all I have." She and Claudia ran the store with the help of several faithful druggists and good employees for seven more years.

******

I went back to Goldsboro, promising that I would return soon. Once at home, I was busy with Mary's graduation and preparation for her to enter college. She had been accepted at Louisburg Junior College in Louisburg, North Carolina. The summer raced by with frequent trips to be with Mother. All too soon, it was time to take Mary to Louisburg.

When we received Mary's first mid-term grades, we were very disappointed. Ollie immediately sat down and wrote Mary the letter of letters.
Dear Mary,

If you can't pull your grades up by the next grading period, you will have to come home and go to work at Woolworth's Five and Ten or some such place. You will not be prepared for a profession. I refuse to pay for you to play.

Your loving dad.

Thank goodness Ollie's strategy worked and Mary was soon on the dean's list. When she graduated, she went to Appalachian State University in Boone, North Carolina, and wonders of wonders, she was on the honor roll and got her Masters Degree in Education at the University of North Carolina in Greensboro. Life is certainly full of surprises.

Chapter Forty
A Wall Banger

Our supper club was flourishing. We were comfortable with each other and laughed at our failures. One thing we decided from the beginning was to be completely honest about how the food we prepared tasted. This became such a habit that we had to remind each other to guard against negative comments when we were not with the supper club. Our fear was that we might attend a non-member's party and blurt out, "Who cooked this awful dish?

One night we were entertaining a supper club that had just been organized. We had an elegant menu, a German meal. I had agreed to stay in the kitchen and keep things rolling, so I was given an easy assignment—an appetizer, hot Sauerkraut balls in a chafing dish.

As always, Ollie and I were running late. Ollie was ready first. He grabbed the large plastic bowl with the hors d'oeuvres and headed to the garage. I heard him yelling, "Betsy, Betsy!" I rushed to see what had happened. The bowl with the appetizers was upside down on the garage floor. He was ringing his hands saying, "What can we do?"

I surveyed the mess, hoisted up my long evening skirt, squatted down and began skimming the little balls back into the bowl. It was a mess but there are times you just have to make the best of a bad situation. We went to the party and served the Sauerkraut balls and no one was the wiser. In fact, we received raves.

Our club also liked to travel. We enjoyed cruises to Puerto Rico and St. Thomas, trips to the beach and Williamsburg as well as other nearby places. Now, we were in the planning stages for a three-week European trip in the future. Good food, good friends, and good times was our motto. Who could ask for more?

******

As we prepared for Christmas in 1971, we had a feeling that something of significance was going on with Georgia. She was having a good time in Atlanta. She liked everything about her life, her roommates, her job, and a new young man that she had met in May. His name was Dick Wieler, and he lived in the same apartment complex as Georgia. She had met him at a party. Dick must have been attracted to her too because in the fall he had taken her to his home in Manhasset, New York, to meet his parents.

Not to be outdone, Georgia invited Dick to spend Christmas with the Toomey tribe. It was fun getting ready for them. Mother and Aunt Claudia came up from Savannah. And, of course, Mary came home from college. Ollie and I were nervous about meeting Dick because we sensed that this was serious. It was. Dick had given Georgia a diamond engagement ring the night before they arrived.

Happily, we liked Dick. He was nice-looking with dark brown eyes and black hair. He was comfortable with our family and seemed to be enjoying himself, so much so that he offered to make Harvey Wallbangers, a drink that we weren't familiar with. He went out and bought all the ingredients and even special tall glasses. On Christmas afternoon we were all in a jovial mood as Dick prepared his HarveyWallBanger concoction and handed each of us a tall glass filled with the colorful drink. It was delicious.

Amid all the frivolity, I ran back and forth to the kitchen to check on our dinner and baste the roasting turkey. Each time I returned I noticed something strange. My glass was always full, but there was no time to ask questions. I just took another big gulp of the cool, refreshing drink.

Finally, it was time to cook the broccoli, make the Hollandaise sauce and take everything up. The biscuits were a golden brown. I placed the broccoli on a silver platter and started to put the Hollandaise on top. It didn't look right. Horrors! I was putting the giblet gravy on the broccoli. I got tickled. I laughed and laughed saying to myself, "Girl, you're tipsy." Ollie always said a thimble full would do me in, and I'm sure I had more than a thimble that day. Somehow, I pulled myself together, rinsed and reheated the broccoli, put the Hollandaise on it, and got everything on the dining room table. Ollie carved the beautiful turkey, and everyone raised their glasses to compliment me on the fine dinner.

Mary had invited a boyfriend and he added to our spirited conversation. Georgia and Mary cleared the table and served our family's favorite dessert, chocolate chess pie topped with whip cream. I was thoroughly enjoying myself when suddenly I realized that I was the only one left at the table. Mother, Aunt Claudia, and Ollie had quietly gone upstairs to their beds.

Mary and her boyfriend were sound asleep in the living room, and in the den Georgia had her head on Dick's shoulder for a nap. Oh well, it had been a great Christmas Day, but I thought we are going to have to watch that tricky Dick Wieler. Mother later confessed that she kept pouring her drink into my glass because she didn't want to refuse Dick's constant refilling. She said, "I didn't want to hurt his feelings."

I said, "Thanks a lot, Bella!"

She just giggled. "That drink was a real wall banger."

******

164

A Wall Banger

Georgia and Dick were married on Saturday, April 22, 1972. What a wonderful time we all had! Dick's mother and Daddy brought ten couples with them from Manhasset, New York. They weren't sure what to expect from a Goldsboro wedding, but ended up declaring they enjoyed every moment of it.

It is the custom in Goldsboro for friends to host a large party the night before the wedding instead of having many showers and parties.

On Thursday night Ollie and I hosted a pick-up supper. Late Friday afternoon the rehearsal took place at St. Stephen's Episcopal Church. Following this, the groom's family entertained the bridal party and out of town guests with a seated dinner party at Goldsboro Country Club.

My supper club buddy, Georgia Tanner, was in charge of the Friday night dance. What a job she did! At 8:30 p.m. the folding doors of the banquet room of the Goldsboro Country Club were thrown open, and the band was playing, "Georgia on my Mind." The lights were dim, and there was the heady scent of flowers. The candlelit room was filled with Georgia and Dick's friends and family. We danced the night away, young and old alike.

The wedding took place at 4 p.m. at St. Stephen's. Georgia was a beautiful bride, but then aren't all brides pretty? Dick was the proverbial nervous groom, so much so that his right trouser leg was shaking in the breeze. To add to the beauty of the day, the choir outperformed itself. The music was heavenly. At the close of the service, Dick looked up at the choir and smiled for the first time. Then, he took Georgia's arm for their joyful walk down the aisle as man and wife.

The wedding reception was held at the country club, but what impressed our guests most was the after party. An informal buffet supper for the wedding party and out-of-town guests was served at a friend's house. Everyone wore informal clothes and enjoyed true down-to-earth southern hospitality. What a perfect time to visit and unwind. That evening Georgia and Dick called from Raleigh where they were spending their wedding night. Georgia said, "Oh Mother, it sounds like you're having so much fun, and we wish we were there too." They left the following day for Bermuda.

Dick's mother and father told us how happy they were to have a new daughter. They said, "One thing is certainly true, the South knows how to party."

Chapter Forty-One
Life Change

Ollie was always glad when fall arrived. It was his favorite time of the year, and he loved his job with the Chamber of Commerce. This was the time when all its activities came alive. It was also the time for his annual check-up. One morning at the breakfast table he told me, "Betsy, today is the day I go to the doctor for my yearly physical."

"You're fit as a fiddle. The chamber is just wasting money on you."

He said, "I really do feel great." He picked up his briefcase and gave me a kiss and said, "I'll see you tonight."

That evening when Ollie got home, I asked, "What did the doctor say?"

"I go back tomorrow for the results."

Late the next afternoon Ollie was greeted warmly by his physician. "Well Ollie, you checked out one hundred per cent, but don't you have anything that bothers you?"

Ollie searched his mind and finally said, "I guess I don't sleep well. I feel great in the mornings, but by the afternoon, I really drag."

"Aha, that's it!" his physician said, "Your compulsive behavior is keeping you awake. You are playing all your meetings over and over again in your head at night. Then, you're planning your next day's agenda. That's why you can't sleep. I have a little pill that will help you. I have all my school teachers on it."

When Ollie arrived home, I asked what the doctor said.

"Well, I'm on a little pill that the doctor says will help me sleep and give me more energy."

That was the last that Ollie and I thought about the medication until the beginning of 1973.

******

New Year's 1973 started out in an unusual way. We had snow for three consecutive weekends. That may not sound like a big thing, but in a town that often doesn't see a single snow flake the whole winter, it is huge. When it snows, everything stops. Schools close and businesses shut down. Everyone takes a holiday. Ollie and I have always loved these occurrences. It is a time to rest and concentrate on each other; however, something strange was taking place at our house. Ollie was unusually quiet. In fact, he didn't speak unless I asked him a direct question. And then he would answer politely, using as few words as possible. He didn't care about looking at the snow, making snow cream, nor did he show any of his usual enthusiasm for an unexpected holiday. Even our two miniature Schnauzers, Snitzle and Fritzle, sensed that something was amiss. They would romp back and forth trying to get Ollie to play with them, but he ignored them. He was in a separate world of his own.

I began to search my mind wondering if I had hurt his feelings, but that was not our way. If anything was ever wrong between us, we sat down and talked it out. I tried building a big fire in the den, mixing up his favorite Martoomeys, chilling the glasses, and having a bang-up dinner when he got home from work. But nothing excited him. He could hardly wait for dinner to be over so he could escape to his bed.

I even found out from his secretary that at work he was closing his office door, so he could be undisturbed. This was something he had never done. He had always enjoyed having his door open and having people stop by to chat. Now, he was isolating himself at work as well as home.

This behavior went on for weeks. I pondered: Could it be another woman? Was he ill and didn't want to tell me? Or could it be financial problems? I was at a loss. Our anniversary was coming up in February, and Georgia and Dick were planning to meet us in Savannah for a celebration. I'd have a chance to discuss Ollie's behavior with Mother and also tell her how proud I was of the way she and Claudia were running the drugstore. Those two amazed me.

Ollie and I set out for Savannah on a gray, chilly day. I looked forward to being cooped up in the car for six and a half hours with him, so he couldn't get away from me. I was determined to find out what was wrong. I finally started the ball rolling. "Honey, I know something is wrong. Can you tell me what it is?"

He just looked sad. I continued, "Are you sick?" He shook his head, no.

"Are we having financial problems?" Again, he shook his head.
I whispered, "Is it another woman?"

He shook his head and slowly replied, "Betsy, I also know that something is wrong, but I have never loved you more."

Tears of relief began to stream down my face. He reached over and patted me. "Betsy, I wonder if it could be those pills that the doctor gave me."

I tried to reassure him, "Ol, we'll find out what it is, just don't worry. Let's try to have a good time this weekend." And we did. Ollie worked hard at being his old self. I don't think anyone noticed that something was wrong. I was alert and very protective. If he was too quiet, I would talk and find a way to bring him into the conversation.

On the way home, I opened my purse and brought out a printed piece of paper. I had made a trip downtown to Clary's and asked the druggist to give me the readout on Stelazine, the drug Ollie's doctor had prescribed. I silently began to read. Fear gripped my heart. Ollie had every side effect that was listed: withdrawal, depression, confusion. This drug was recommended for psychotic patients in mental institutions. I briefly told Ollie what I had read. "You must go back to the doctor," I said.

"First, I'll just try taking one pill at night instead of two—one in the morning and one at night. I love the sleep it gives me."

He is hooked! Oh, no! I thought.

Several mornings later after we had finished breakfast, Ollie went upstairs to get ready for work. I was drinking coffee and reading the paper when suddenly I sensed something was wrong. I raced upstairs and found a white-faced Ollie hanging onto the chest of drawers. "Betsy, I feel like I'm going into a million pieces. Help me please!"

I went to the phone and called the doctor's office. I told the receptionist my husband was having a reaction to medication. She told me to have him there at 10:30. Ollie calmed down, dressed and said he was capable of going by his office and to the doctor. He said, "I have an important luncheon meeting at noon, but I'll call you when I get a chance."

About noon I was in the kitchen when I heard the front door open. It was Ollie. He said, "Betsy, I'm in trouble, real trouble. The doctor told me he has misdiagnosed me. I am not a compulsive person and now he is going to have to reverse the medication. He either wants to put me into the hospital for a week or I can go to the beach alone, walk the beach and try to break the cycle. What should I do?"

I called the doctor and told the receptionist that I would like to talk with him. She said, "What do you want to talk about?"

"I want to talk about my husband," I answered.

"Oh, he won't do that. Your husband will have to tell you what he wants you to know."

I said, "Look, I want to talk with the doctor, and I mean right away." Then I hung up.

Ten minutes later Ollie's doctor called me. He said, "Mrs. Toomey, I hear you're a little upset."

"Yes, I am, very upset. Which treatment do you recommend as the best way to correct my husband's condition—the hospital or the beach?

"I don't think it will matter. Either one will do.

"How long do you think it will take to straighten Ollie out?"

His reply sent cold shivers down my spine, "Mrs. Toomey, it might be a week, a month or a year or, in fact, it could be never. Just let me know what you decide, so I can make hospital arrangements, if necessary."

I put the phone down and in an instant I turned and said, "Ollie, you're not going to the hospital and you're not going to the beach alone. You're going to Libby and Gene's in Florida."

Ollie wailed, "They won't want me. They'll be afraid."

"No, they won't be afraid. They've known you since you were a young boy in Ohio. You don't need to be alone. You need to be with them. Since Gene has retired from running his funeral business in Ohio, they will enjoy having you there while they're spending the winter in Florida. Dear friends and sunshine will do you good."

I picked up the phone and called Sarasota, Florida. Libby and Gene had been Ollie's lifelong friends. And once when they had had some marital problems, we had stood by them. I knew that I could ask anything of them. Libby answered the phone, and I quickly explained the problem.

She said, "We want him." So I made plane reservations for the next day, a Saturday, and Libby and Gene planned to meet Ollie.

It was with a heavy heart that I put him on the plane in Raleigh. He seemed so pitiful and confused. I had to fight back my tears.

Once at home I called the girls. They were shocked. It was spring break and Mary cancelled a trip to come home and be with me. That was the longest week of my life.

I called Florida and talked to Ollie, but I knew no more when I hung up than before. He always said, "I'm fine and I love you."

Finally, I called Sarasota once more. Libby answered. "Oh Libby, how is Ollie?"

Her reply was, "He's just fine."

When she said this, my heart leaped for joy. I knew that Ollie was going to get well. "How can I ever thank you and Gene enough?" I asked.

She said, "We thank you, Betsy, for this great privilege. Only this morning we picked up Ollie's ticket. He is coming home Saturday."

When I hung up, I danced around the den. My husband was coming home.

I was up bright and early that Saturday morning. I wanted everything to be perfect for Ollie's homecoming. On the way to Raleigh, I felt that I had to prepare Mary. I knew Ollie was better, but I thought that he would need time to recuperate"

I said, "Mary, your dad may not be quite like you remember him. We'll just have to give him a little time."

Mary and I stood looking out the huge glass window as Ollie's plane landed. We held our breath as we watched the steady stream of people coming down the stairs. At last, we saw him and I couldn't believe my eyes. This was not the man I had put on the plane a week ago. He had more bounce to the ounce than I had seen in years. He came through the door and quickly spotted us.

Mary ran to him and he threw his arms around her covering her face with kisses. Then he slowly walked to me and, with a radiant smile, he hugged me and softly whispered, "Betsy, I'm home."

I'll never forget that ride back to Goldsboro. Mary drove and Ollie was like a spigot that was turned wide open. Words flew from his mouth. He told us the following strange, wonderful account:

"Betsy, when you put me on that plane, I was so confused I was fearful I wouldn't be able to change planes, but you had taken care of that, just like everything else. Someone met me in Atlanta and helped me get to the next plane. Thankfully, Libby and Gene were there in Sarasota waiting for me. They took me to the little house they had rented for the winter on Siesta Keys. As we walked into the house, I noticed there were all kinds of spiritual books, Bibles, and tapes lying about. I said, Gene, the folks you rent from must be very religious.

"Gene smiled and said, 'These are ours.'

"I thought, that's odd, Libby and Gene had never been too churchy.

"About that time Libby came in with cookies and lemonade saying, 'Okay, Toom, we want to hear the whole story.'

"When I got to the part about the prescription drugs to reverse the Stelazine, Libby interrupted me.

'Do you have the drugs?'

"I nodded, 'Yes.'

"She said, 'Go get them.'

"She took them and immediately flushed them down the toilet.

"'Ollie, we won't need these,' she said.

"When my tale was over, Libby told me to stretch out on the sofa and get comfortable.

"Then she said, 'Something very wonderful has happened to us. Last summer we heard about an Episcopal priest named Dennis Bennett. He came to Oberlin College to speak, and we signed up for a three-day seminar. Those were the most incredible days of our lives. For a long time we had felt something was missing in our lives. Father Bennett's teaching led us into a new spiritual dimension, the Baptism of the Holy Spirit. We were already Born Again Christians, but the Baptism of the Holy Spirit is by the Lord Himself. You must ask for it, and it is given to strengthen you in your service to the

Lord. Ollie, we were thrilled when Betsy called us. Our feeling is that the Lord sent you to us.'

"I felt a little uncomfortable and sat up. I didn't know what to make of all this, but I was open to anything and I was desperate.

"After dinner, Libby and Gene explained to me that their lives had new meaning and how happy they were. They had met a group of people who loved the Lord as they did. They met every Tuesday evening and asked if I would be willing to go with them.

"I answered, 'Yes,' even though I didn't want to go. But in no way did they pressure me. Our days were relaxing. We walked the beach, took long naps and talked about our childhood days. Libby and Gene gave me time to be alone which I needed. I was fighting the confusion and the depression.

"Tuesday arrived and I was apprehensive. We had an early dinner and drove to a typical Florida bungalow. My nerves were on edge. I had no idea what to expect, and I found myself fidgety. Gene opened the door and I walked into a large living room filled with people. There were all kinds of folks, young and old, two Catholic nuns, several ministers, and a man was seated in the middle of the floor playing a guitar. Libby told me that he was the host and the leader. Everyone was extremely friendly and I enjoyed the robust singing. There was a short Bible teaching followed by a long prayer time. I heard strange sounds, and I surmised this must be what is known as speaking in tongues.

"The host asked if anyone needed prayer. Someone said, 'I feel that a person in this room is in terrible trouble.' I was seated between Libby and Gene, and they punched me in the ribs. I sat there like a choir boy.

"When I wouldn't get up, Libby whispered, 'It's that silly Toomey pride.'

"Finally, the meeting was over and we were invited into the dining room for refreshments. I was enjoying a glass of orange juice and glad that the whole thing was over when three men walked over to me and asked if they could pray for me. I felt trapped. But I nodded, 'yes.'

"One man said, 'We sense that you are in some kind of trouble.'

"I nodded, 'Yes.'

"Another man asked, 'Do you believe in Jesus?'

"I nodded, 'Yes,' again.

"Then the man asked, 'Would you like for us to pray for you be baptized in the Holy Spirit.?'

"I mumbled, 'Yes.'"

"They quoted the following scriptures: Matthew 3:11, Mark 1:8, Luke 3:16. Then they placed their hands on my head and began to pray. They prayed and prayed. I thought they would never stop. One of the men finally whispered, 'Open your mouth and speak.'

"I knew they would never stop until I spoke. I gathered my courage and said, 'Abba.'

"They stopped praying and hugged me. They said, 'You've received the Baptism of the Holy Spirit. You'll never be the same again.'

"My fear had disappeared and I was calm and peaceful. But that was all. There were no bells. No nothing. Libby and Gene and I went home and stayed up almost all night talking.

"On Thursday morning Libby and Gene took me to St. Boniface Episcopal Church to a midday communion service. The church was beautiful. The service was familiar. I was comfortable, and after the communion, there was a special healing service. There were physically handicapped people and young mothers with deformed children all waiting to go to the altar rail and many, many old people. We waited our turn and at last I was kneeling at the altar. A kind old priest whispered to me, 'What is your problem, my son?'

"I answered in a quivering voice, 'I have a drug problem and my mind is cloudy.' He laid his hands on me and prayed the most beautiful prayer I've ever heard. Instantly my mind was clear and I was filled with unspeakable joy.

"Libby and Gene were thrilled.

"They said, 'Now you're fine and we can get your ticket home.'

"They repeated the words that the man at the prayer group had said. 'Ollie, you'll never be the same again.'"

We were almost home when Ollie finished. Mary and I were in tears. I was so thankful; however, I wondered what direction our lives would take from now on. But the one thing I knew was I had put Ollie on the plane as one person, and he returned home a new person.

On Sunday Mary left for college, and on Monday Ollie returned to work. His one desire was that I would have the same experience. I was not so sure about that. I loved my friends. I liked my life, and I didn't want to lose any of my friends. I knew how people could ostracize you saying, "They got religion."

All of this was going through my mind as I drove down Ash Street when I suddenly heard in my heart, "Who are your friends? Your friends are only your friends when you do what they want you to do." I was startled. I knew I could never have thought that up. I told Ollie, "I'm ready. He found a minister who laid hands on me and asked the Lord to baptize me in the Holy Spirit. Life has never been the same since. It has been better and better.

Afterwards, things that were once so important lost their fascination. We were enjoying each other and many simple things. In this new life we were like babes learning to crawl before we could walk. It's strange to say and may seem like a cliché, but we did look at things in a different light. The sky seemed bluer. The birds sang new songs, and the grass was greener.

I was anxious to make a trip to Savannah to give Mother and Claudia an account of all that had happened. On the way to Savannah, I told Ollie, "It's like after you've read a good book. You want to share it with those you love." After I related the whole story to Mother, I sat quietly waiting for her reaction.

Bella was not impressed. She raised her eyebrows. "Bettye Lorraine, a little religion is a good thing, but too much is ridiculous."

I was crushed. I knew that the subject was closed and not once during our visit did I mention it again. She just didn't understand.

On the way home I said to Ollie, "Our trip to Europe is fast approaching. It's only a few weeks away. Do you think we should go? Perhaps we will make some of our friends uncomfortable."

Ollie said, "I think we need some help with this." So we made a trip to see the minister who had laid hands on me. We told him about our European trip with people who were very dear to us and that we were fearful in some way we might spoil it for them.

He told us that we must go. That surely God had prepared this trip at this time for us. You'll see things that they won't see. Go and be gracious and loving. Just be yourselves.

******

On May 1, 1973, ten of the supper club members left the Raleigh-Durham Airport on the first leg of our journey to Europe. We joined a group of thirty-five people in London. It was supposed to be a leisurely trip, but it was fast-paced. Our guide was good, and he didn't want us to miss a thing in England, France, Switzerland and Italy. It was tiring and almost everyone seemed to have a down day when they were just plain exhausted and nothing looked good to them.

Georgia Tanner had hers in Lucerne, Switzerland. We were all going to a special dinner party one evening. I popped into Georgia's room and found her crying. I put my arms around her and said, "What's wrong?"

"I don't have anything to wear. My hair won't do and Hal took me to buy a ring. I didn't like any of the ones he had picked out. I was so ungrateful, and I feel mean and horrible." Later, after a short nap, Georgia pulled herself together and was fine.

While in Paris, Ollie and I and Georgia's husband, Hal, decided to make a second trip to the Louvre. During the trip we viewed the *Mona Lisa* painting and the statue of the Winged Victory.

Ollie and I laughed at Hal's reaction to the Winged Victory. When he saw it, he stared at the headless work of art and said, "If that's victory, I would hate to see defeat."

Italy was my favorite foreign country. Ollie and I purchased a sparkling crystal chandelier in Venice for our dining room. It would be our keepsake of the trip.

Rome was the most fascinating place to me. On the Spanish steps I was pinched by a native behind me. When I turned around and gave him a startled look, he bowed low and said, "Madame, it is a compliment." We thought it was a hoot. Even Ollie laughed.

In Rome at night even though I was dead tired, I read from the Book of Romans in the Bible. Paul was my hero. One afternoon Ol and I took a cab to St. Paul's outside the walls. I was enthralled. Tradition tells us that Paul was buried under the altar inside the church. I kept saying, "Do you really mean Saul who became Paul?" I was thrilled.

A day or so later one of the men on the tour stopped me and said, "May I ask you something? Why is it we all seem to be getting weary, but you two seem to be going strong, better than when the tour began?"

I smiled and thanked the Lord that we had not spoiled anyone's trip. I was learning that when you walk with the Lord, things just work out.

******

After returning home from Europe our first task was to get rested and put the slides of our trip in order. The heat of summer was upon us and eastern North Carolina was hot and muggy. We decided to take a break from the heat and go to Kanuga, an Episcopal retreat center high up in the North Carolina Mountains. It is a perfect hideaway situated on a lake surrounded by mountains. My favorite activity was sitting on the porch in a big rocking chair taking in the beauty.

Kanuga featured prominent speakers, but we had never heard of the guest teacher for that week. It had not mattered to us. Our interest was a respite from the hot weather.

The first morning we were there, Ollie said, "Let's skip the lecture and go for a hike."

I shook my head and said, "No, let's try it once. The priest was the Reverend Terry Fullam. Everyone called him Terry. I had never heard anyone explain the scriptures in the manner he did. He made it interesting as well as fun. Wild horses could not have kept us away after that first morning.

Terry was a large man with a vibrant personality and a twinkle in his eye. His home parish was in Darien, Connecticut, a suburb of New York City.

174

I bemoaned the fact that I wouldn't get there often. Happily, I learned of his tape ministry. All of his sermons and teachings were recorded and for the next several years Terry became an important part of my life. I listened to his tapes while I did household chores, and I actually looked forward to ironing when I could listen uninterrupted. Once when Ollie was joking with me, he said, "If I died I don't think you would even notice. You'd just go on listening to Terry."

We always listened to tapes while we traveled and once when taking Mother and Claudia back to Savannah, we were, as usual, listening to Terry. In a grumpy voice, Bella said from the back seat, "Does that man ever shut up." Bella never realized we were listening to tapes.

In 1977 Ollie, Mary and I felt very fortunate that we were able to go on a trip to Israel with Terry Fullam. It was the most meaningful journey of my life. Terry taught us to see Israel with our hearts not with our eyes. "You have to experience it," he said. On this trip I fell in love with the Jewish people. On our second trip two years later, my heart was captured by the Arabs. The Lord was teaching me how to love.

Chapter Forty-Two
Clary Drug Company – For Sale

While Ollie, Mary and I were preparing for our trip to Israel in 1977, Mother was making plans for retirement. She and Claudia were weary, and they were ready to leave the drugstore and spend the rest of their days at home.

In January of 1977 Mother put an ad in the Georgia Pharmaceutical Magazine: FOR SALE Clary Drug Company in Savannah, Georgia. Mother told me that reading the ad in the newspaper gave her a queasy feeling in the pit of her stomach. The drugstore was like an old, old friend. How could she sell it?

Several months passed before she received a call from a Mr. John Drinkard who made an appointment to see the store. Mr. Drinkard was from La Grange, Georgia. He and his wife wanted to come the following weekend.

Bella told them yes, and they settled on a time.

Mother said she and Claudia were both sad and glad. The store had been their baby after Kelley died. It was like putting their only child up for adoption.

On Wednesday at 11 a.m., Betty and John Drinkard arrived. They were a young couple, and they had their cute little girl with them. It gave Bella a start as she remembered long ago when my daddy opened their first drugstore at 242 Bull Street.

The Drinkards liked the Abercorn Street store, and the druggist and Bella answered all their questions. This was the first of many meetings, and the more Mother saw them, the easier it was to let "her" store go.

Bella's legal counsel was John Ranitz, a staunch friend and advisor. And so it was that in September 1977 Mother signed the final papers selling the Clary Drug Company. Mother said she gave a sigh of relief. She had run the good race. It was time to relax and enjoy life. No one knew how old she was. When anyone asked, her reply was always, "Ladies never tell their age."

******

Mary never shared Bella's views on telling her age. In 1978 she was teaching special education in Winston Salem, North Carolina. It was a friendly city. She didn't mind saying she was twenty-seven, but she did bemoan the fact that Mr. Right had not appeared. Finally, she met that man one Sunday at church. He was a student at Wake Forest University working on his doctorate.

They started dating, and several months later. Mary called and said, "I'm bringing someone home to meet you. His name is Jim Johnson, and he just might be the right man for me. "

These words caused us to be a little anxious. Mary had had many suitors, only to say, "He's not the one."

Ollie and I sat on the front porch waiting for them. At last, they drove up and we could see Mary laughing. Later, Mary told us what was so funny. Jim had spied us and said, "Mary, your parents are really munchkins."

Jim is six feet four inches tall, and the Toomeys range from five feet to five feet five inches.

Jim proposed in 1980, and Mary said, "Yes."

We had another Goldsboro wedding, but this one was different. Mary and Jim were older. They had definite ideas about the kind of wedding they wanted. The wedding was held at St. Stephens Episcopal Church. It was long, spiritual, and beautiful with communion for all, plus a few surprises. Jim's younger brother, David, one of the groomsmen, fainted. He is as tall as Jim, and he went down like tall timber. Everything stopped while they carried him out, and then the minister cleared his throat and continued. The loveliest moment of the service was when the entire congregation sang "The Lord's Prayer." They sang with such gusto it seemed as if the roof would fly off the church.

Mary and Jim's wedding will always be remembered as the day many loyal Carolina basketball fans sat through a long wedding while their beloved UNC Chapel Hill played in the NCAA Semifinals. Carolina defeated Virginia, only to lose in the national championship to Indiana.

The reception was a great celebration! I wondered if all the jubilation was that Mary had chosen a mate or that Carolina had won. After the reception, Mary and Jim left the wedding for the Cloisters at Sea Island, Georgia.

The bridal party and the out-of-town guests made their way to the famous after-party at a friend's home. Jim's mother and dad to this day talk about the fine time they had in Goldsboro.

Folks will never be able to forget this wedding. First, there was David's fainting, then the NCAA semi-finals and on the following Monday, March 30, President Reagan was shot. Thanks to the quick acting and nimble bodyguards, the President was only wounded. Later, when we were discussing the wedding, Ollie said, "You know, Betsy, this wedding was just like Mary, exciting, never a dull moment, and best of all, filled with love."

******

177

Bella's retirement must have started the ball rolling because Ollie also began to think about retirement. He told me about his plan.

I said, "Oh, Honey, how can we live, if you don't work?"

He smiled and said, "Believe me, it can be done."

I immediately went out and bought a good basic black suit. I thought to myself, "I need something I can wear for years!"

Ollie had made up his mind and went to his board of directors. He was sixty-five years old, and he thought it was time to make room for a younger person.

Later, Ollie told me they were shocked. He had been at the helm of the Chamber of Commerce for twenty years. He was like a reliable, permanent fixture.

Never, was a retiree treated so royally!

On his last day of work Ollie left me saying, "Well Betsy, this is it."

To his surprise a large billboard caught his eye as he was driving down Ash Street. It said: HAPPY RETIREMENT, OLLIE.

A crowd turned out for his retirement dinner at Walnut Creek Country Club. Ollie was truly overwhelmed and surprised with the unexpected gift of a brand new Century Buick.

All he could say was, "There never was a town like Goldsboro!"

It seemed as if the whole town was wishing him well and asking him not to leave. And so we didn't. We decided to finish our days in Goldsboro, but in our hearts, we've never left Savannah, and we never will.

******

Ollie's retirement brought new freedom. Savannah became our second home which was good because Bella and Claudia needed us more and more. Ollie and I finally said, "Hey, how about you two moving to Goldsboro? We'll find you a small house close to ours. We'll all be together."

You'd have thought we said a dirty word. Bella scowled at us, and Aunt Claudia shook her head saying, "No."

Ollie and I decided to let it slide and hope for the best.

Chapter Forty-Three
The Fourth Knowing

Even though Bella wouldn't tell her age, I thought she was in her late eighties. She was still driving her car, but now she was having little fender benders which she kept to herself. She had a tendency to drive too fast which was particularly dangerous in the heavy Savannah traffic.

One day while thinking about Mother, I had a *knowing*. I called and told her Ollie and I were coming to Savannah. She was overjoyed. She said, "I'll be watching for you." But she wasn't.

Usually when we drove into Mother's driveway, she was looking out the window, and she would rush out to greet us. But not this time.

George Blood, her neighbor, walked out to greet us. He said, "Lorraine, the girls have been in a wreck. It happened on the corner of Habersham and Washington Avenue. They begged not to be taken to the Emergency Room but go to Doctor Williams' office. They said, 'She'll take care of us, and we can go home. You know Lorraine's coming.'"

Ollie and I quickly drove to Dr. Williams' office. We were shown into a room where Bella, Claudia and the doctor were in deep conversation.

The doctor quickly said to us, "They're all right, just shaken up and frightened. You can take them home."

As soon as we walked into the house, Mother did as usual—the unexpected. She got angry. In fact, she got downright mad. She kept saying, "That woman hit me, and my car had to be towed away."

"I know, Mother, but just think, you and Claudia weren't hurt, and the other woman is all right too. What a blessing!"

In a fractious and irritable voice, Mother growled, "I don't think being hit by a woman is a blessing."

Aunt Claudia nodded her head in total agreement.

This went on for several days. And instead of Mother calming down, she got worse, repeating, "It's all that woman's fault."

Finally, I gently said to Mother, "It's not her fault. You and Claudia went through a red light. We're so thankful it wasn't any worse."

Dear Mother crumpled like a balloon that had been pricked by a pin and started crying. "Oh, no, I'm so sorry. Are you sure the lady is all right? What can we do?"

Ollie and I stayed on and took care of Mother's business. But the worst was yet to come. We decided that Mother must not drive anymore. She was, in our opinion, a danger to herself and others.

Ollie said, "Betsy, I'll tell her. Let her be mad with me, not you."

And so it was. Bella was hopping mad with poor Ollie. But he was firm. "Bella," he said, "Thelma has the car you gave her. She can take you grocery shopping, to the doctor's and wherever else you need to go."

We stayed until Mother calmed down, and we were sure she was comfortable with Thelma chauffeuring her around. When Ollie and I left, I promised Mother I would return soon.

Mother and Claudia stood in the driveway and sadly waved good-bye. I cried all the way home. I knew life would never be quite the same again.

Chapter Forty-Four
Bella and Claudia leave Savannah

After Mother stopped driving, things were not as bad with Mother as I had feared. She still had friends who were driving. They visited with her, played Canasta several times a week, and every Saturday went to the Oglethorpe Mall for lunch. They liked to sit in the mall and watch the shoppers stroll by.

One morning in 1984 Mother called me. She was so excited. "Have I got news for you?"

"Slow down," I said.

"Okay," Mother replied. "But I just found out some news about John Drinkard who bought the drugstore from me." She paused, out of breath, then continued, "He sold Clary's to a local pharmacist, John Leffler. Now what do you think of that?"

Before I could answer she said, "When are you coming again?" That was always the question.

Over the next several years I began to realize things were slowly but surely going downhill in Savannah. Each time I visited Mother she complained about how strange Aunt Claudia was acting. Thelma overheard our conversation and piped up with, "That's the truth, Miss Bet."

They went on telling me how Claudia couldn't remember things. Mother said, "She doesn't even want her toddy at night before dinner. The strangest thing is that after we eat, she just gets up and goes to bed without saying a word, not even goodnight. That's very unusual."

Finally, I said, "Mother, it's time for you two to come close to us."

She shook her head, "No, Savannah is my home."

I became frustrated but took solace in the fact that my childhood friend Nita stopped by Mother's every morning before going to work at Desbouillon's Jewelry Store. This became a ritual. Mother had coffee ready, and they had a little visit. How grateful I was to Nita. She kept me informed and agreed Claudia was as sweet as could be, but she just wasn't herself.

My journeys to Savannah became more frequent. Sometimes I felt like a yo-yo. Each visit I pleaded with Mother to make the move to Goldsboro.

Finally, in 1988 Mother called and in a frantic voice said, "I can't take it anymore. I'm ready to come to you."

Mother had found Claudia striking matches trying to light an electric lamp on her dresser. She took Claudia to the doctor who diagnosed her with

181

dementia. Yes, it was past time for them to come to Goldsboro. We should not have asked. We should have told them what they had to do.

Ollie went into high gear. We decided that Mother would live with us and Claudia would be placed in a nursing home. Ollie was pinch-hitting as the executive director of the United Way of Wayne County, so the big move was up to me.

All of the nursing homes in Goldsboro were full. Luckily, we found an opening in Smithfield which was twenty miles away. We had to strike while the iron was hot for fear Mother would change her mind. We made a reservation for Claudia.

I went to Savannah, packed their clothes, and after they were in bed, put things in order. The next morning we locked up and left Savannah. As we drove over the high bridge leaving town, I had an ache in the pit of my stomach. Aunt Claudia was sitting in the back seat. She had no earthly idea where she was going.

After we had driven over a hundred miles, Aunt Claudia said, "We certainly are taking a long ride."

Ollie met us at the nursing home in Smithfield, and Aunt Claudia was as happy as a lark. As the nurses got her into bed, she said, "This is a nice motel." With that, she pulled the covers up and went to sleep.

It was really surprising how cheerful Mother was. I suppose she was relieved not to have the responsibility of Claudia anymore.

Each day we went to see Aunt Claudia. She seemed contented and completely satisfied. She was so sweet that the nurses made her their pet patient.

Things were going well. Mother and I decided to drive to Savannah to check on her house and put it in the hands of a realtor. Once there, old memories flooded Mother's mind. Kelley's death seemed to haunt her. She asked me to call her Bella all the time, just as Kelley had.

Ollie volunteered to go to Smithfield and visit Aunt Claudia each day while we were away. One afternoon he found Claudia in her wheelchair and he asked, "What have you been doing?"

"Oh, a bunch of us went downtown to the baseball game."

"Well, who won?"

She smiled and said, "You know, the local team."

Her imagination was good and not once did she ask for Mother or me.

Thank God she was happy. In November 1988 dear, precious Claudia died in her sleep, just eight months after the move from Savannah. We took her home to Bonaventure Cemetery.

How can you comfort someone else when your heart is breaking? Aunt Claudia was a second mother to me. She taught me little songs, bought Nancy

Drew books for me and held me tight when I had one of my terrible earaches. She always loved me and was a playmate for a lonely little girl, but my grief could not compare to Mother's. She and Claudia had been best friends since childhood. Their love only increased as they aged.

Thankfully, Bella's house in Savannah sold. When we signed the final papers and closed the house, it seemed to me that we were dismantling a lifetime of memories.

Bella picked out the furniture she wanted, a four-poster bed, dresser, chest, TV and a recliner along with her other personal effects. I had promised her our master bedroom and bath, and told her we would furnish it with her own familiar things. Family and friends were given gifts. Then I called in antique dealers, but there was tons of stuff left. As I filled black plastic bags for the Salvation Army, Bella went behind me rummaging through them, declaring, "I just have to keep this."

In desperation, I decided on an "in house" sale which I never could have done without my friend, Eleanor. I was nervous about how Bella might react to seeing her possessions sold and carted away. She fooled me. She enjoyed the mob of people who came. She was a super saleslady. She did not shed one tear.

By the end of the day, the house was practically bare. I was amazed at the large amount of money we had collected. Eleanor's husband George handled all of the finances. When he told us the final figure, we were flabbergasted. I guess the old saying is true—one person's trash is someone else's treasure.

After completing our business, Bella and I headed back to Goldsboro. I was glad to have Mother with me, and we did everything possible to make her feel happy, even refurbishing her wardrobe. She had always loved pretty clothes, so we went shopping. Ollie made a big fuss over her purchases. Bella modeled them for him, giggling like a school girl.

There were many good times, but there were hard times too. Ollie had become accustomed to my undivided attention. Sometimes I felt I was being torn apart by the two of them. Then the Lord gave me a scripture: "Therefore by the mercy of God you do not lose heart." 2nd Corinthians 4:1

And I would remember what a privilege it is to care for those we love. Bella was my constant companion for breakfast, lunch and dinner, which was fine. At night when Ollie and I went to the den to watch TV and discuss the day, Bella sat right beside me on the loveseat. She was my second skin. I knew I had to make some time for my husband.

Mother and I had always been able to be honest with each other. I took the bull by the horns. I said, "Bella, you know how much I love you and how much I love Ollie. I feel that I have to give him a little bit of my time. "Don't you agree?"

"Of course you should," she replied.

"Mother, you and I can be together all day long, but after dinner what would you think about going up to your nice room and watching TV?"

She smiled and said, "Like I always left your house in Savannah by five o'clock so you and Ollie could have time together."

I nodded and Bella continued, "Of course, you and Ollie should have time together," and with a twinkle in her eye she said, "Remember, I was married twice."

After that, life was smoother for Mother, Ollie and me. I knew she missed Savannah, so when Mother and I received an invitation to spend a few days with Eleanor and George Blood, Bella's next door neighbor and my dear friends, she was very excited. The Bloods had moved to Long Point on Wilmington Island. Eleanor was anxious for us to see her new home. Ollie encouraged us to go.

As Mother and I breezed down Interstate 95 to Savannah, we harmonized and sang lustily. I teased Bella, "I love your country alto."

She replied, "Your soprano is not bad either."

When we approached Savannah, I put my window down and began to sniff the air. I always did this. I loved the salty, sweet smell of the marsh.

Bella made a face and turned up her nose, "It stinks."

"Oh Mother, you're not a Geechee like me."

Our days in Savannah were a tonic for Bella. We shopped, ate at Johnny Harris', strolled through the squares, sat on park benches feeding the pigeons, and visited old friends. The last place we went was Bonaventure Cemetery. We took flowers and placed them on family graves. As always, there was a sense of beauty and tranquility that enfolded us.

Eleanor is a great cook. We enjoyed her delicious meals which George spiced up by teasing Mother. He had always loved Bella and Claudia. He thought they were rare, funny characters. He said, "Bella, I never thought we could pull off your in house sale. You were one persuasive saleslady."

She gave a little chuckle and said, "George, you just do what you have to do."

On the way home Mother said, "The trip was fun. But it's time to go home. I'm glad I'm with you."

My heart sang.

******

As we pulled into our driveway in Goldsboro, the front door opened and Ollie came out to meet us. He had really missed us. After dinner he proudly told us about having a new security system installed.

I smiled and said, "That's nice." I wasn't very enthusiastic. I was tired and I really didn't think we needed a security system.

That night in bed Ollie said, "I thought with the security system we would be able to occasionally leave Bella alone and go out to dinner. We can turn it on when we leave, and she'll be safe and snug upstairs in her room. Should it go off, our next-door neighbors said they will check on her."

Sleepily I murmured, "That sounds fine. I'm tired, honey, but thanks for being so thoughtful."

Only minutes had lapsed when the most horrible, ear splitting sound roared like a banshee. Noise filled the house. I thought the world was coming to an end. Ollie and I both leaped from the bed. He screamed, "It's the alarm. Someone's in our house." I was so flustered I couldn't think or move.

Ollie shouted, "Call 911."

I stumbled into Bella's room where the phone was. Bella was standing in the middle of the room. Even without her hearing aids she had heard the noise. She was rubbing her eyes and saying, "Is it time to get up?"

I tried to get past her to reach the phone. If I moved to the right, she moved too. In desperation, I wiggled around her and with shaking hands I dialed the emergency number. Nothing happened. No one answered. I must have dialed it wrong. I tried again. Still nothing. I grabbed the phonebook and found the number for the police. Thank God, they answered. "Our security system's going off. Someone's downstairs in our house."

The policeman replied, "Why didn't you call 911?"

"I did. They didn't answer."

And then I knew. In my fright I had dialed 919, our area code. I caught my breath and said. "Will you send someone?"

The policeman took the information and replied, "They're on the way. Now don't go downstairs."

He didn't have to worry about that. I ran to tell Ollie and there was that dear man standing at the top of the stairs clad in his shortie pajamas holding a big shotgun that had belonged to his father. He was going to protect his women.

The police came and discovered someone had attempted to enter through our front double doors. The alarm must have scared them away. We went back to bed. Then I confessed my 919 mistake.

The next morning Ollie had the system hooked up to the police department.

******

A few days later Bella came to me with a very serious look on her face and asked if we could talk.

I nodded, having no idea what was coming.

"Once you told me what happened with you and Ollie spiritually. I told you that a little religion is fine but too much is ridiculous." She stammered, "I've changed my mind. I don't know what you two have, but I want it, too."

I simply couldn't believe my ears. I let out a squeal of joy, and we began to laugh and cry together.

That night Ollie laid hands on Mother and asked the Lord to baptize her in the Holy Spirit.

Life continued on as usual, but Bella seemed more peaceful. She looked forward to going to church with us on Sunday mornings. She was constantly saying, "Tell me about heaven. What's it going to be like?"

We had long talks, and I read scripture to her and sang a song that Ollie and I used to sing with the young people when we taught Sunday school. It was an upbeat jazzy number about Heaven being a wonderful place. By the time I finished my vocal and dance, we were both laughing. But something kept nagging at me. What if Bella got sick and I couldn't care for her and I had to put her in a nursing home?

I would feel so guilty. Finally, I decided to talk it over with Mother. She listened intently. Then she said, "Getting old and death are just a part of life. I am no longer afraid. I know that you will take care of me no matter where I am."

I asked Mother if she would visit all the nursing homes in the county with me and tell me which one she liked best.

After our careful survey, Mother said, "If anything happens to me, I like Brian Center."

I tucked that bit of information away, praying that I would never have to use it.

Chapter Forty-Five
Lady Godiva

It was early August, 1990. I was in the kitchen preparing dinner. The little TV was on giving the latest war news. The United States was at war with Iraq. It all began when Iraq (under the command of Saddam Hussein) invaded the tiny country of Kuwait.

I was mumbling under my breath, "Another war. Why can't people learn to get along?" The war was called the Gulf War or Operation Desert Storm. Airmen from our base Seymour Johnson were on the way to the war zone. It seemed we could hear the huge Air Force transport planes flying overhead day and night.

Mother was completely focused on the war. She was glued to the television. She watched CNN from morning until bedtime. I tried to explain that she was hearing the same news and seeing the same pictures over and over again.

She said, "Bettye Lorraine, you don't understand, I've never seen a war before.

That night after dinner, Mother quickly excused herself and went upstairs to watch the war. Ollie and I went down to the den to discuss some business. Ollie said, "There are some papers upstairs you need to sign. I'll get them."

When he returned he had a shocked look on his face. "Betsy, you need to go upstairs and check on Bella. Something is definitely wrong."

I ran upstairs. Mother's door was wide open. She was sitting in her recliner without a stitch of clothes on. She had taken the pins out of her long red hair, and it was hanging down on her shoulders. "Bella, what in the world are you doing?" I asked.

She motioned for me to be quiet.

I couldn't believe my eyes. Bella was always so modest. At last a TV commercial came on. She muted the TV.

I asked, "What are you doing watching television naked?"

"My goodness," she replied. "I was just getting ready to get my gown out of the closet when CNN started showing a big explosion. I wanted to see it, so I sat down for a minute. I guess I got so interested I forgot all about my clothes."

"Mother, did you know Ollie came upstairs and saw you?"

"Oh no, I'm so embarrassed," she said.

"We're just so thankful that you're all right. You get into your nightie and go back to your news."

187

The next morning Ollie and I were at the breakfast table drinking coffee when Mother appeared.

Ollie had his nose in the newspaper. He glanced up and said, "Good morning, Lady Godiva."

I held my breath. I hoped that he hadn't hurt Mother's feelings. There was a long silence.

Bella broke into peals of laugher, "That was a good one on me."

Lady Godiva was Ollie's nickname for Mother from then on. She seemed to like it.

******

I said before there are good days and there are bad days and then there are the worst of days. Things were going well in March 1991. I was puttering around upstairs when I heard Mother calling me. She wanted me to watch TV with her. I walked into the den and sat beside her on the loveseat. It was getting late in the afternoon. I said, "Bella, I need to get dinner started."

"I'll set the table," she replied.

We got up, and as we reached the steps to the kitchen, a strange thing happened. Mother started going around and around in a circle like a teddy bear doing a jig. At first I thought she was kidding. Then I saw her face. Her mouth looked like an ugly gash and had an unnatural position. Her eyes were rolled back. Then she started to fall.

In my fright I had superhuman strength. Screaming for Ollie, I got her up the five stairs that led to the kitchen.

Ollie took one look and called 911. Mother had suffered a stroke. There were days in the hospital when she couldn't speak. She became angry when she could only say. "So, so, so.—"

The doctor recommended that we place Bella in a nursing home. He said, "Betsy, you are not physically able to give her all the care that she needs. I have found it is far better to take a patient from the hospital to a nursing home than to try it at home, only to find it is necessary to go to a nursing home."

Ollie and I listened to the doctor and prayed. The only saving grace for me was that Bella had picked a nursing home. With tears in our eyes we took Bella to the Brian Center. It was a huge adjustment for Mother and me. I devoted myself to helping her make the change. I must say she was wonderful. Not once did she make me feel guilty. She grew stronger and her speech improved.

We fell into a schedule. I went to the nursing home every afternoon after lunch and stayed through the dinner hour.

Brian Center had a big front porch with rocking chairs. Sometimes we rocked and chatted the afternoon away.

Occasionally, I took Mother out to lunch or for a ride in the car.

Mother refused to admit that she was handicapped in any way. Once I took her to the mall and got a wheelchair. I was pushing her around when suddenly she said, "Stop. Now you get in and I'll push you." Her mind was stronger than her body.

Finally, I got brave enough to take her home one afternoon. I was uncertain how she would react. But I wanted her to see that her room was just as she left it. She enjoyed spending the afternoon rummaging through her clothes and costume jewelry. She looked at her watch finally and said, "It's time for you to take me back to Brian Center. I don't want to miss my dinner."

How happy that sentence made me. From then on I brought Mother home often.

Bella liked to look stylish and her one request was that I would keep her hair colored. Once a month I got the key to the beauty shop at Brian Center on the day it was closed. I colored her hair a soft auburn, and this would always pick up her spirits.

One afternoon when we were driving down Berkeley Boulevard, she said, "I have something I need to talk to you about. You keep telling people how old I am, and you are all mixed up."

I questioned her, "Mother, how old are you?"

She pulled herself up and said, "I'm sixty-five years old."

"Well, Mother, that's funny," I said. "I'm older than you are."

She put her hand over her mouth giggling. That was the end of that.

One Sunday night Ollie and I returned home from the beach to find a message on our answering machine from Brian Center. They asked if we wanted to take Bella to the oncologist in the morning, or should they. I was not aware that anything was wrong with Mother. This frightened me.

We took Mother to the doctor's office the next morning. And in typical Bella style she had a grand time enjoying all the attention. It was confirmed that she had Aplastic anemia, a disease that we knew nothing about. We were told that in time she would become deadly tired. Her age made a bone marrow transplant impossible.

Bella wasn't a bit concerned. She said, "I've lived a grand life in my beloved Savannah, and I am thankful for each day I've had."

In July 1992 we were in the midst of a heat wave. The temperature was a sizzling one hundred degrees. People were advised to stay indoors if possible, but I had promised to take Bella to lunch. When I arrived at the nursing home, she was all dressed and ready to go.

I said, "Mother, it's just too hot to venture out. Let's have lunch here."

She seemed relieved saying, "Will you help me into my night gown? I'm so tired."

That was on a Thursday. My precious, fun-loving mother never got out of bed again. On Saturday she passed away from congestive heart failure.

******

Mother's death was a special gift to me, strange as that may seem. How else could I have endured the separation? I remember her telling me long ago, "When your mother dies you have lost your best friend." Now, I know that to be true. Her death was so beautiful, I was able to rejoice.

It was the morning of July 18, 1992. The telephone rang. It was Bella's favorite nurse. She said, "Betsy, I think you'd better come over here. Your mother needs you."

I dashed over to the nursing home. As I walked into Mother's room, the nurse was putting a fresh rose-colored gown on her and brushing her hair. I thought she looked beautiful.

I said, "Hey there." She opened her eyes and smiled. She looked at me. Then she slowly closed her eyes again.

I sat beside the bed holding her hand. The nurse came in regularly to check her vital signs. Finally, the nurse shook her head, and I knew we were approaching the end.

I called Ollie and he came right away. He walked over to the foot of the bed and said, "Hello, Lady Godiva."

Mother opened her eyes and her face lit up. When the nurse came back, she didn't leave again. She held one of mother's hands and I held the other. I kept whispering in her ear, "I love you," and singing, *Jesus Loves You this I know.*

She was serene and peaceful. Then all three of us, Ollie, the nurse, and I, felt Mother's spirit soar away. The nurse said, "She's gone." Ollie was visibly shaken. He said later, "It was like she sailed into the blue."

The nurse said, "I've never seen anything quite so beautiful."

I couldn't cry. It was as if I had seen the hand of God.

Her funeral was held at St. Stephen's. To my surprise, the church was full. Mother was an unusual character, and many people had grown to love her. Did I weep? Yes, I wept for me. I would have to learn to live without my closest friend, my mother, my Bella.

We took her to Savannah and buried her at Bonaventure Cemetery next to those she loved: Daddy, Kelley, Claudia, and her infant son.

Was it a coincidence that on September 17, 1992, my birthday, Clary Drug Company was purchased by Revco? The days of the independent pharmacies were ending. The Clary Drug Company was the oldest drugstore in continuous operation in Savannah. I thought it strange and rather wonderful that 1992 marked the end of Clara Clary Kelley's life and the closing of Clary's Drugstore, an institution.

EPILOGUE
The General Oglethorpe

It was June 1993, and Ollie and I were breezing along down I 95 on our way to Savannah for my 50th high school reunion. The class of 1943 had been very close, perhaps because of World War II. Our young men had graduated one day and gone off to war the following day. We had lost classmates and that had grieved us, but we were strong. We celebrated each other and life.

What a strange twist of fate it was that our 50th reunion was being held at the refurbished General Oglethorpe Hotel which my father had invested in so many years ago. I closed my eyes and began to recall the story he had told me.

Well, it was back in the 1920s. Daddy's friend Paul came bouncing into the store. "Good morning, Luther. I have some big news. It's about a Dr. Pemberton who invented a soft drink in 1886. Now after all these years, it's up and running. And the exciting thing is the stock is for sale. You can get in on the ground floor. It's a real winner. They have named the drink Coca Cola. What do you think of that?"

Daddy smiled and shook his head. "Thanks for thinking of me. But several years ago I had a little extra cash, and I invested in Savannah."

He had invested in the new luxury hotel, The General Oglethorpe that had been built on Wilmington Island. "It's going to be good for Savannah," he said. And it should have been because it was a handsome, huge building. It was opened in 1927. The setting was perfect. It overlooked the river where he was sure tourists would dock their boats and spend time in Savannah. The General had it all: An eighteen hole golf course, a huge swimming pool, tennis courts, boating, stables, luxury living with fine dining and dancing. The whole setting was breathtaking. There were live oak trees with silver moss swinging in the breeze, magnolias and azaleas. I was just a little girl, but I could remember how we would drive out on Sunday afternoons.

My daddy was like a school boy. He showed us every nook and cranny, and we would sit in the bar where he ordered me a Shirley Temple and declared that the General Oglethorpe was equal to any New York bar. Everything was perfect. There was only one thing wrong— where were all the paying guests? Daddy was sure they would come. They never did. The hotel went into bankruptcy and closed. All the lovely furniture was shrouded with white sheets. Daddy took it in stride. He shrugged and said, "I'd better stick to the drugstore business."

My heart began to race as Ollie pulled into the circular drive of the Oglethorpe. I had an eerie feeling to think we would spend two nights here, but then I heard, "Hey, Lorraine, we're glad you're here."

The weekend was a huge success, and I smiled to myself thinking how happy my daddy would have been to see the General filled with happy, dancing people. I was ecstatic that the class of 1943 was still a bunch of dancing folks.

******

I hate to admit it, but I'm an old lady. People say that Ollie and I look young for our ages and act even younger. Maybe it's because we enjoy each other and every day, or perhaps, it is the influence of our new younger friends. They don't seem to mind our age. But the fact is we go to more funerals than weddings. Our beloved supper club friends have left us one by one. Once we were twelve strong, and now we are two. Please don't accuse me of being morbid, I'm not. But I know that I am in the sunset of my life. In modern terms, I might say it has been a great ride. I wouldn't change a thing.

As of 2008, Ollie and I have been married sixty-two years. We are not whole without each other. We are comfortable together, and we know each other's thoughts.

Looking back, I can see that this was God's plan for my life. Many people say that you can only love one man. That has not been true in my life. I have truly loved five men, each in a different way. Sidney was my first love, the love of my youth. Danny was my grown-up war-time romance. Roy was the sweet, beloved brother I never had. Ollie was my soul mate. And, of course, there was my dearest Dad. They have all played an important part in my life. I thank them for that. They will always be in my heart.

Dear Roy died of pancreatic cancer in 2000 and recently I learned through research that Danny died in 1983. I grieve for him and his years in a German POW camp in World War II and for a life that was all too short. Ollie and I continue to see Sidney and Beth, his pretty wife, when we are in Savannah.

Numbers have always blown my mind, but they don't lie. Ollie is ninety and I am eighty-four. When I was a little girl, my father told me that there was a beautiful sunrise just as I came into the world. I thought, isn't it wonderful that when the sun sets in my life I will return to my beloved Savannah. I will have had sunrise and sunset. When the Lord calls, I will make the final journey.

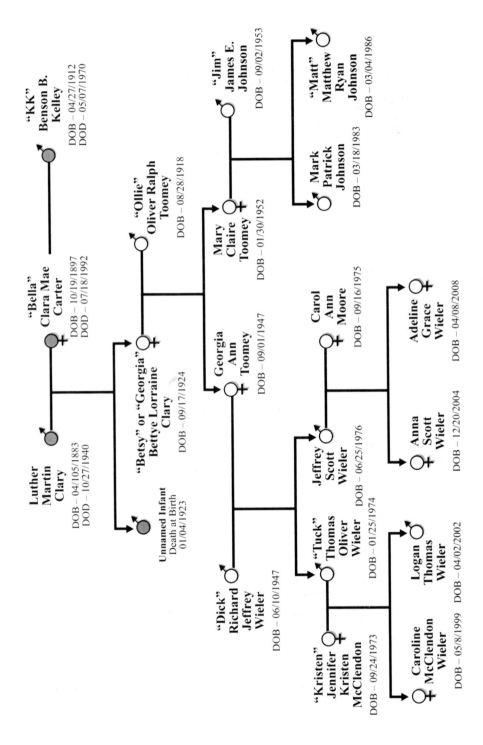

"KK"
Benson B.
Kelley
DOB – 04/27/1912
DOD – 05/07/1970

"Bella"
Clara Mae
Carter
DOB – 10/19/1897
DOD – 07/18/1992

"Ollie"
Oliver Ralph
Toomey
DOB – 08/28/1918

Luther
Martin
Clary
DOB – 04/105/1883
DOD – 10/27/1940

"Betsy" or "Georgia"
Bettye Lorraine
Clary
DOB – 09/17/1924

Unnamed Infant
Death at Birth
01/04/1923

Georgia
Ann
Toomey
DOB – 09/01/1947

Mary
Claire
Toomey
DOB – 01/30/1952

"Jim"
James E.
Johnson
DOB – 09/02/1953

"Matt"
Matthew
Ryan
Johnson
DOB – 03/04/1986

Mark
Patrick
Johnson
DOB – 03/18/1983

"Dick"
Richard
Jeffrey Wieler
DOB – 06/10/1947

Carol
Ann
Moore
DOB – 09/16/1975

Jeffrey
Scott
Wieler
DOB – 06/25/1976

"Tuck"
Thomas
Oliver
Wieler
DOB – 01/25/1974

Adeline
Grace
Wieler
DOB – 04/08/2008

Anna
Scott Wieler
DOB – 12/20/2004

"Kristen"
Jennifer
Kristen
McClendon
DOB – 09/24/1973

Logan
Thomas
Wieler
DOB – 04/02/2002

Caroline
McClendon
Wieler
DOB – 05/8/1999

Katherine Wood Wolfe and Bettye Clary Toomey

Katherine Wood Wolfe grew up in Raleigh, North Carolina. She graduated from Meredith College and has graduate degrees in education and Library Science from East Carolina University and has completed further studies in Library Science at the University of North Carolina at Chapel Hill. She has worked as a teacher and media coordinator in the North Carolina Public Schools and as a college librarian at Chowan College and Wayne Community College. Since retiring in 1999, Katherine has actively pursued her creative writing interests and worked part-time at Mount Olive College. She lives in Goldsboro, North Carolina.

Bettye Clary Toomey was born in Savannah, Georgia, in 1924, the daughter of Clara Carter Clary and Luther Clary, owner of Clary Drugstores on Bull Street and Abercorn Street. "Betsy" graduated from Savannah High School in 1943 and continued her education at Rollins College in Winter Park, Florida. While at Rollins, she married and moved to Ohio. Happily though, she returned to Savannah in 1956 where her husband served as administrative assistant to the Executive Director of the Savannah Chamber of Commerce. She currently lives in Goldsboro, North Carolina, but keeps Savannah on her mind through her travels to Savannah to visit friends and relatives.